T0285010

WORK DIFFERENT

KATE BRAVERY ▪ ILYA BONIC ▪ KAI ANDERSON

WO RKDI FFER ENT

10 TRUTHS FOR WINNING IN THE PEOPLE AGE

WILEY

Copyright © 2024 by Mercer (US) Inc. All rights reserved.

Published by John Wiley & Sons, Inc., Hoboken, New Jersey.
Published simultaneously in Canada.

No part of this publication may be reproduced, stored in a retrieval system, or transmitted in any form or by any means, electronic, mechanical, photocopying, recording, scanning, or otherwise, except as permitted under Section 107 or 108 of the 1976 United States Copyright Act, without either the prior written permission of the Publisher, or authorization through payment of the appropriate per-copy fee to the Copyright Clearance Center, Inc., 222 Rosewood Drive, Danvers, MA 01923, (978) 750-8400, fax (978) 750-4470, or on the web at **www.copyright.com**. Requests to the Publisher for permission should be addressed to the Permissions Department, John Wiley & Sons, Inc., 111 River Street, Hoboken, NJ 07030, (201) 748-6011, fax (201) 748-6008, or online at **http://www.wiley.com/go/permission**.

Trademarks: Wiley and the Wiley logo are trademarks or registered trademarks of John Wiley & Sons, Inc. and/or its affiliates in the United States and other countries and may not be used without written permission. All other trademarks are the property of their respective owners. John Wiley & Sons, Inc. is not associated with any product or vendor mentioned in this book.

Limit of Liability/Disclaimer of Warranty: While the publisher and author have used their best efforts in preparing this book, they make no representations or warranties with respect to the accuracy or completeness of the contents of this book and specifically disclaim any implied warranties of merchantability or fitness for a particular purpose. No warranty may be created or extended by sales representatives or written sales materials. The advice and strategies contained herein may not be suitable for your situation. You should consult with a professional where appropriate. Further, readers should be aware that websites listed in this work may have changed or disappeared between when this work was written and when it is read. Neither the publisher nor authors shall be liable for any loss of profit or any other commercial damages, including but not limited to special, incidental, consequential, or other damages.

For general information on our other products and services or for technical support, please contact our Customer Care Department within the United States at (800) 762-2974, outside the United States at (317) 572-3993 or fax (317) 572-4002.

Wiley also publishes its books in a variety of electronic formats. Some content that appears in print may not be available in electronic formats. For more information about Wiley products, visit our web site at **www.wiley.com**.

Library of Congress Cataloging-in-Publication Data is Available:

ISBN: 9781394181292 (cloth)
ISBN: 9781394181308 (ePub)
ISBN: 9781394181315 (ePDF)

Cover image(s): Courtesy of the Author
Cover design: Wiley

SKY10057404_101223

Contents

Preface

Ten new truths about work: They were sparked by the pandemic. They have withstood the fraught economic and geopolitical landscapes that have elapsed since. They will define our futures. These truths are more important than ever for leaders to embrace as we prepare to navigate the next seismic change: the emergence of generative artificial intelligence (Gen-AI). These starkly unique and epochal events—that occurred within the space of just a few years—are demanding a pivot in how we work and how we work together. This book charts the reverberation of these events and discusses the implication for leading and working in the People Age.

Introduction: The Pivot

...And Just Like That, Everything Changed

At the beginning of 2020, we'd shake a stranger's hand without a second thought. We'd go to a restaurant without caring how close we were seated to our fellow diners. We'd go to a movie, unconcerned about whether the person doling out our popcorn had sanitized her hands.

That was the beginning of 2020. Come the end of Q1, it was game over.

We went from *on* to *off*.

We became separated from pretty much *everybody*.

International borders were closed off.

Flights were grounded.

Travel was halted.

The largest cities in the world shut down.

The world's most famous gathering places fell silent. Times Square—empty. Trafalgar Square—empty. Place de la Concorde, Saint Peter's Square, Mecca, Tiananmen Square—empty, empty, empty, empty.

Governments instructed residents to stay home, to minimize social interaction, to cancel scheduled activities, to wear masks, and to isolate. Quickly—virtually overnight—this became the new norm.

This became our lives.

There were whispers about the virus as early as November 2019, so maybe, just *maybe* we should've been better prepared... but we weren't. All we could do was stare at our televisions and doomscroll on social media, and we watched in horror as the story unfolded.

With the health, safety, and well-being of people around the globe in jeopardy, healthcare workers quickly mobilized. Despite their heroic efforts, it was an uphill battle. After all, we knew little to nothing about what some called COVID-19, and others called the coronavirus, and still others flippantly called The 'Rona.

As the virus raged, we in the business world were forced to rethink our priorities. For most companies, the immediate need of securing the safety and well-being of their people (first) and humankind (second) skyrocketed to the top of the charts. Offices were empty and business districts were ghost towns, but economies had to keep going. As most workers retreated to the safety of their homes, the digital shift began in earnest.

Emergency personnel and the newly named category of *critical* or *essential* workers kept the physical economy running (i.e., groceries, retail, shipping, and waste disposal). They put their own safety at risk, in part for the greater good, and in part because they didn't have much of a choice. In sharp contrast, companies that were either nonessential or dependent on close human contact went dark (i.e., construction, hospitality, tourism, entertainment, and professional sports).

From face masks to ventilators, new priorities emerged, and the smartest, most compassionate businesses were there to meet the most unprecedented demand. Many tech-savvy companies and individuals were able to adapt overnight.

There was a reason for that.

During the digital evolution of the late 2010s and early 2020s, a new infrastructure emerged and provided us with tools to react quickly to meet global communication needs. Video platforms like Zoom, Slack, and Google Meet became our new conference rooms. Our basements, our extra bedrooms, and our kitchen tables became our offices. The 9-to-5 workday became the 7-to-10, then the 5-to-9 workday. The salient question was: *In this new setup, how well could your organization rearrange its work, its workflow and its workers?*

As we accepted the fact that the virus would be with us for who-knows-how-long, work truths were rebooted and new work realities set in. The most immediate realization was that—save for such frontline, essential workers as medical personnel, growers, packagers, and deliverers—*not all employees needed to be physically present in the workplace to get their work done.*

Remote working worked. Small consolation, but a consolation, nonetheless.

The success of remote working represented the first of many business dominos to fall. Short-term thinking gave way to addressing the bigger picture. Before the pandemic, some executives estimated that about 45% of their workforce could pivot to the future of work.[1]

They were wrong.

Turns out they wildly underestimated our ability to adapt, as tens upon millions of people changed *where* they worked, *when* they worked, and *how* they worked.

People Get Ready

American business icon Jack Welch passed away at the beginning of March 2020, a loss that gave us business nerds an opportunity to reflect on the evolution of the large corporate CEO mindset as well as the priorities that drove Welch's success.

Dubbed the "Manager of the Century" by *Forbes* in 1999, the late chairman and CEO of General Electric was driven by shareholder primacy and stock returns as the measure for success. Welch's view was that short-term focus would cumulatively deliver for the long term. Arguably, his early-career success and late-career celebrity made it feel okay for corporate CEOs to use workforce restructuring as a go-to solution for cost cutting.

Economic cycle after economic cycle—we're talking 1987, 2001, and 2008–2009—business playbooks hammered one point home: *Reduce people costs to protect shareholder returns*. Overuse of workforce restructuring as a tool to deliver financial results ultimately broke the *Loyalty Contract* between employer and employee. COVID eventually took the employer/employee relationship full circle, shifting the balance of power, and with a hard punch, it reset the employer/employee deal.

The People Age had arrived.

The People Age isn't a direct consequence of COVID, but COVID accelerated many of the trends associated with the future of work, everything from flexible working to total well-being, to investments in artificial intelligence (AI) and automation. As global demographics shifted and fortunes diverged, they collided with a pandemic-induced reset of values.

By most projections, global population growth will peak around 2040. Currently, it's growing at a snail's pace; in parts of the world, death rates are actually outpacing birth rates, meaning some local populations are in the early stages of decline. There are fewer people of working age to support retirees and keep things running, and fewer young people to fuel and renew the workforce. It was no coincidence that most economies around the world entered the COVID era with unemployment rates at record lows. The situation hasn't been helped by the fact that most foreign workers returned to their home countries during the pandemic and stayed there. From then on, immigration restrictions around the globe only exacerbated the situation, an issue that's hurting organizations already short on people and skills.

As a result, many companies' responses to these economic challenges played out differently than traditional management practices would have foretold. A few large and influential employers were quick to break the mold: Rather than reducing their headcount to manage costs, they gave their employees security by assuring them that as long as the pandemic prevailed, their jobs would be safe. Economics and short-term shareholder returns took a backseat. Empathy became a top priority.

Empathy. Embrace that word. You'll be reading a lot about it here.

It wasn't long before companies like Apple, PepsiCo, Medtronic, and Marsh McLennan preached that the wisest long-game play was to protect employees (and, for that matter, society) during this unprecedented time. They saw it as necessary to secure the future of their firms.

This was the new thinking.

Here's Your New Reality. So Now What?

This people-first response was an outcome of a multi-stakeholder alignment model that had already begun to take hold in the boardroom and in society. In 2019, this shift went mainstream—kind of like when Green Day went from playing for six people at punk clubs in San Francisco to selling out Wembley Stadium—and companies became more vocal about putting People and Planet at the heart of their business models. That same year, the Washington-based nonprofit lobby association the Business Roundtable released an updated "Purpose of a Corporation" statement, expressing a need to move from shareholder primacy to a multi-stakeholder model of success, one that delivers positive outcomes for society, customers, employees, and shareholders.[2]

Here, in the second decade of the twenty-first century—as we write this—the urge for sustainability has emerged as a response to the increasing, existential threats to humankind. Environmental risks were articulated by Fridays for Future activists, and the Black Lives Matter movement called out centuries of passing the buck on social injustice and racial violence.

This all created a business powder keg.

Then COVID-19 lit the match.

COVID-19 was the ultimate test and, perhaps unsurprisingly, a number of the Business Roundtable companies failed to meet their pledge once the virus was firmly entrenched in society. Some employees were let go, while others were asked to take a pay cut, all to protect potential dividends to shareholders.

Suddenly, the watchful eye of the public was on businesses worldwide, and one work truth became ever more self-evident: Companies that demonstrated genuine concern for *all* of their employees—*not just those at the top*—stood a better chance of coming through these successive shocks stronger than before.

Where Workers Were and Where Workers Want to Be

As the working world navigated its way through COVID-19, a new power dynamic emerged between employers and employees. And this time, the rebalancing was not skewed toward the high end of the income scale. . .for a change.

The pandemic gave people at all levels, from admins to the C-suite, an opportunity to reflect on their work/life priorities. With that new outlook came empowerment, especially when combined with emerging labor shortages in many industries. Voluntary turnover skyrocketed as employees proactively chose work options that better suited their needs and values. Quitting a seemingly good job became a Thing, and *The Great Resignation* (or *The Great Reassessment*) provided a clear blueprint of the new world of work.

Expectations were being redrawn. Big-time.

For decades up to the pandemic, we all had to go above and beyond to be recognized and promoted. Workers threw aside work/life balance to (hopefully) get to a better financial place. Many eventually realized that their efforts were leading to success for their companies and their bosses.

But not for them.

Leading up to and during the pandemic, a huge number of people learned to stand up for themselves, to call out discriminatory or exploitative behavior, to establish an acceptable work/life balance.

To be respected for who they are as human beings.

They were willing to walk away from undesirable jobs, low pay, and unrelenting supervisors, even in the face of economic uncertainty. And this sentiment is reflected in the emergent values of those first entering the workforce. They don't want to sacrifice a happy today for a (potentially) brighter tomorrow; 75% said they would walk away from an employer who didn't share their values.[3]

Ch-Ch-Changes

There has never been a more impactful, interesting, and challenging time to lead people or to be a part of The People Function.

The pandemic opened the eyes of decision-makers to the reality that even with the proliferation of technology, people are still the heart and soul of the company. As Morgan Stanley Senior

Advisor Jeff Brodsky said, "If the financial crisis was the CFO's crisis, 2020 was the CHRO's crisis"[4] And step up they did, with 76% of executives saying HR was the hero of 2021.[5]

HR as heroes? It's about time!

The immediate focus was to protect people's health under the most challenging of circumstances. Now, the challenge for people managers is to win, retain, and upskill talent in a world that has fundamentally changed. The good news is that trust in organizations is at an all-time high,[6] and employees are eager to partner with their employers and their digital assistants to build a future of work that is less exhausting, more meaningful, and more inspiring. Surely, this is not too much of an ask.

So, what does this all mean?

In a nutshell:

- Business has never been more competitive.
- The world has never been less predictable.
- Talent has never been more in-demand.
- Top talent has never been more difficult to find, attract, and retain.
- People have never had more choices about work.
- The ChatGPTs of the world are pushing us to realize the unique value that people bring to the table.

That all being the case, The People Age is here to stay.

This begs the question: "Hey, Team Mercer, what the hell is The People Age?"

Excellent question.

The People Age is a brave new world built around human-centric values, a world full of opportunities and challenges in service of advancing prosperity for all. Navigating uncharted territory requires accepting and adapting to new truths, as many of the old rules and accepted practices no longer apply. Today, *business as usual* is anything *but* usual, and that's not a bad thing.

Before, during, and after COVID-19, businesses were forced to pivot, and they'll need to keep pivoting if they want to thrive and remain relevant in the world that lies ahead. The litmus test of resilience will be their ability to read market signals early, then effectively respond to employees' wants and needs. Market-sensing and employee-sensing lay at the heart of balancing economics and empathy. Companies that are thriving are already figuring out how to design more human-centric work models, focusing on how to make the adoption of technology easier, and caring about their employees' work experience. But as economic headwinds bite in the mid-2020s, it's clear that staying the course on these newfound learnings takes intentional redesign and courageous leadership.

This brave new world is scary, no doubt, but as David Bowie told us, when there are ch-ch-changes, you have no choice but to *turn and face the strange.*

Speaking of facing the strange—just as the worst of COVID-19 was behind us, along came a chatbot that sounds almost. . . human. The next colossal change had arrived.

When OpenAI released ChatGPT in November 2022, we witnessed the fastest consumer adoption of any technology ever.[7] While it took Uber 70 months to reach 100 million users per month; Spotify, 50 months; and Instagram, 30 months; ChatGPT only took 2 months to reach these user numbers.[8] BAM!

ChatGPT was not the first generative artificial intelligence (AI) solution. But it was the easiest for consumers to use. With the most impressive results in content quality and interaction. With ChatGPT, AI had its iPhone moment. And the world of work has reached another historic pivot in the journey we call digitalization.

The enthusiasm is as great as the skepticism. While 75% of companies say they plan to adopt AI technology, many business players are critical about the path it will set us on, with vocal calls from many for greater regulation and governance.[9] Bill Gates heralds generative AI (Gen AI) as "revolutionary."[10] Elon Musk calls AI the "greatest risk we face as a civilization,"[11] while Warren Buffett and Charlie Munger are cautious about the hype. During the most recent Berkshire Hathaway annual shareholders' gathering, the two high-ranking executives displayed a certain degree of pessimism when it came to the potential of robotics and AI impacting the stock market and society in general.

Munger, in particular, seemed to dismiss the enthusiasm around AI, favoring instead what he referred to as "old-fashioned intelligence."[12] To his point, and despite ChatGPT's utility, there's no substitute for decades of real-world expertise.

While the critical approach to the big change issues of our time is justified, we are reminded of the discussion about flexible working. What was long considered impractical is now rapidly becoming a reality.

And this is where our confrontation with the new realities of the world of work begins.

New Truths Might Set Us Free

This book presents a whole lot of new truths that emerged during this short period (2020–2023). Truths that served as the trigger event for a fundamental shift in how we work, what we work on, and why we even work in the first place.

These truths displace age-old beliefs about what people want and which organizational cultures and leadership styles help them thrive. Together, they signal a radical one-eighty from traditional notions of management reality. They demand a pivot in how we strategize, learn, and lead. Because they impact every aspect of work, they require new ways of thinking and demand action from organizations, leaders, and even employees themselves to adapt and stay relevant in a changing world.

This book seeks to deliver a fresh perspective on today's *people agenda*, a paradigm (see Figure I.1) that recognizes not only the shifts in labor models and employee sentiments, but also looks ahead to how operating models and organizational cultures need to adapt to stay relevant for a new era.

Under this model, we'll look at how the traditional employer/ employee relationship has shifted as well as the new paradigms under which people are operating. We'll also touch on the challenges of meeting employees' lifestyle needs in an environment built for a different time; what people fundamentally expect from work today; the fables that can hold everybody back; and how to attract and retain motivated talent.

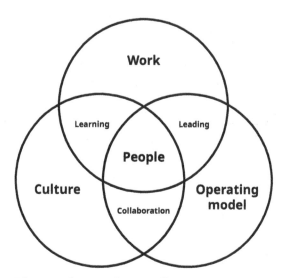

FIGURE I.1 The people agenda paradigm.
Source: Mercer

We'll underscore the importance of purpose and empathy in delivering an inclusive organization, and how firms can outgrow the legacy traits of *command-and-control* to create an organizational culture that breathes with its people and benefits everyone.

We'll muse as to how AI will impact The People Age. Some folks argue that AI will marginalize the human contribution to work and change our operating models like never before. We'll hold against that and outline the opportunities for individuals and companies alike to amplify their intelligence.

We'll focus on how to manage the most valuable resource in an organization—the people—in a more sustainable way. We'll discuss how to deliver on *decent work* and embed healthy work habits into a company's DNA. We'll discuss what sustainable people management looks like in practice.

And finally, we'll share the blueprint for a successful people strategy that enables all leaders and executives to deliver on their future-of-work and sustainability agendas.

Listen, change is never easy, and sometimes our only choices are to opt in or to opt out. The People Age presents an opportunity to adapt or be left behind. For those who embrace these new realities, there is now the chance to innovate further, to be bolder in business and social ambition, and to create a sustainable talent advantage like no other.

Why Us?

These are world-altering concepts, so why should three members of Team Mercer be the ones to write about it? Well, our experiences—especially during the pandemic—bring different perspectives on the new realities of work around the world, and we are united in our passion for The People Agenda.

Kate, an organizational psychologist, draws from her time living in China and the United Kingdom during the pandemic and working with global firms on their talent strategies. Leading on Mercer's *Insight & Advisory* agenda globally, she stays on the pulse of workforce trends, emerging tech. and leading people practices. During this period, she was the incumbent partner of the World Economic Forum (WEF), helping Chief People Officers innovate and respond as the Future of Work agenda reset overnight.

Ilya, an Aussie native who's based in New York, brings a global executive's view. As Mercer's Head of Strategy, he worked with the leadership team to secure Mercer's business continuity response to the pandemic. He is similarly focused on Mercer's business evolution as we adopt various Gen AI tools to augment our own workforce, enhance our business competitiveness and continue to make an ever increasing positive impact for our clients.

And Kai, a seasoned strategist, who, starting with his own company and now leading Workforce Transformation for Mercer, has spent years guiding organizations throughout Europe. His book *Digital Human* (2017) championed the concept of prioritizing humans in the digital transformation. Amid the pandemic's upheaval, Kai continued his mission, helping clients reimagine their work and navigate decisions in a time of immense pressure and uncertainty.

Diverse experiences, diverse perspectives, but a clear recognition by us all: That once we unfreeze how we have worked for centuries, what lies ahead is a once-in-a-lifetime opportunity to reinvent how we work and to define what it means to win in The People Age.

CHAPTER 1

Goodbye Employees, Hello Contributors

Work Different

By the time businesses (kind of) (sort of) figured out how to navigate the pandemic, approximately 50% of the worldwide workforce found itself, as Steve Jobs might have said (with his creative use of grammar), working *different*.[1]

For those who had already worked remotely—be it at home, at a café, or in a local park near a router from which WiFi could be easily stolen—it was just a matter of rearranging their schedule. Work-from-home newbies, however, had to set up their workspace, upgrade their technology, and figure out how to simultaneously make their daughter a grilled cheese sandwich while leading an international Zoom meeting. The truth was that we humans all learned to be more *enterprising*, while enterprises started to become more *human*.

Looking back, this all seemed simple, even quaint.
Back then, not so much.
Those who *had* to work in an office during the pandemic were faced with challenges of their own. *When do I wear a mask? How often should I get tested? How close is too close? If I'm exposed to the virus but I don't have symptoms and I've tested negative multiple times, should I stay home?*

Again, today, that all seems relatively simple. Again, at the time, not so much.

But clever companies adapted. (We like to think we adapted well because we like to think we're clever.) Adaptation was not only born out of necessity, but also because there was a real opportunity to innovate and to accelerate our thinking around work and working.

The pandemic forced (clever) business leaders to listen to their employees harder than ever before. The working world became a massive brainstorming session, and no idea was taken off the table, whether it came from the long-time CFO or the 19-year-old in the warehouse, who'd only been with the company for two weeks.

The employees were leading the leaders. Listening, learning, and looking around was happening at an unprecedented scale. It's impossible to quantify if or how well this approach worked, but one thing is certain: It made for a work environment where people felt heard, and executives started to close the chasm in work outlooks that had been building up over the years.

Anecdotally speaking, the mobile workforce at Mercer seemed to appreciate the newfound flexibility. (Folks also enjoyed the fact that the commute from their bed to their desk was about 45 seconds, and their dress code allowed for hoodies.) They were able to create their own work environment and a comfortable schedule. They were able to configure a home work space that allowed for minimal interruptions and offered good lighting, all while remaining a safe distance from that tempting two-pound bag of chocolate-covered raisins on the kitchen counter.

But it wasn't a pajama party for everybody. Suddenly the size of your home mattered. For many, remote working was not utopia. People in shared flats had no privacy. Ironing boards made for less-than-ideal desks. Access to WiFi and the quality of broadband meant access to employment. The difference between those living in small apartments and those with a spare room to adapt was palpable.

That was the shift experienced in the office world, and probably a disproportionate amount of time and focus has been given to the plight of knowledge workers. Other industries had different challenges that forced a *different* kind of thinking different. Frontline workers were battling the pandemic around the clock, from healthcare workers to police officers, from teachers to cashiers, from garbage collectors to pizza distributors. They kept our lights on, cleaned our streets, educated our children, and delivered our dinners. And Mercer's research showed that while knowledge workers became burnt out, skill workers became fed up.[2] The voices of the divided were deafening and The Great Resentment was brewing.

But like any great period of change, it was also a time of rapid advancement in thinking and technological adoption. We learned that one teacher could educate a group remotely, with parents as intermediaries. We realized phone calls from doctors could be far more convenient than trips to their offices. We saw how a health system in crisis could be alleviated as pharmacists and care workers took on responsibilities previously held by other experts. We watched in awe as digital payment and automated delivery mechanisms exploded, challenging our assumptions around which tasks needed in-person interactions.

While we may never want a bot to tell us that we have a terminal illness, we might not need a face-to-face chat with a doctor to receive other test results. We started to realize the work that rests within jobs today could be done in different and new ways. We could deconstruct a job and reconstruct it differently to solve problems of scale, talent shortage and efficiency, and to build learning in for potential successors. These new ways of working prompted a rethink about jobs, who does those jobs, and what parts of those jobs are truly valued. As we began to see jobs in terms of what *really* adds value to the firm, we also discovered that not all jobs are created equal. Not all jobs are *good* jobs.

Contracted Contributors

It was clear to everyone that *times they were a-changing*. These new realities were getting everyone thinking about what might come next regarding work. For folks in the people business, like us, it was clear that we would need unprecedented amounts of empathy to understand the vast diversity of experiences within these new realities. It was clear that employees' health and well-being was now part of the employment equation. And it was clear that as we sought to figure out what was next, the employer-employee relationship was already being reset.

In the traditional employment contract, employers typically control *where*, *when*, and *how* work is done, and in return, the worker is paid to execute the role according to these parameters. Clarity of job description, clearly allocated tasks, and non-negotiable ways of working were hallmarks of a good employment contract. However, at the end of this period of *working different*, after this period of intense innovation and employee introspection, workers started to value *different* things at work.

During this period, workers and their bosses worked in partnership (no one had more knowledge than the other about the virus, about the future), and they were galvanized behind a common purpose, that is, fighting the pandemic, keeping the lights on, learning and innovating together. This set a new tone for how people wanted to work. People wanted to be viewed as true partners. They made a conscious choice to give their time, skills, and knowledge, and they wanted it to count beyond just a paycheck. And a buoyant labor market gave voice to this ask.

Call them associates, affiliates, colleagues, collaborators—contributing to a firm emerged as the new mental model for how employees and contractors viewed the relationship with those who write their respective paycheck.

Contributors are not just part of the process; they're invested in the outcome. Instead of counting down the hours until end of the workday, contributors are busy figuring out what they can achieve before they end their day.

While contributors may be performing the same tasks as the employees before them, they expect more autonomy in how they do said tasks. Their input is heard—and, more often than not, taken to heart—which results in new levels of self-motivation.

Leading companies *get* this.

Those who were already on this path before the pandemic fared best. Take the global pharmaceutical firm Novartis, which, prior to the crises, had instigated a campaign to build an "un-bossed culture," a paradigm that essentially flipped the traditional employment model. Centered around "servant leadership" principles, this approach was based on enhancing leaders' ability to be inclusive and empower their workforce. Managers were to support their teams, rather than the other way around. Empathy was critical to making this work.[3] When Novartis needed to ramp up innovation and production of vaccines, it already had a culture based on curiosity, outside-in thinking, and innovation with its talent—or *associates*, as it calls its employees—ready to up their contributions and help solve the pandemic crisis.

Setting the Table

Team Mercer loves tables. All consultants do.

Figure 1.1 is one we particularly like, which shows 10 dichotomies between employees and contributors that we hear from our people and our clients.

Working in Partnership Is about Hearing, Not Listening

The buoyant labor market post-pandemic—and the job switching it sparked—certainly encouraged leaders to listen more; digital focus groups, pulse surveys, and workforce sentiment analyses all burst onto the scene in response. As the data came in, it was clear that many employees felt their companies didn't respect their lives outside of work, failing to appreciate the sweat, angst, and safety risks that workers endured through the pandemic. As the workforce made way for the next generation—one that really *got* digital working, breathed equity and inclusion, and learned at school to call out the bullies—it was clear that the old working habits and mindsets were no longer fit for purpose.

We needed to operate under a new paradigm. Welcome to The People Age!

As jobs became more complex and new technology tested everyone's adaptive capacity (and sometimes their patience), it

Employee mindset	Contributor mindset	People leader implications
I plan to progress in my career here for the next 10-plus years and I expect to be trained for my job.	I'd like to contribute for the next few years and learn valuable, transferable, skills along the way.	Motivation has moved from staying employed to remaining marketable. This increases the need to ensure learning occurs in the flow of work. Training for a new role, not just for their role today, is part of the new employment deal.
I'll fit in with the defined work pattern to oblige with the company's culture and shift outside commitments to make this work.	I want to bring my best self to work, and this means not working unsustainable hours and/or being able to work around my existing lifestyle commitments as necessary.	Moving from a sense of workplace obligation to an accommodating work/life schedule lessens the tension between work and non-work responsibilities, creating a stronger and more long-term commitment to work.
My worth is defined by my role and level at work. I expect perks and opportunities to reflect these achievements.	My worth is defined by my contribution. I want to be appreciated for the skills and experience I bring to the table on day one, and I expect to have access to the resources I need to deliver on my goals.	Determining the worth of employees based on tenure or status can lead to disengagement. Knowing what skills and abilities contributors bring to the table provides a better sense of each person's ability and drives a more future focused view of contribution.
I joined a company, and am part of a department/team, and I work for my boss to contribute to the company's success. I want to ensure I meet my job expectations.	I joined a brand and am motivated to contribute to a purpose. I want to do work I am proud of and meet our stakeholders' needs.	For a more inclusive workplace, focus on brand affinity and purpose, with defined success metrics for all stakeholders—customers, society, employees, not just shareholders
I expect to be compensated in line with my level in a way that is benchmarked to the job that I do, not how I do the job. I expect parity in my package.	I want to be recognized in a way that reflects my contribution to team achievements/outcomes and reflects what I value most (benefits, training, pay security, flexibility, etc.).	A reset is happening around how talent is recognized and rewarded. A one-size-fits-all rewards structure leaves individuals looking for greener pastures as we stick to programs we offer, rather than reward packages that excite.

FIGURE 1.1 Ten dichotomies between employee and contributor mindsets.
Source: Work Different: Bravery, Anderson, Bonic

Employee mindset	Contributor mindset	People leader implications
If I am a dedicated employee, who displays good citizenship behavior, and delivers solid performance, I will progress up the hierarchy which will lead to better pay prospects.	If I am a high performer with potential to contribute further, I will be given opportunities to realize my potential and will be incentivized to remain with the company.	It's vital to evolve the view that, "The only way is up." Climbing the proverbial ladder is not the goal for everyone, nor tenable in our flat, networked structures. Ensure a component of rewards is tied to skills and contribution and find opportunities to keep talent engaged and moving forward—even when they may want a change of pace.
Being a good employee means doing work you might not always agree with, or don't see the immediate value of—such work supports the hierarchy and is akin to paying your dues.	Don't give me busy work or boring work. Explain why we are doing what we are doing. I will then take responsibility for doing my work effectively and will ensure stakeholders are happy with it.	Design jobs to be more appealing by leveraging tech to replace repetitive tasks, enable options to contribute in ways beyond pure profit generation. Offering meaningful and engaging work will always help retain goal-orientated contributors.
As an employee I respect the expertise of my seniors and/or of tenured bosses and I defer difficult decisions for them to solve.	As a contributor, I recognize that expertise and coaching rests in multiple quarters. My role is to help decision makers make informed decisions. I expect to be empowered to make decisions within my array of competencies.	Today managers typically have less knowledge about a topic than their team members and are often time-poor, limiting their insight. Therefore, effective decision-making rests on efficient knowledge sharing and engagement.
Being a good employee means staying within the lines and emulating what my boss or my prior incumbent did before me. Stepping out of the norm typically means stepping up or out.	Contributors are clear about what they want to offer, when and how much. They come with diverse interests and skill sets and don't want to be boxed into a role.	Our preferences and skills are always evolving, and we might want to make different types of contributions at different times. Make it easy for people to contract for the volume of work to which they can commit and vary your engagement style toward them.
I separate work and life. I understand that to succeed here, I need to embrace the company/team culture and learn to "play the game." This is true even if I don't feel the culture or the companies' values fully align with my beliefs or allow me to be true to my authentic/whole self.	When I join a company/team, I want to play an active role in shaping its culture. I expect my opinions and suggestions to be acknowledged. I expect my company to use its power for good and I will be vocal (even externally) about how I am being treated and walk if my values are misaligned.	A culture constructed intentionally around diversity and inclusion is critical for innovation and reputation. Enabling employees' voice and individuality to shine through means that your culture is more likely to represent your customer profile and reflect the values of the times and the issues which resonate for your people.

FIGURE 1.1 (Continued)

was clear that knowledge was no longer residing at the top of the house. Traditional decision-making structures threatened to stymie corporate agility. To survive, organizations would need to operate as sensing organisms rather than hierarchical institutions. It was clear that organizations needed less directive leadership and less siloed working to keep up with the demands of a faster-paced working world born out of crises. At the same time, workers also needed clarity on direction, more accountable teams, and leadership that was centered around enablement. The prevailing sense was: *Yes, we survived the Pandemic Apocalypse, now give us a roadmap to Utopia.*

By way of example, as contributors showed interest in fully flexible work schedules, compressed work weeks, job-sharing programs, or various hybrid options, many companies listened and empowered their workers to make it happen. And that empowerment was *huge* because if contributors didn't believe their asks were being taken to heart, there would have been a heck of a lot less contributing.

At Mercer, we sought to listen, and our colleagues seemed happier and more productive with work-from-home options. But being a partner is not only about meeting employees on their terms—it's about working together for a shared outcome and about being honest as to which jobs lend themselves to different work models, all while being open to considering new ways to deliver results. An unexpected benefit of this listening practice and discussion of flex working was that it drove more conscious thought about where we spend our time, who we spend our time with, and an examination of how we work together asynchronously across temporal and physical boundaries.

But it was hard. Great cultures don't just emerge, they're intentionally designed, and they only stick with shared values and multiple discussions around ways of working and interacting. Like any good relationship, it takes work to go the distance. People who felt their companies were lagging on these new *a-ha's* sought to take their skills elsewhere, and those who stayed voiced their dissatisfaction. Employers around the world realized they'd better change things up and, if they hadn't already, become vastly more employee-friendly. They needed to take the lessons in empathy honed during the pandemic and give them solid form (metaphysically speaking) with more effective partnering skills for every people leader.

While we needed greater partnership and design thinking to solve problems at the height of the pandemic, we had differing views on how we should partner in the aftermath. Take the much-talked-about chasm in expectations around flexible working. In 2022, 66% of executives globally believed that work essentially gets done in the office, with 78% concerned about employees' ability to build solid interpersonal relations if these new practices remained.[4]

Employees, however, saw it differently, with 74% globally believing their organizations were more successful with remote/hybrid working, and 80% confirming that their teams collaborated well with a mix of remote and onsite contributors.[5]

Many leaders recognized this disconnect in outlooks immediately, while others sat on their hands. . .and the hand-sitters got burned. Look at what happened in the United States: According to the U.S. Bureau of Labor Statistics, the average employee turnover rate in 2021 was a staggering 47%, which included both voluntary and involuntary turnover.[6] In 2022, the cost of voluntary turnover set businesses back over $1 trillion.[7] And guess which industries were most impacted globally? According to LinkedIn data, it was Professional Services, so we at Mercer had a vested interest in figuring out a new way to partner.[8]

Don't get us wrong, we are not naïve *work-from-anywhere* advocates; we are champions of dialogue and testers of *the art of the possible*. Amid the economic headwinds in late 2023, the pendulum swung back again, and many organizations started bringing their people back into their work sites. The effects of large-scale virtual work are complex and not necessarily positive—cultural, learning, and engagement issues all sprung forth. The question is how leaders tackle these issues and preserve the opportunity that flexible work models can deliver for contributors, for organizational agility, and for companies' diversity and inclusion ambitions. The genie is already out of the bottle, and when digital-first workers combine with digital-first businesses, the true cost of turning our backs on this opportunity to work *different* will become more evident

Dancing to a Different Tune

Leading up to 2020, the working world was evolving in a more contributor-centric direction, albeit slowly. Social media ensured that accountability for bad practices went viral, and younger candidates asked questions about culture, diversity and skill development in their interviews. But the pandemic forced everyone to shift into high gear or be left in the dust.

We all learned through on-the-job training what was possible regarding new ways of working. It wasn't just employees' views that changed, executives also developed a more positive approach to their organizations' ability to adapt. The majority of workers thrived within this new paradigm, one defined by collaboration, empathy, and of course, pajamas.

Companies also learned that much of what we did at work could be done different. (More lousy, but strangely compelling, Steve Jobs-ian grammar.) For instance, a Mercer colleague in China told us that their normal two-day turnaround for a monthly report turned into just a few hours of remote collaboration, as necessity drove the team to uncover more efficient ways to handle the task, part of which was evaluating what stakeholders really valued from the report. Others found that with new technology, they could configure jobs differently, leveraging intermediates to relieve skilled workers and splitting jobs so that more junior people could step up and learn.

Further, we all came to realize that moving talent around to deploy their skills elsewhere wasn't a bad thing. Some of this was pandemic-induced, that is, French cosmetics giant LVMH pivoting from manufacturing high-end perfume to hand sanitizer.[9] And McDonald's in Germany loaned it's restaurant staff to the grocery chain Aldi while restaurants were forced to close or reduce their hours of operation.[10] But by 2023, just 7% of companies confirmed they were still part of a talent consortium, that is, sharing talent with other firms.[11] Not all innovations were adopted, but the seeds of new talent practices, such as talent marketplaces, were sown.

Finally, organizations learned that newfangled tech is moving things along quite nicely—both initially, with Teams, Zoom, and Slack changing how we share and collaborate, and later on, with Gen AI and Microsoft 365 helping us work smarter. It's becoming clearer by the day that a skilled workforce will leverage new technology across the firm, not solely where the tools were meant to be used, and the resulting boost to knowledge and creation will forever change how we contribute.

Steve Jobs would indeed be proud of everybody for figuring out just how *different* work can be.

More Ch-Ch-Changes

Throughout the 21st century, the unwritten contract between employers and their workforce has steadily evolved (see Figure 1.2). Traditionally, businesses' number-one goal for their contributors has been to *retain* them. Contributors have been seen as assets working under a transactional *Loyalty contract* in which pay, benefits, and security were exchanged for time and output, all of which were determined and dictated by the company.

That system was fine, but far from perfect. The need to increase workplace productivity while focusing on employee motivation morphed into an *Engagement contract* centered on achievement, camaraderie, and meaning. More than ever, employees were considered humans, not just assets to be optimized. In a perfect employer/employee relationship, that meant better pay, better benefits, and a better work experience. Employers had to buy into the notion that employee satisfaction was what retained talent, and a whole industry emerged to measure and drive up engagement levels.

What we saw before the pandemic was a break in this model. Engagement was becoming less and less of a driver of retention, and the pandemic quickened the pace toward what we call the

Evolution of the Psychological Contract at work

Past Focus: **Retain**	Past Focus: **Motivate**	Current Focus: **Recover**	Future Focus: **Energize**
Loyalty Contract (transactional)	**Engagement Contract** (work and workplace centered)	**Thrive Contract** (whole person consideration)	**Lifestyle Contract** (Lifex—life experience)
Basic needs: Pay, Benefits, Security	**Psychological Needs:** Achievement, Camaraderie, Meaning	**Well-Being Needs:** Purpose, Equity, Impact	**Fulfillment Needs:** Choice, Connection, Contribution
Workers are assets to be retained	Employees are assets to be acquired and optimized	**Human led, Technology enabled** People and machines work together for maximum value creation	**Human centered, Partnership built** People across the talent ecosystem partner to build sustainable systems
Pay and benefits in exchange for time and output	Broader set of rewards (pay, benefits, career, experiences) in exchange for organizational engagement	Healthy experiences in exchange for a commitment to organizational renewal	Total rewards that include flexibility and employability in exchange for continued relevance

FIGURE 1.2 Evolution of the psychological contract at work.
Source: Mercer

Thrive contract—an employment model anchored in purpose, equity, and impact. Employees demanded a healthier experience in exchange for a commitment to the organization's renewal. Concerns about equity, skills, and total well-being all took center stage during this period.

Working for the Weekend

As we started to rebuild following the years of introspection about work and lockdown frustrations, lifestyle issues were clearly on the rise. Health, well-being, and a greater respect for the whole person are now very much front and center. Mercer's research now confirms the emergence of a Lifestyle contract, an unspoken agreement about the trade-offs people will make. In 2022, one in three employees said they would sacrifice a pay hike for greater flexibility, one in three would trade additional days off, another 29% would take better benefits, and one in four would trade pay for time to focus on CSR (corporate social responsibility) activity.[12]

In 2022, Citibank hired analysts from the United Kingdom into an office in the south of Spain at half the starting salary that they would earn in London or New York.[13] Interestingly, the chance to live in a warm, sunny locale was not the primary motivator. Instead, the guarantee of not working weekends or more than an eight-hour day during peak periods was what made the deal a swipe-right offer. Respect for people's lives and enhanced employability in exchange for continued relevance is the new deal. What employees want in return for their time and energy has clearly changed. A just-good-enough paycheck, two weeks of vacation, and taco Tuesdays aren't enough to mitigate consistently unfulfilling, pressure-filled, 50-hour work weeks.

Research by Oliver Wyman shows that Gen Zers (people born between 1997 and 2012) are prioritizing their life and want to contribute in new ways. They want to work for companies that are focused on sustainability and said the opportunity to engage in socially responsible activity would motivate them to stay.[14]

Companies that are already engaging this group—in designing the future of work—are ahead of the curve. In 2023, 69% of companies report they are recognizing the whole person by building a culture where employees feel comfortable bringing their authentic selves to work.[15] And then there's the issue of *actual* rewards, as tacitly promised by the phrase *Total Rewards*. Does the individual who's in the office three days a week have a better chance at a promotion than a colleague who's fully remote, even if the latter is just as (or even more) productive? Again, no easy answer, our research findings suggest presenteeism matters. In 2022, 75% of HR worried that those who elected to stay remote would struggle to get promoted and 74% believed their manager would be incentivized to move remote workers onto freelance contracts.[16] Unfettered use of AI in talent decisions may also fuel this bias, as historical data favors full-time, onsite workers. Monitoring this type of adverse impact is partly why advocates demand that tech *informs* decisions, but does not *make* hiring or promotional decisions autonomously—a risk when bot delegation is so alluringly time-efficient.

And then there's the issue of upskilling. In 2022, one in three employees reported that the last time they wanted to learn a new skill, they were deterred by not having enough time during—or even after—work to dedicate to the process, and many just didn't see the payoff for this personal investment in terms of pay and promotion.[17] So, how can upskilling and training be worked into the *Lifestyle contract*? This is a relatively huge question because if you live for 100 years, that means you'll spend about 50 of them working, therefore we'll need to learn and relearn to support multiple career transitions—if only to keep us all engaged.

The emerging *Lifestyle contract* is taking a variety of forms depending on where people live, their financial realities, and what they value in life. The key is that it remains unbiased and prioritized around people first—their choices, their connections, and their contributions. Partnering to unpack these needs is an investment in the future of individuals that in the long run will increase retention, bolster job satisfaction, and significantly benefit businesses.

A Proposition You Can't Refuse

In building a people-centric business environment, a starting point is to ensure that your employee value proposition (EVP) resonates with your target contributors and differentiates your organization from the zillion others out there.

As a refresher, the EVP is designed to help organizations draw the attention of the talent they want to attract and galvanize their commitment once they've joined. Typically, an EVP might include information about compensation (comp), work/life balance, employee benefits, stability, career development, work environment, and company culture. Every company adds their own unique flavor to these statements or commitments as they strive to address the wishes, needs, and passions of their past, present, and future workforce. Long story short, it answers the potential employee's primary question: *Why the hell do I want to work here?*

A compelling and honest EVP lays the foundation for the Lifestyle Contract. As research from Gartner points out, "Organizations that effectively deliver on their EVP can decrease annual employee turnover by just under 70% and increase new hire commitment by nearly 30%."[18] In essence, the value proposition is the *promise* while the experience is the *reality*. And if the promise and the reality are as far apart as a catfisher and their picture on Tinder, you're in serious trouble.

One company that not only has a compelling EVP but has worked hard to counter its past reputation challenges is Nike. Nike is now seen by many as an innovative, worker-friendly, straight-up-cool entity. Their promise, *We see the power of sport to move the world,* is emblematic of their values around elevating human potential. What sets apart Nike is their commitment to creating an environment that is focused on equality, inclusion, empowerment, and respect; a mission that deeply resonates with their target population of engaged contributors, and one that the company fought hard to establish by revising their factory codes and leading the charge on sustainability.

A centerpiece of Nike's EVP is "Win as a team," a sentiment that all but defines the Nike vibe. The company culture emphasizes a team mentality for innovation. Benefits and compensation are approached with the same perspective. Employees get gym discounts, relocation benefits, competitive pay, retirement plans, advanced learning opportunities, and a 50% discount on Nike merch for themselves and their families. But it's the company's focus on the environment and worker rights that keeps them an employer of choice.

And then there's the British consumer goods company Unilever, which not only puts sustainability at the heart of their value proposition, but uses it as a rallying cry to inspire their employees to become leaders of change. Below are four pillars[19] designed to bring Unilever's EVP to life for their people:

1. **Purpose Power.** Unilever tells its people and prospects "this is more than a job"; it's an opportunity to follow their purpose while changing the world and the business for good.
2. **Be the Catalyst.** The firm urges its talent to explore, challenge the status quo, and be proactive to change the world.
3. **Brilliantly Different Together.** Here, the organization stresses the power of the collective, combining each individual's strengths and differences to make a bigger impact.
4. **Go Beyond.** Unilever positions itself as a haven of high-quality touchpoints that help contributors realize their full potential.

A Quick but Important Digression About Ch-Ch-Change

If our friend David Bowie were still with us, he might tell us that *change rests with the people*. If dissatisfaction with today (D) is coupled with a clear vision of tomorrow (V) and tangible first steps (F), our power to change can overcome any resistance (R) to new ways of working; this is the DxVxF>R change equation.[20] Companies that are made up of vibrant, diverse talents are likely to be progressive in welcoming in nontraditional talent and non-traditional ways to do work. Knowing who is joining, who is leaving, who is progressing, and who is stagnating can help leaders tackle those aspects of the work experience that don't live up to the EVP (the Vision), while helping to uncover critical first steps (F) to drive change.

It's not just about how many people are leaving or how long they're staying; it's about understanding *why* they go when they go, and *why* they don't come back. Knowing what different people want from the work experience is paramount, especially if we don't want to find ourselves out of people.

Between slowing population growth and protectionist migration policies, the future could be decidedly *out of people* if we limit our companies' attractiveness to those who are in our organizations today, or fail to address the blockers holding certain segments back from progressing, such as preventing their return to work through lack of childcare, targeted training or systemic biases. Leading a people-fueled business means being open to radically different talent models and looking at nontraditional hires. Cutting the need for apprentice hires to have a four-year college degree, double blind CV submission, and skills hiring are trends happening across finance, business management, engineering, and healthcare occupations, which is not only increasing job appeal and diversity, but is also changing managers' mindsets on who can do a job. Research by the Burning Glass Institute showed that between 2017 and 2019, employers in these sectors cut degree requirements for 46% of middle-skill and 31% of high-skill jobs.[21]

Businesses spend an incredible amount of time and money on understanding customers' preferences—why not spend a fraction of this to *x-ray* the workforce? Group them by shared interests, look at internal labor flows to see where you might have inherent biases in your policies and practices as well as where the EVP is not resonating for different groups of workers. Conducting listening exercises, and figuring out what they expect from their employer (as well as their thoughts on your labor market competitors) can help you be a swipe-right employer.

Creating internal labor flow maps is easy—taking action on what you learn is harder. The needs and concerns of young workers, remote workers, tenured workers, veteran workers, different ethnic and gender groups, and even workers in high-stress positions will differ. And different target groups will share different preferences, so while IT specialists might favor the latest digital tools and equipment, finance experts might prefer old-school software. Microsoft Excel, anyone?

What we really need to keep an eye on is underrepresented groups. Yes, you might be growing today, but think how much faster you could be growing if you didn't have a leaky pipeline, didn't lose talent at certain levels, improved knowledge sharing, or upped your attraction factor to vital untapped populations.

You're Gonna Hear Me Roar

"But Mercer," you might be saying, "I'm not an insights or marketing person. Who's funding this quest to get inside my dream candidates' head?"

Fair question. While we can't help you get buy-in (though you might make the case that it's an extension of market research), we can give you a head start. Here's what employees *really, really want* (see Figure 1.3), based on our Global Talent Trends research.

41%	Feeling valued for my contributions
39%	Work that fulfills me
34%	Having fun at work
32%	Feeling a sense of belonging
32%	Having a manager whom I trust/who advocates for me
31%	Being empowered/having autonomy to make decisions
31%	Abundant opportunities to learn new skills
30%	Being able to integrate my life with my work
30%	Working for an organization with a purpose I am proud of
29%	Having leaders who set a clear direction

FIGURE 1.3 What employees say helps them thrive at work.
Source: Mercer

People Leaders Beat Leaders of People

Great People Leaders appreciate the difference between managing a *person* and managing a *business*. Their focus is on ensuring that teams have what they need to succeed, that they're being treated fairly, and that they're gaining something from the work experience besides a paycheck. You can't do this without a cold hard look at your own biases and preferences.

Great People Leaders understand human behavior. They can balance economics and empathy when making decisions, an area that high-growth companies are consistently rated higher on in our research.[22] They're concerned not just about having the right number of people on the bus, but making sure the passengers are seated and comfortable.

Great People Leaders tap into what matters most to each individual, regardless of whether they are in a project role, expert role, or people manager role. They know what skills people bring to the table today and what they want to develop, and they have pretty honest conversations about what is possible in terms of opportunities and development. They champion the *Lifestyle contract* throughout the organization and play an important role in delivering on the EVP.

And companies with great People Leaders get more potential contributors to swipe right.

And swiping right, as you know, can lead to the love of your life.

People Leaders' Calls to Action (CTAs)

1. **Have a conversation around lifestyle goals**. It's easy to get locked into unsustainable work patterns, without stepping back and asking yourself or your team: What do I want in return for my contribution, and what are the tradeoffs I am prepared to make to meet my own lifestyle goals? Be honest about what roles, work schedules, and career paths can meet different worker's expectations.

2. **Cultivate an inclusive talent culture**. It takes work to build a vibrant team that nails cross-functional collaboration across various work patterns and work models. Team charters and ways of working all help, as does having one person focused on inclusion to call out blind spots. But nothing beats knowing your own biases and preferences, and how they inhibit contribution and progression in your team.

3. **Keep challenging your and others' worldview**. New generations bring a more gender-fluid outlook (one in 10 in the U.S. and U.K. identify as cisgender),[23] along with a more cognitively diverse perspective and a preparedness to challenge the status quo, especially on matters of equity, inclusion, and mental health. Don't miss out! Ensure that everyone in your business is exposed to the stories, insights, and ideas from your workforce, and that younger talent speaks up—reverse mentoring/shadow boards/coaching across demographic divides can all help.

Executives' and HR's Calls to Action (CTAs)

1. **Cultivate an EVP that resonates with future talent.** What people value is changing and the experience of work is evolving at breakneck speed. Map out critical experiences for various persona groups and validate these regularly against the reality of working at your firm. Talk to talent who don't take up an offer to join, and make it a habit to review social media and engagement comments about real work experiences.

2. **Double down on fun, flex, and futures**. Our research shows that workplaces that are able to deliver on the promise of an enjoyable work experience today and help contributors make a difference tomorrow are winning out. What this looks like by country and generation varies. Engage your workers to define what this looks like for them and their co-workers, and bake it into your promise and your reality.

CHAPTER 2

Stressed Out, Burnt Out, and Quietly Quitting

Anxiety.

Exhaustion.

Depression.

Unsustainable work habits.

Unrealistic work expectations.

One trillion dollars in lost productivity, yearly.[1]

Yes, this is a rough way to start a chapter, but there are people at your company who experience all of that on a daily basis due primarily to their job situation. Imagine how rough it is for them.

We're often asked if it's true that a notable percentage of workers across the world feel overworked, underappreciated, and undervalued. Unfortunately, from what we've seen—and we've seen a lot—the answer is a resounding *yes*. To that end, Mercer's research told us that workers' energy levels around the world dropped by 11% from 2019 to 2021. Perceptions of burnout risk rose from an already unpalatable 63% of workers globally feeling at risk pre-pandemic to a shocking 81% just two years later![2]

With one in two workers reporting that they feel exhausted on any given day, medical claims on the rise, and a significant proportion of workers failing to return to work from their long-term sick leave, it's clear that not all workers are thriving.[3]

The challenge, though, is that by the time we see signs of distress, it's often too late to turn it around.

Not good. Which begs the question: What are organizations getting wrong?

Has work really become such a health hazard, or are people just less resilient than before? Is this mental health crisis more evident simply because workers are speaking up more? Or is there something seriously wrong with our workplaces? Is there something managers are collectively missing?

The honest answer: it's all of the above.

We Did It to Ourselves and We Need to Fix It

Our new ways of working are certainly part of the problem. Yes, individuals became more enterprising and independent during the pandemic, which led to that *thinking different* we talked about, and that was fantastic. For others, however, the isolation of working at home, or the sheer fatigue of working multiple shifts, or the increased pace of remote work—compounded with the frustration of being pushed out of their comfort zone—added to an ever-growing mountain of stress, which was very much not fantastic.

Some disliked feeling that they had to be glued to their computers because if they missed a Slack message, bad things would happen.

Some disliked Zoom meetings because bosses and colleagues could see how messy their homes were; others, because staring into people's faces all day is taxing.

Some disliked the lack of meaningful contact remote working results in, something that we as human beings aren't (or at least weren't) used to.

Some disliked bearing the brunt of covering for their absent colleagues. Others resented having to return to their worksite.

Some disliked working unsustainable hours.

Pre-pandemic, the working world had boundaries and structures that had been the norm since, well, since work became *a Thing.* Suddenly, the norms went out the window, and we were all forced to rethink our lives, to take ownership of more work stuff than ever before. But not everyone was equipped to self-manage, nor did they have the space in their calendars to fully adapt.

No wonder so many people are fatigued. We're getting exhausted just writing about it.

Managers were at a loss on how or when to intervene: *Do I offer up a pep talk? Do I revamp their current position? Do I move them to a new position? Do I stop their work altogether?*

The challenge is that, on the one hand, we've been banging on about empowerment—"Hands off, managers, workers have got this"—and now we're saying, "Hey, managers, you need to lean in and fix this."

For individuals, if the support, input, and communication they need isn't forthcoming, stress only ramps up, increasing the chance of burnout and further disengagement. And it's not just about new ways of working or unsustainable work hours; these feelings also arise due to cognitive dissonance between what people believe in and what they are asked to do. This could be when that awesome EVP you've created is picked apart by a stressed-out boss, or the company narrative around inclusion or time off is not the day-to-day reality workers are living in.

The good news is that people are talking about mental health and workplace stressors more, 'fessing up to feelings that they're indeed drained, disillusioned, and at risk of burnout. This is progress, but also new ground for many people managers—from spotting issues, to talking about them, to effectively responding to personal and cultural issues that might be impacting a worker's mental health and well-being. Add to this the fact that many are tackling these issues with diverse teams that might be remote, hybrid, or new to work altogether, and this is very much a "today" problem.

And, as is the case with many today problems, there are no easy answers.

The Human Energy Crisis

You signed on to work a 40-hour week. But every week exceeds 50 hours. A few months of working longer hours, and double duty has now become the norm. All without a pay bump.

You signed on to be a coordinator. Two weeks after your first day, you were doing the job of two coordinators. Two months later, you were doing the job of a manager because they left and were not replaced. All without a promotion.

You work all week to get through your to-do list, but on Friday you've not gotten to any of the big items and feel overwhelmed. You need a minute (maybe two, maybe three) to breathe, to think, to be a human being, to be creative—and you're not getting it. All without any change in sight.

This. Is. Not. Sustainable.

This is why organizations, at the dawn of The People Age, are facing a Human Energy Crisis.

Truth be told, none of us should be surprised. How can contributors be expected to perform their best when they're wiped out, frustrated, and wanting (read: deserving) a long-sought-after break or raise? We see it, we know it, and we need to do something about it.

The Human Energy Crisis in question came about from the combination of new ways of working that have not yet been fully adopted, and old ways of working that have not been effectively abandoned (i.e., "Why am I getting the same document via Outlook, Teams, *and* Dropbox all at once?") as well as a lag in moving to a more human-centric work environment. All the while this creates an unsustainable cognitive load, typically on top of a tall set of goals and a never-ending to-do list. In other words, some contributors are *losing their mojo* because they can't get behind remote working and digital collaboration, while others are *going mojo-free* à la Austin Powers due to those extended work weeks and unpaid, unacknowledged pseudo-promotions.

Many people have flagged this mess as an unhealthy feature of the modern digital workplace, an illustration of unresolved tension between the new school and the old school. Think of it as a rap battle between the Sugarhill Gang and Drake—except that the Sugarhill Gang wants to work a solid 9-to-5 gig so they have time to hippie to the hip-hip-hop (and they don't stop), while Drake doesn't want to deal with the 60-minute commute to his office because he won't have time to do one dance before he goes.

Microsoft found that since the start of the pandemic, the length of the typical workday increased more than 13%, while after-hours and weekend work is up 28% and 14%, respectively.[4] The pandemic opened up flexibility as to how, when, and where people work and accelerated digitalization, but if we're not careful, these innovations will further feed this crisis. But even if our work hours are sustainable, complexity, constant learning, and an underlying psychological fear of not keeping up are wearing us all down.

The Human Energy Crisis calls for a new kind of workplace sustainability. An increasing number of companies are taking that to heart by experimenting with such concepts as no-meeting Fridays, a four-day work week, and using direct polling or passive data to get real-time checks on energy levels. They're also ensuring that large transformation projects are fed into their workforce planning models to forecast the impact of these initiatives on various teams' capacities, allowing them to staff up and/ or look at new ways to pace and deliver their projects.

Speaking on the Human Energy Crisis, Cathryn Gunther, Global Head of Associate Health at Mars Inc., said, "Mars. . .views energy as an output of holistic health. What is special about Mars—that I've not seen in many other companies—is this intentional focus [we have] on individual and team energy. Mars data shows that our associates' energy is strongly related to engagement and job satisfaction, and that high-energy managers lead more engaged teams."[5] Mars utilizes a signature program called Energy for Life, which originated in the Johnson & Johnson Human Performance Institute.[6] The program asks associates to stop and think about their purpose in life. It teaches people how to build energy management practices across the four domains of energy (physical, mental, emotional, and spiritual) to help associates bring their best selves to the office. Making the link between personal motivations and passions and the mission of the firm makes sense, but you can love your job and still be exhausted at the end of the workday.

Perceptions of exhaustion and thriving, of course, are not mutually exclusive, but if we don't address work habits that are no longer serving us well—especially those that deplete our energy—we won't create the healthy work environments that inspire and retain our talent. We now have a responsibility to look at how sustainable our workplaces and work habits really are. The good news is that many are waking up to this call. In 2023, 37% of HR leaders said they were working to redesign work with well-being in mind (e.g., realistic workloads, no-meeting days, reduced complexity, positive work environment, a culture of trust, and more). Progress, yes, but what about the other 63% of companies?[7]

A Quick Science Lesson, Part 1: Energy Is Finite

The laws of science tell us that physical energy is a finite resource. So, too, is workforce energy. People get fried, so it would stand to reason that work teams get extra crispy.

That all being the case, we can be more deliberate in how we deploy talent and in addressing what saps workforce energy. It takes a concerted effort to keep contributors happy and productive, and that means figuring out what's getting in the way. The challenge is that as many businesses become hyper-localized and launch projects in isolation, they sometimes fail to realize how these new projects tax employees' time, from emails, to learning new tech, to broader transformation projects for which they might volunteer. And this complexity is not easing off. Solving this requires organizations to treat energy as the finite resource it is, and better anticipate stress and pressure, and to be empowered to act when they sense trouble.

Through this energy lens, it becomes clear that the post-COVID return-to-work preoccupation with counting *badge swipes* misses a critical point: Physical presence alone doesn't lead to equal or better performance. Equal to, if not *more* important than people returning to a physical workplace, is bringing people back *emotionally*. We've been in firefighting mode for way too long. We need to find our way back to a more sustainable mode of working.

A Quick Science Lesson, Part 2: The Perma-Crises Mindset

And speaking of firefighting. . .

In 1999, NASA's unmanned Mars Climate Orbiter was charred to a crisp in the Martian atmosphere. NASA basically wasted $125 million on the project, and hundreds of scientists, engineers, and leaders saw their reputations destroyed.[8]

In a *Harvard Business Review* article entitled "Stop Fighting Fires," Robert Bohm wrote, "The crash was traced to a simple communication problem—one engineering group used metric units of measurement; another used imperial units—but that explanation masks a more complex underlying problem. Root cause analysis of the orbiter crash holds lessons that have never been more relevant than today."[9]

According to a NASA report published shortly before the crash, the early Mars Climate Orbiter project subcontractor's workforce numbers was substantially smaller than planned. This led to delays as well as a cascade of poor technical decisions. To catch up, engineering staff numbers were boosted by borrowing from other projects that were in their early phases. Engineers worked 70-hour weeks to meet deadlines, a factor that likely caused more errors in the short run and declines in effectiveness in the long run. Early warning signs of catastrophe were missed or ignored. An investigative report after the crash implied that the navigation error that caused the crash could have been corrected with what rocket scientists call a contingency burn.[10] That's a fancy name for a test run—but a decision on whether to perform the burn was never made because of the crush of other urgent work, what Bohm called "firefighting."

"Sometimes even a well-managed organization slips into firefighting mode temporarily without creating long-term problems," Robert Bohm, writing in the *Harvard Business Review* explained. "The danger is that the more intense firefighting becomes, the more difficult it is to escape from."

Fast-forward to today. One of the modern workforce challenges is an increasingly prevalent perma-crisis (or perma-firefighting) mode that has taken hold in many organizations. We're moving at a much faster pace than ever before, and this is wearing, but also we are not equipped to make good decisions under these conditions.

There are greater expectations from investors, a constant influx of new *enabling* technology, and the simple truth that many of us just don't have the skill set or experience to prepare accordingly. Predicting the impact of multiple risks in a BANI world—that's brittle, anxious, nonlinear, and incomprehensible—is a challenge, which is why some managers have given up on longer-term planning altogether.[11] We've certainly fallen out of the habit, and this muscle has atrophied. As a result, *everything* is urgent. Higher stress and depleted energy in the workforce are the results of constantly putting out blazes. Thing is, most of these fires aren't really conflagrations, just sparks that require a spritz of water rather than a fire hose, six firefighters, and a bunch of axes.

To mitigate this bad habit, we first need to get back to basics. Good objective setting and goal cascading can help. These are core levers for executing business strategies, but too often this process is poorly executed. Robust expectation-setting and risk assessments, as well as defining the RACI (who is Responsible, Accountable, a Contributor, Informed) at the beginning of project kickoffs, can lead to greater alignment to departmental goals—especially when they come with honest conversations about the need to balance financial metrics (i.e., revenue, profit, or cash flow) with human capital metrics (i.e., well-being indicators, absences, hours worked, or untaken paid time off) on scorecards. Constantly reacting, especially if stimulated only by the investor and executive perspectives, is a recipe for living in a perma-crisis. If we want more sustainable work and more human-centric workplaces, we need to stop firefighting.

Go Easy on Me

As Adele famously sang, "There ain't no room for things to change when we're both so deeply stuck in our ways." So, who's responsible for this situation? Workers? Managers? Leaders?

And more to the point, are our wellness interventions making a difference or adding to our workers' to-do lists?

Whatever your thoughts on these questions, the fact is there's something in our cultures and organizations that is driving people to need more personal days, more sick leave, more time out.

Younger generations are more willing to talk about mental health problems (good news) and managers are more alert to the issues (also good news). But the harsh reality is that stress is amping up healthcare costs, there's immense pressure on budgets due to health inflation, and there's an estimated $1 trillion in lost productivity each year due to absences and rising benefit premiums.[12] We *all* need to take action.

And there is a range of factors adding to the mix. In Europe and around the world, a prolonged cost-of-living crisis caused a squeeze on household incomes, sparking worries about being able to cover the bills, make mortgage payments, and fund retirement. This hit the most vulnerable the hardest. And more recently, many young people have begun asking if the value of education is worth the debt they would incur.

In Asia we saw the Tang Ping, a vote against unsustainable hours in China, influence the desirability of companies. But despite the youth advantage that many South Asian nations still had in 2023, the impact of an aging workforce in countries such as Japan, China, and South Korea fueled urgent talks about providing healthcare and funding retirement.

In the United States, a strong labor market clouded other signs that American workers were not well and that the days lost to productivity were on the rise. Rates of anxiety, depression, and burnout in 2023 were all at all-time highs, despite the pandemic being behind us, and labor participation rates that year were lower than pre-pandemic levels.

In South Africa, the unemployment rate in Q1 of 2022 was 35%, and was much worse for those aged 15–24 (64% unemployed). While graduates enjoyed a relatively lower unemployment rate, the biggest driver of joblessness was discouragement—many young people have "lost hope of finding a job that suits their skills" or ability to commute, according to Statistics South Africa.[13] Wherever you turn, angst, work-related stress, money worries, and various reactions to these stressors are mounting.

The Link Between Stress and Performance

At the 2021 Summer Olympics in Japan, the world watched as gymnastics legend Simone Biles withdrew mid-competition. She had a case of what sports pundits refer to as "the twisties," the gymnastic version of *the yips*, a phenomenon that messes with an athlete's ability to nail something they've done on the field a zillion times. In Biles's case, that meant she couldn't properly see the floor while twisting in the air, thus a proper landing—or even sticking a *safe* landing—became nearly impossible due to her mental state.

We all know that stress is subjective, personal, and complicated. What stresses you out might spur performance in your co-worker. As we've seen in sports and in the workplace, the same situation can drive one person to peak performance and cause another to freeze. When one person succumbs to stress, the physical and psychological demands on the rest of the team increase as they shoulder the demand/supply gap. The team-wide stress level can increase and create a group of under-producing, bummed-out contributors. Add to this incessant news stories of escalating world events, and the effort required to keep our heads above water during the cost-of-living crisis and the new work agenda, and it all wears us down.

In other words, stress can be contagious.

Increasingly, things like uncertainty, change fatigue, picking up the slack for other team members who themselves are stressed, balancing multiple roles (such as being a parent or taking care of elderly relatives), working excessive hours, adapting to new ways of working, coping with digital fatigue, and being available 24/7 can lower morale, create a toxic environment, and undermine performance.

All that said, a healthy amount of arousal can spur some on to greater performance. According to Mercer's own workplace health expert, Wolfgang Seidl, "[Some] individuals thrive on having enough stress to keep them engaged, and stress provides signals that one is growing in their career."[14] Remember that delicate balance we need to strike to feel like we are thriving?

But prolonged stress alters our mood, which can lead to burnout. In our study into the drivers of burnout, despite men and women citing pay as the top aggravating factor, women also blamed an increased workload and an inability to juggle work and life as the next-highest causes of frustration.[15] Men, on the other hand, cited the loss of their network as they embraced new ways of working, and a growing sense of inequity at work as drivers for their mental health concerns. Clearly, how we respond to and support workers' needs should look different for different contributors. Ivan Ivanov, head of Occupational and Workplace Health at the World Health Organization (WHO), cites workplace practices and poor job design as contributing factors to this rising healthcare epidemic. In a global health panel hosted by the WEF, he shared, "We cannot treat people with cognitive behavioral therapy, antidepressants, and clinical care and then return them to the same work environment that made them sick. This is absolutely ineffective—and a waste."[16]

Many other stress-related issues were apparent before the pandemic, and many were simply tolerated. Some such as fear of missing out (FOMO) at work were exacerbated by job uncertainty. Many are deeply rooted in hierarchical models of work, with tenure-based notions of promotion and what it takes to get ahead. This often revolves around a belief that going above and beyond will accelerate career trajectories, help secure promotions, drive pay increases and result in a state of fulfillment from work success. And while a strong work ethic and self-discipline is commended, work at the expense of a fulfilling life. . .well, maybe not so much.

There has to be another way to work—another way to live.

When It's More than Just Stress

According to the WHO, "[Burnout] results from chronic workplace stress that has not been successfully managed." It adds that increased mental distance from one's job and related feelings of negativity or cynicism and/or reduced professional efficacy are characterized by feelings of energy depletion or exhaustion.[17] (It's worth noting that the WHO only recognized burnout as an occupational issue in 2019.) Signs they suggest we all watch out for include an emotional loss of control, fatigue, feeling down all the time, social withdrawal, lack of appetite, and feelings of hopelessness. They also flagged that Emotionally Sensitive People (ESPs) experience these factors more readily and have to be hyper-vigilant with regard to trigger situations. So, what are these burnout triggers we all need to know? And how can we help our people to stay on the right side of the arousal curve?

The new world of work has impacted and accentuated many stressors. Studies show, for example, that many of us feel work has intensified as we've condensed our commute time, with some of us using those minutes (or hours) of transportation that were baked into our workday for, y'know, *work*. That means an eight- or nine-hour workday becomes a 10- or 11-hour workday, and that usually doesn't come with a pay bump.

Unless we properly reward our workforce on every level, we might find ourselves without a quality workforce to reward. The Maslach Burnout Inventory (MBI) highlights six underlying factors that can cause burnout—the following are some thoughts on their implication for people managers worried about burnout.[18]

MBI Burnout Factors	Mercer Recommendations
Workload	Check in regularly with team members to see if expectations are manageable; establish ways for people to flag when workloads unexpectedly rise. Build skills around project management and self-awareness. Ask questions on workload in your engagement surveys. Watch out for poor prioritization, delegation, and perfectionism.
Perceived lack of control	Look at the balance between predictable work and unexpected requests. Build skills around boundary setting and scope creep. Ensure no one is an island and designate buddies as needed. Watch out for decision-making that overlooks the downstream impact on others' workloads and pressures.
Lack of reward and recognition	If others are not feeling valued, consider how to make their work recognized and their contribution more visible to others. Build skills around empathy and gratitude across the team. Watch out for people who fail to utilize or take up rewards and time off effectively.
Poor relationships	Audit your, and your team's, significant work relationships in terms of quality and frequency of interaction. Build skills around stakeholder management. Watch out for partnership patterns where a lack of trust or respect is pulling down team energy or morale.
Lack of fairness	Consider how members in similar roles are treated, especially with regard to opportunities and airtime. Build skills around performance management, transparency of work, and team accountability. Watch out for times when praise or accommodations favor some members, but not others.
Mismatched values	If you feel that values and beliefs are misaligned with the way the organization makes decisions, speak up and be part of the change. Build skills in value-based leadership and reconfirm the reason why team members are being brought together.

*Source: **Work Different**: Bravery, Anderson, Bonic*

I'm Fired Up and Tired of the Way That Things Have Been

The guys from Imagine Dragons is not the only one reflecting what the masses are thinking. Bryan Creely has been pretty vocal, too. Creely spent several years as a corporate recruiter until he was laid off in 2020 and became a career coach—and, as he puts it, "to live more worry-free and independently."[19] In 2022, he dropped a TikTok video in which he discussed a phenomenon called Quiet Quitting: a worker putting in the job's minimum requirements, and no more.

The video garnered over 400 million views, clearly resonating with generations of frustrated workers. (For what it's worth, Quiet Quitting begat Bare Minimum Monday. No need to explain that one, right?) It put an exclamation point on a new workplace trend and had many more people than ever thinking *there's more to life than going above and beyond in my job.*

To elaborate, Quiet Quitting is not physically leaving one's place of employment, but rather leaving it emotionally. The gist of it is that workers choose to no longer do anything more than what they're specifically expected to do in their jobs. And with Gallup estimating that half of U.S. employees are already close to Quiet Quitting, we'd all better listen.[20]

Quiet Quitting questions the unwritten employer-contributor contract and asks: *Why should I go above and beyond what I was hired to do with no greater remuneration and/or recognition?* (Translation: *What's in it for me?*) This often stems from situations where the psychological work contract has been broken. Countless people went above and beyond during the pandemic period, and willingly so. While some have thrived taking this approach, and even learned new skills, many have not seen adequate recognition, reward, or reciprocation for their efforts. Yes, we all stood outside of our doors on a Thursday night in the United Kingdom in 2021 and clapped for our National Health Service (NHS) workers, but did it help them secure a pay raise in 2022? The strike that spilled into 2023 would sadly suggest not.

The actual *extra* work is also a point of consideration, as workloads vary greatly.

But workers do wonder if they're doing somebody else's work.

They wonder if they're expected to take over for someone who left the company or is on leave, and if so, are they doing so without a pay increase?

They wonder if they're wasting their time with busy work rather than something that adds value to the company or their resumes.

Mercer's Melissa Swift suggests organizations take a searching look as to where they might be encouraging performative work. In her book *Work Here Now: Think Like a Human and Build a Powerhouse Workplace,* Swift says, "It's worth auditing everything you do to make sure you're not unconsciously egging on performative work, either through your own behavior or through what you reward. Are you giving higher performance ratings to people who schedule meaningless meetings to show off? Are you over-reporting to your own bosses? It's often striking how much performative work can be stopped simply through one individual in a leadership role calling out their own counterproductive behaviors."[21] Even before Creely came up with the label, workers had been Quietly Quitting for years and no one was any the wiser. And if a worker could get the job done with minimal effort (and without anyone noticing), well, good for them. But ever since Tim Ferriss made the case for a shorter work life in his 2007 book *The 4-Hour Workweek,* the globalization and uber-delegation it takes to get there have drawn criticism. People are questioning where the work really gets done in organizations, and whether AI and automation have truly added capacity and expertise. Other contributors are changing their approach to work by taking a stand against what they see as unreasonable requests or untenable work cultures. Some folks are not Quietly Quitting over being assigned extra tasks (the genesis), but rather because they believe they've been treated unfairly, disrespected, ignored, or overlooked. Sound familiar? Call it stress, exhaustion, burnout, or Quiet Quitting: The antecedents of these phenomena are incredibly similar. These are all just different ways of pulling back to protect oneself in the new world of work. And depending on people's personality profiles, some will withdraw, some will push against, and some will develop other physical or mental health symptoms.

It's Okay to Not Be Okay

For years, mental health issues in the workplace went unacknowledged and/or ignored, especially in markets where presenteeism is valued and/or with lower labor protection. Stress is often stigmatized because it created discomfort among workers and managers, most of whom had little-to-no understanding of its consequences; but it also went unmentioned because people were scared of the impact on their careers, for example, being seen as *not cutting it*, or not being considered for important projects and promotions.

Most companies now boast a workforce that isn't afraid to speak up. But like generations before, this openness will be closed off if corporate cultures slide back to the macho attitude that there are those who cut it, and those who don't.

Due in part to the pandemic—when we were all stressed the hell out—mental health found its way into C-suite conversations at companies around the globe. Today, leading organizations are making mental health and well-being a key pillar of their workforce strategies, and it's about time.

Take Dell Technologies. Dell's brain trust saw the need for mental health support for their workers, especially outside the United States, where over half of their team members resided. The company piloted localized and personalized solutions within their existing international employee assistance programs (EAPs). They kicked it off in Singapore and Malaysia, where an analysis of Dell's medical claims history found that while workers were similarly impacted by burnout and stress, fewer reached out for support compared to workers in other countries.[22]

So what would motivate contributors to utilize the resources available? The company focused on four key areas:

1. Reduce the stigma associated with mental health.
2. Raise awareness of the importance of emotional well-being.
3. Provide a comprehensive program.
4. Ensure the program was readily accessible to all.

Digital by nature, Dell turned to technology. It built a solution around local needs in multiple languages that integrated with Dell's existing benefits ecosystem. By combining preventive care (i.e., digital self-care sessions and virtual coaching sessions) with critical care (i.e., immediate clinical support when necessary), Dell elevated the visibility and importance of mental health, making it a crucial element of its people strategy just as vital as any other aspect of its benefit program for workers.[23]

It's understood by many that mental health issues, along with all aspects of well-being—financial, social, physical—need to be front and center in The People Age, especially given the time we spend at work and the cost to individuals and the organizations if we get it wrong. There is now a higher duty for managers and co-workers to be vigilant for signs of stress and distress, listening for changes in tone and sentiment, and being ready to take action.

Thing is, not everyone is prepped for this responsibility.

A manager at an insurance firm with whom Mercer works observed, "I've never had so many staff out on mental health leave and this is putting pressure on the rest of the team. What I worry about is that when we fully remove people from the workplace for prolonged periods of time, we struggle to bring them back. We need to intervene earlier and partner around alternative options such as part-time working, gig arrangements or job sharing. We need to actually redesign our jobs and get better at prioritization and flagging when people struggle. We are just not good at having these discussions."

It's The People Age, folks. It's time to get good at those discussions.

The Calm After the Storm

Burnout, exhaustion, Quiet Quitting, the Human Energy Crisis, and the perma-crisis all share two things in common.

- They're all the result of an increased cognitive and emotional load.
- They're people-centric issues demanding a people-centric response.

This isn't easy—paradigm shifting never is—but we all need to recognize that the new world of work requires active work redesign, stress vigilance, and constant work renegotiation as we explore various models of flexibility and remote working. We certainly aren't there yet, but on the plus side, data and tech can nudge us in the right direction. We need more intentional work to get our employee experience back into a healthy place.

While there are no clear-cut, one-size-fits all solutions to any of these problems, the seven trends that follow are what we see leading firms following in the quest to make well-being a right, rather than a privilege:

1. **Identify unsustainable work practices and take action on the root cause.**

    Many companies know where they have risk exposure to stress-related illnesses from turnover rates, longer work hours, and from targeted questions in their engagement studies. When that's the case, speaking to workers about their experience is a good place to start.

    A Big Four professional services firm came to Mercer with just such a challenge. For one of their critical departments, we reviewed where and how value was being created in the team and specifically who was doing the work. Then we explored how the work was getting done, what could be augmented by tech, and what might be better done by other contributors—inside or outside the firm, all in service of a vision to return workers to what they did best (often what they studied for or why they joined in the first place). We then audited the prevailing work culture and supported a cultural change program to address those work habits that were getting in the way of efficient, asynchronous collaboration.

A combination of increasing work intensity, an unsustainable percentage of time spent on performative tasks such as reporting and presenting, and a relentless work culture all made many of the jobs challenging for even the best and brightest to succeed at. A total work redesign and a resetting of cultural norms not only brought joy back to the team, but it also helped people in these roles see a sustainable pathway to promotion—one that didn't risk their health. There were costs to automate parts of the job, redistribute the work, and reset goals, but the impact on retention has been a significant off-set.

2. **Manage energy as you manage budgets, with forecasting and discipline.**

   New initiatives, learning new tech, and unforeseen events all get layered onto workloads and sap our energy. Left unchecked, we go down the spiral. Improving objective-setting and *go/no go* decision-making, especially around new initiatives and transformation asks, can make a huge difference. Setting aside a fund to help teams manage absence-related shifts in workload, as well as capacity constraints, can also help mitigate near term energy issues and stress-related risks. Robust Capital Expenditure (CapEx) and Operational Expenditure (OpEx) processes that take into account the downstream implications of signing-off on new projects is also critical. And if the impact is unknown, formalized *test and learn* pilot teams can take project-based work offline or evaluate what resources will be needed for a successful enterprise-wide deployment later. This tactic allows robust workforce planning practices (both strategic and operational) to offset capacity and bandwidth limitations.

   One financial institution utilized a dynamic workforce planning platform to enable managers on a quarterly basis to reevaluate the upcoming load on their people. This enabled them to not only map changes in the demand drivers of their business (external) and see how these played out on their talent supply (given internal turnover and absence rates), but it also enabled them to model the potential impact of broad transformation plans on their people's capacity.

When executives saw the systemic bottlenecks and potential breaking points within under-resourced departments, they opened a discussion on the use of *always-available* contingent pools and better planning for projects at an enterprise-level, rather than loading up busy teams. One executive commented that just seeing the real-time impact of proposed projects on workforce capacity changed his view on project priorities. Companies are filled with smart people, and everyone's project in isolation has a sound business rationale; it's the aggregated impact of these siloed decisions that can turn bad if not checked.

3. **Know what motivates your people and make redesigning the employee experience (EX) a priority.**

Contributors have made it clear that they want purpose, belonging, and a healthy work environment—both emotionally and physically. They want psychological safety, flexibility, and transparency under good economic conditions. (A fat paycheck wouldn't hurt either.) Respect for their time, good meeting etiquette, sustainable workloads, and ways to voice their expectations are also high on the list for a winning EX. And moral burnout can occur if the grind outweighs the give.

If we want to inspire the next generation in our workplaces, we need to redesign workplaces around their diverse needs and interests, tackling head-on what demotivates and disengages them. This means paying attention to values and culture; this means identifying the moments that matter in a worker's life; this means building a value proposition that is both sustainable and equitable. We can't do this without being honest about what gets in the way. One manufacturing firm admitted that they introduced 22 new tech processes during an 18-month period. It was no surprise that many leaders described "managing" at the firm as a burden, rather than a privilege. What many of these tech enhancements effectively did was pass work from internal teams, like finance and HR, directly onto managers. Yes, this increased self-service but it also transferred a time load to do these tasks. Treating managers as clients of these internal groups and defining their desired interaction with experts and technology changed the game, leading to some features of the tech being turned off and some activities being returned to human teams to better engage their human workers.

4. **Cut the chatter so we can focus on the conversation.**

To make this new order of work feasible, we need to embrace the modern workplace rather than force the old world of work onto digital platforms. What we know about the digital natives entering our workforce is that they want to *work different*. They don't use email like previous generations, they don't use social platforms as punctuated events, they don't consume media in the same manner—heck, they don't even use emojis in the same way. They might, however, use quips like "Okay, Boomer" to call attention to these differences. In the workplace, everyone needs to get on the same page.

Cutting through the noise will take communication channels and strategies ... channels that work across generations. This is still very much a work in progress, but being clear on which channels to use, good content architecture, and internal communication protocols will ease the pain of these transitions.

Making change stick requires rules and direction to be embraced by leaders *and* workers on the ground. This structure helps foster a culture that's geared toward defining the most logical channels of communication, sharing the rationale so people can make informed decisions around which systems to use (and when) and for which purpose. Digital collaboration communities are not broadcast communities, collaborative workspaces aren't content repositories, and benefit portals aren't the same as mobile apps in helping you choose the right benefits, which aren't the same as face-to-face knowledge-sharing on what's right for you—but all have their place. Lack of attention to channel strategy, and to where digital aids can really help, not only adds to the exhaustion that people feel but prevents us from bringing the true power of our people and our people offerings to the fore.

Contributor input is critical, but flexing for *everyone's* preferences will have us all pinballing between countless apps and forums all day just to keep up. One pharmaceutical firm found a better use of people's time by embracing *radical simplification* across all internal processes and functional policies. As part of this shift, the company set guidelines for meetings and rules for training length, and strengthened their internal communication strategy. The HR team cut lengthy policy statements by two-thirds and demanded the same from their business partners.

Another company doesn't record meetings on designated *in-office* days so that people cannot dial in or listen from home. They have found that this change, along with sending pre-reads in advance, results in their time together being spent on high-quality conversations and decision-making. And a third company cuts all standing meetings each year so they can be intentionally reset (or sunset) if needed.

5. **Tackle ways of working between team members, and make time for tech adoption.**

When it comes to determining how and where to spend work time, we all need to better our intentions. This often demands a close look at our companies' working habits as well as our own. The good news is that in a data-driven world, professionals often have many opportunities to reassess how they work. From activity reports in Microsoft Viva to feedback on our schedules from Gen AI tools to old-school DIY timesheet reviews, there are several ways to figure out where and how we spend our time—and if we might want to work different in the future.

Addressing persistent team-based work stressors, helping contributors voice their concerns, and setting boundaries are all especially critical now that the walls of traditional workdays and meetings have come down.

A Mercer employee commented, "Our biggest issue on the team is that some members are using new digital tools to collaborate, while others are persistently emailing decks and working offline. This makes the rest of us work double time and some members feel they are doing other people's admin chores as they put offline work back into online systems."

Formalized processes for informal communication, agreed-upon tools for collaboration, and innovation are all key. Just as critical is ensuring that peers respect and hold each other accountable for keeping team members informed and delivering quality outcomes.

6. **Role model healthy work habits and create a climate where workers can manage their lives and get to know others socially.**

As we transition from the old world of work to the new, we need to take a holistic look at well-being and be honest about how well we role model what we say on this topic.

Much of the stress and anxiety in today's work environment is fueled by social isolation and a reduced sense of belonging. For the most part, these feelings were brought about by remote working, but these are continuing as we put the brakes on travel and meetings. Just because we can work independently, remotely, asynchronously, doesn't mean it's the best approach for the task at hand, nor for laying good partnering foundations.

Anxiety and a reduced sense of belonging are also appearing in agile teams—especially with young talent who might struggle to master their trade as they flit from opportunity to opportunity. Socializing can be a tonic for collaborating with people who have different work styles, and active buddying can counter the loss that often comes with new work models and role switching. But people need a *home*, be it a team with a shared purpose, a functional or professional allegiance, and/or a people manager/coach who is personally invested in their career.

A good number of companies are finding that returning to the office is restoring some of the structure of work that some colleagues have craved, and it's having a positive impact on contributors' mental health. Other firms are finding that *flexing loudly*—encouraging staff to be clear when they need to pick up the kids, or when managers are taking time to go to the gym—has set a new tone for what's acceptable as *time off* and how to do it. For those that are heavily hybrid or remote, ground rules are helping. And let's not forget the four-day workweek that many employers are testing to off-set stress and restore energy.

What is becoming clearer is that we often don't know what we've given up, nor what we are missing out on as we evolve our work habits. One company is mandating that new hires work their first three months entirely in the office before they adopt any new work modes, so that they can build their networks, assimilate into the company culture, and figure out how they can balance their mental, social, and physical well-being needs, both at home and in the workplace.

7. **If you want a human-centric work environment, co-create with humans.**

While flexible schedules and remote work are significant aspects of the new work world, finding creative solutions to new challenges is at the crux of this renewal. Business as usual gets stale after a while, and workers want to be part of a company that embraces and runs with new initiatives. One hairdressing chain is closing at five o'clock on a Saturday, their busiest day, to see if they can return more time to workers, especially in the summer months. It's an experiment, and if their associates can bring in clientele earlier in the day to offset the loss, they will keep these *summer hours*. Companies that are constantly listening to requests from those who are new to the organization, new to the business world, or hail from spheres outside their typical field of vision—and engaging them in co-creating the future of work together—are already ahead of the curve.

People are attracted to, and remain with, companies that have a reputation for treating their workers well. Young talent is not going to put up with the work climate of the past, nor should they. They want to see equal attention to matters such as palatable work hours, decent jobs, and an investment in employees as human beings.

When the real experience of working for a company is discussed openly on Glassdoor and social media, businesses cannot afford to lose prospective hires because they read an angry post from a disgruntled employee about how lousy the company is.

Now is the time for leaders and employers to use all of the tools at their disposal to create and maintain a thriving, people-focused workplace. And we have the tools, from apps that help us evaluate how work gets done today to methods for redesigning work in light of how AI, automation, and a contingent workforce might relieve pressure and further improve how work gets done. We have tools that help us listen to our workforce and evaluate work patterns and stress indicators to help us intervene early when well-being (and productivity) is at risk. We have well-being apps and on-demand EAP systems for support. We are not lacking the tools, but we are sometimes hesitant to open Pandora's box. Yet the mere fact that we needed to write this chapter is a sign that the box is bursting, and these are some of the most important conversations to have.

And we don't know about you, but we're ready to quit the Quiet Quitting.

People Leaders' CTAs

1. **Stress and exhaustion need airtime and action**. Talk to your team about stress, encourage self-reflection on work habits, share coping mechanisms, and make it easy to flag difficulties around workloads and stakeholders so these can be addressed early on. Ensure there are mechanisms for people to check in with those who might feel disconnected, and that everyone has ready access to mental health support (e.g., employee assistance programs, well-being apps).

2. **Clarify goals and tackle work intensification**. Ensure everyone is clear on their deliverables and identify the energy sappers in your business, your department, and/or your team. Be honest about work habits and tech, innovations that are adding to other workers' stress, and the time needed to learn new technologies. Design work to ensure that jobs are manageable in the time allocated and encourage people to lean into tech to enhance how they work.

3. **Belonging and agility need to find their rhythm.** As we migrate to more agile jobs, internal talent marketplaces, and adopt more fluid ways of working together, it's vital to ensure that workers have a place, a team, a tribe where they feel they belong—and flexible work doesn't come at the expense of social connection. Ensure they have somewhere to consolidate their learning and track their progress with someone invested in their career.

Executives' and HR's CTAs

1. **Pace and coordinate transformation plans**. Decentralized work models have many advantages, except when people are trapped responding to: enterprise-wide transformation, country-sponsored growth plans, local-team priorities, and personal goals in unison. Figure out how to have visibility into this intersection and work with those in impacted roles to pace the various initiatives hitting the workforce's energy and bandwidth at any given time. Mapping *demand* stimulated from internal projects, alongside modeling of external demand, can help visualize capacity

2. **Develop insights around health and well-being.** We're living in the age of data science and predictive models. Many of us probably already have the data needed to make the next generation's life a whole lot better, *if* we turn data into insights and take action on red flags: be it managers with too many direct reports, workers clocking constant overtime, workers failing to take their vacations, negative sentiment in social posts, failure to take up preventive healthcare, or lower-than-desirable health outcomes with certain providers. We sit on this data today, so use it and make it available to others.

CHAPTER 3

The New Rhythm of Work

Drop the Beat, Y'all!

Some music nerds feel that the ultimate in modern rhythm comes from James Brown's late-1960s rhythm section, which featured not one, but two funky drummers (Clyde Stubblefield and John "Jabo" Starks) and the funkiest bassist ever (William Earl "Bootsy" Collins). You can't get much funkier.

Some point to the sounds of the 1980s: the Eurythmics, the Pet Shop Boys, Michael Jackson, Erasure, Depeche Mode, Duran Duran, Spandau Ballet, and Simple Minds. Also excellent choices.

Others roll with the old-school producers who made hip-hop what it is today: DJ Premier, Marley Marl, the Bomb Squad, and Rick Rubin. Makes total sense to us.

More recent generations will stump for the various electronic dance music (EDM) subsets: Downtempo, drum-and-bass, trance, dubstep, acid jazz, and techno. Good call, as we'll support a quality beat drop any night of the week.

Those are for the music nerds. But what about the business nerds? Like us.

Business nerds like us appreciate the awesomeness of a fat beat—just look at our Apple playlists—the kind of rhythm that brings people to the dance floor, the kind of rhythm that creates a feeling of oneness. This is why we choose a variety of (metaphorical) beats and apply them to our modern principles of work.

After all, an office with a good groove has a considerably better chance of succeeding than an office that works to the sounds of paper shredders and battery-operated pencil sharpeners.

You see, work *does* have a rhythm. Every company's rhythm is different—sometimes the rhythm is stated, while in other cases, it's implied—but the good companies tend to find a consistent groove. The thing is, thanks to the (metaphorical) deejays who lord over the world's business dance floors, that groove is constantly changing, and as much as we enjoy consistency, there's nothing wrong with change.

Company beats have to change because the world of work is constantly evolving. At the start of the Industrial Age, it was the drone of conveyor belts on the assembly line. By the late twentieth century, offices plodded along to the rigid, mechanical downbeats of punch clocks, typewriters, printers, and paper workflows. Then came the internet, breaking the old rhythms and making room for individuals to create their own. These new tastes and tools became even more diverse during the pandemic.

Today, we stand on the precipice of Gen AI and quantum computing, possibly the most complex beat the business world has ever heard and felt. The tech is ever-changing, so if we want to stave off stagnancy, we have to acknowledge the beats, embrace the beats, and incorporate the beats.

What's equally if not more exciting is the ability of AI entities like ChatGPT to funk up virtually every industry. Bots like this can help professionals to write a close-to-ready press release, or suggest potential KPIs, or even find images for a branded campaign. (For what it's worth, Google also developed an AI song-maker called MusicLM. Insert your own music industry punditry here.)

Today, these technologies are working in ways that, back in the day, weren't possible and/or economically viable. Creative AI is again changing how we work and whom we work with, offering both efficiency and the option to drive up (or drive down) the human component. No longer is creativity the sole domain of us humans; the premium on human skills to add context, shape searches, interrogate validity, and evaluate relevance has never been so high. Ironically, the more we lean into tech, the more we learn about our own uniqueness.

Yes, every employee at every company needs to accept and embrace the new grooves because they're not only here to stay, but they're going to keep changing. Just look at the music revolution circa 1980, when cost- and user-friendly technologies made the production and consumption of music more accessible. The explosion of hip-hop, new wave, EDM and other genres can be traced back to synthesizers, drum machines, and multitrack recorders. Meanwhile, the Sony Walkman not only allowed for on-the-go listening, but also empowered more people to create their own mixtapes. We still see these trends today via streaming platforms, curated playlists, mobile recording apps, and more recently, AI-generated music. To quote mega-producer Calvin Harris, when asked why musicians are so eager to incorporate new technology into their process: "What do you expect [musicians] to do? Sit at home and cut up bits of recording tape?"[1]

If fresh tech can improve dance floors and recording studios, imagine what it can do for your workscape.

Due, in part, to the ever-changing demographics of the work world, an increasing number of executives are learning that they can't fill the vacancies on their teams, oftentimes because their tech—or their attitude toward tech—is behind the times. For this reason, they're increasing their efforts to digitalize their businesses and build a workforce that's augmented with new, powerful tech.

The challenge is that different generations of workers often have different preferences and habits in terms of adopting and adapting to the new work rhythms. Furthermore, we need to guard against the *haves* and the *have-nots* in terms of access to new tech. Assimilating new practices into an already overloaded schedule is like a set from a deejay who can't match tempos. It just doesn't feel right, and without a proper feel, it's difficult to deliver a proper rhythm.

But when you get right down to it, the best beats, the best grooves—whether it's at the Deptford Northern Soul Club or the Mercer offices at Tower Place West—are created by *people*. It's about how we work individually, with each other, and with technology, and why we work together. It's about getting in sync with the company culture and the day-to-day work environment.

If the beat is on point, people will thrive.

The Importance of Being Nsync, Er, in Sync

We've come a long way in recording, mixing, mastering, and of course, accepting the new rhythm of work. But the rhythm in question is fresh, and freshness, more often than not, brings challenges.

For example—and pardon us if we're again diving into the work-at-home well—working remotely was seen to be a time-saver, but in many cases, the missing commute time to and from the office created a new, unhealthy rhythm.

Many leaders, teams, and individuals compensated for the lack of being together in one place by overloading daily schedules with a ton of virtual meetings, some of which were as important as a new single by Beyonce, while others were as unimportant as the 58 remixes of said Beyonce single. The incessant Zoom calls, Teams meetings, and Google Meets left workers with zero downtime, zero time to think, and zero time to sip on a Mocha Cookie Crumble Sugar–ccino. Time saved in commuting turned into early or late meeting hours since availability was a given. But here is the rub: despite the apparent increase in productivity, very little of this translated into higher output.

For remote workers, back-to-back-to-back meetings are oftentimes the norm. Since February 2020 to 2023, according to Microsoft, the average team saw a 252% increase in its weekly meeting time, and the number of weekly meetings has increased 153%. As a result, the workday span for the average team has increased more than 13% (46 minutes) since March 2020. After-hours and weekend at-home work is more mainstream than ever, clocking in at 28% and 14%, respectively.[2] The only thing that's decreased since remote work became completely common is the use of the phrase "You're on mute," as we've all figured out how to navigate Zoom. (We've FINALLY become so adept at the technology that many workers not only mute their audio, but also turn off their video *so they can do actual work during a meeting!*)

The new work grooves have given workers the opportunity to take care of business on their own schedule, which further funks up the beats. New parameters create the opportunity to work 24/7, begging the questions: *How do we not spiral up expectations of workers?* And: *How do we negate the potential loneliness of asynchronous work?* And: *Has efficiency won out over engagement, learning and innovation. And: Will our back-to-office directives be an effective salve to some of this pain?*

One would think that squeezing more work into our working weeks would lead to increased productivity—in fact, reports from the beginning of the pandemic indicated that very thing. Such an increase, however, dissipated with the influx of endless meetings, and there's no let-up in sight, although it is rumored that some companies have planned additional meetings to address the abundance of meetings.

We're not kidding. Meetings about meetings is a thing.

In early 2022, *Harvard Business Review* reported, ". . .92% of employees consider meetings costly and unproductive." They also noted a couple of new techno-stress factors, explaining that countless online interactions often lead to "Zoom fatigue,"[3] which leads to a workforce filled with "Zoom-bies," a condition neuropsychologists say is a big contributor to techno-stress.[4]

So next time you schedule an unnecessary meeting (or two) (or ten), realize that if you keep it up, your colleagues might start looking like the cast of *The Walking Dead*.

"Boss, Why the &$%* Are We Having All These &$%*ing Meetings?"

We don't have stats on this, but if we were to guesstimate, we'd say that about one-third of all work meetings could be shortened, consolidated, or cancelled altogether. That's just an estimate, mind you, but a quick look at our Microsoft calendars tells us that number is relatively on point.

Part of the reason businesses have so many confabs is because they're really easy to schedule and really, *really* easy to attend. It's simple to add your entire team to a meeting—all it takes is a single click. And they have no excuse to not be there, unless they're in another meeting. Part of it is also the flattening of new work models and a lack of decision-making discipline—leading to suboptimal meetings that are all talk and no action.

And then there's the FOMO, which has contributors believing they need to be in regular meetings they've never attended before because they might fall out of the loop. Oftentimes, leaders make matters worse by emphasizing the importance of this specific meeting; thus, contributors feel obligated to attend. Presenteeism in all forms is still very real.

In many cases, old (bad) meeting practices have also been transferred into the virtual space. Instead of taking the time to rethink how we interact with one another under these new circumstances, we simply turned to our Zoom, Teams, or Slack meetings and kept plowing forward. Adding insult to injury, we missed out on the socializing aspect of in-person meetings—the moments when, while waiting for the attendees to gather, we chatted about private stuff, dropping anecdotes to lift spirits and create connections. We might even exchange some off-the-cuff work ideas that weren't yet *meeting-ready*. (This vibe feels like a thing of the past, a vibe that many contributors miss, kind of the way beat junkies miss deejays who know how to spin a quality set of old-school drum-and-bass.). On-site workers are also feeling the pressure to deliver on attendance, training and work goals.

And then there are hybrid meetings, a different beast entirely. Many of us have mixed feelings about meetings in which some attendees are remote and others are together in the same room. Yes, there are pitfalls: They often don't start on time because at least one of the remote attendees has trouble logging on, a massive frustration for those in the room, in real life (IRL). Or those in person are chit-chatting and forget to engage those online or are just too muffled to be heard. Oftentimes, in order to not disadvantage the remotely connected participants, on-site participants will use their laptops—the flow of speech is more or less the same as a virtual meeting, and we are missing out on the in-person social interaction, still.

It's kind of like clubbing with your friends, except half of the group is dancing at the venue, while the other half is watching a feed from somebody's smartphone. Fun for some, but not for others. Address this or, as Gloria Estefan would say, "the rhythm is gonna get ya."

Tweaking the Tempo

Can this be fixed? Can we turn a meeting from a meandering 67-minute ambient track to a three-minute banger?

Of course we can.

Streamlining the decision-making processes—which can be aided by cutting down the number of meetings, reducing the number of people involved, and delineating who is or isn't a decision-maker in the room—will free up a significant amount of time for both the organization and the individual. It'll also speed up decision-making considerably, creating competitive advantage to companies that have slowed down in this new world of working. (To that end, some companies have removed all standing meetings to force this change.)

Next, you'll want to apply good meeting practices, both old and new. Old-school meeting tenets that we all know (but often forget or ignore) include:

- Invite only those who will benefit from, and add to, the meeting.
- Make an agenda with pre-set times for each topic, decision, or update.
- Share the agenda up front, along with the meeting's purpose.
- If it's a decision-making call, call out the decisions at the start of the meeting.
- Ensure minutes are taken; capture the facts and cut out the BS.
- Open the floor for questions.
- Review the outcome and follow up with action items, names, and deadlines.

That's old-school. That's Fatboy Slim. Still good. Always will be.

Here's the new set of rules. Let's call them the Martin Garrix set:

- Share key-but-lengthy details in advance to make the most of your actual meetings.

- Set up *everything* prior to meeting (i.e., virtual whiteboards, roles and responsibilities, co-creative exercises).
- Create channels that hold notes, material, and actions, with set processes for reminders prior to the next meeting.
- Turn off recording. If you want people in the office, make it mandatory. Don't give them the option to dial in or listen post.
- For sessions of 10-plus people, and/or get-togethers where ideas or direction need to be captured, use Slido, Menti, or a similar tool to open out brainstorms like: *What's concerning you about Q4?* Or: *Given the discussion, which option do we take?* Or: *What do you think of the new Taylor Swift album?*
- End with a three-question, five-minute session to garner input from everybody. Take polls through appropriate tools.

Yes, deejays can fill dance floors all by their lonesome, but oftentimes the best musical (and business) rhythms are created by a group—Blur, anyone?—all of which is why, when appropriate, you should try to build a social aspect into your meeting's agenda:

- If you called the meeting, kick things off with a personal anecdote, that is, what you did over the weekend or your upcoming vacation plans.
- Shorten the meeting.
- Share who's celebrating a special occasion like a birthday or work anniversary.
- Carve out time for nonmeeting input from other teams.
- Shorten the meeting.
- Have one person share what's on their mind, maybe work-related, maybe not.
- Did we mention shortening the meeting?
- End the meeting 10 minutes before the hour so contributors can catch their breath before the next meeting. (This takes discipline and requires issues to be parked, moved to bilateral, or tabled for a future meeting.)

Simply put, the goal of each meeting should be to make the most of each contributor's hour, aiming for each session to be productive, informative, and as mindful of all attendees' time as possible. The impact on the company's collective satisfaction with well-constructed and well-executed meetings will rise significantly.

To Quote Post Malone, "Go Flex"

For some contributors, the primary attraction of a flexible work environment is the freedom it allows in terms of performing their jobs. Autonomy is a key motivator for contributors who prefer flexible work models to rigid work constructs. The sometimes very different expectations of contributors and employers regarding flexible work requires an honest assessment of how much autonomy there actually is at home, and what dependencies make collaboration different in hybrid setups.

Those working from home have experienced how the rhythm of work has changed. Here are three examples:

- The elimination of setup and travel time often resulted in more free time. (On the surface, that's great, but starting meetings at 8:00 a.m. rather than 9:00 a.m. wasn't always so great.)
- For those craving a nine-to-five, many have long struggled to down tools at 5:00 p.m.
- Our online calendars—directly viewable and bookable by many colleagues—are divided into 30-minute segments ("manager time"), which are the new units of measurement at work. This reality can interrupt what Amantha Imber at Inventium calls "maker time": three to four hours to actually produce work that is creative in nature.[5]

During the pandemic lockdown—when all contributors were forced to work at home—the new work rhythms felt pretty darn good, as everybody was in the same remote boat. The following is some of Mercer's research on this state of affairs:[6]

- 59% of employees said their work/life balance was great, while 15% said it was terrible.
- 58% said remote working improved their work/life balance, while 14% said it made balance harder to achieve.
- 57% said remote working positively impacted their well-being, while 12% said they were negatively impacted.
- 57% said they felt less stress when working remotely, while 14% said they felt more stress.
- 55% said they were more productive when working remotely, while 14% said they were less productive.
- 46% said they worked fewer hours when remote, while 20% said they worked more.

But with the end of lockdowns and the ad hoc return to the office, the world of work has become segmented. Contributors are now working from home, from offices, from work sites, and thanks to the ease of mobile devices, from wherever they find a time and place to sit down. . .work-from-Spain, anyone? The phone thing has its downsides; we've all had calls drop out as we drive through a tunnel or intermittent connections as we dial-in from remote offices.

It's also a generational thing: Gen Yers have often commented that they find it rude when someone calls them out of the blue; today's business etiquette dictates that you book an appointment or send a text to check if it's okay to call them. As we know, Gen Zers are more likely to listen to an influencer than they are to read your email. Gen Xers and Boomers will need to communicate in way that works for the younger generations to be *heard* in the new world of work.

The problem is that home, office, on-site, and mobile workers have work rhythms that might differ from one another. The home contributor has a five-second break between meetings, while the office contributor may need a few minutes to switch rooms, and even more time if someone stops them in the hall with a question. Bumping into people—a term that has been used to express how coincidences spark new ideas and innovation—is something that organizations were missing when going remote (which is why Apple always wanted their contributors to spend more time in their worker-friendly offices).

The office contributor may have a computer glitch that in-house IT can fix in five minutes, while the home contributor may be waiting for a techie on the company help line for 20 minutes.

Home office contributors may miss interactions with colleagues, while on-site contributors may miss out on some *family moments,* a challenge that the hybrid norm of 3 days a week on-site aims to address.

On-site work might feel like a parallel universe to those who've gotten used to having more control over when they work, how they work, and how they dress for work. And the divide is showing: in 2022, many frontline workers expressed that they were fed up with their deal, most notably around flex, whilst, while a large percentage of knowledge workers showed signs of burnout.

It was clear nobody was winning. Not the company. Not the leaders. Not the contributors.

But the fix might not be as difficult as one might imagine.

I Want You Back

With the WEF's release of the Good Work Framework (which we—Team Mercer—partnered on[7]), we have guidance on what human-centric work models look like in a post-pandemic world, and one aspect of the situation is clear: flexible, hybrid work is a right for all, not just a privilege for a few. If all contributors can figure out what best suits their needs—and what allows them to perform at peak efficiency while maintaining a quality work/life balance—and leaders balance these needs with organizational necessities, companies will naturally fall into a tighter, more positive rhythm.

The point is that we're experiencing different working models across different groups, each having its own pace, and each exacerbated by spatial, temporal, and digital boundaries. Many contributors agree that there's more energy when in the office or on-site, but greater concentration often happens at home or another remote setting. These are new realities we all need to work with to unlock the full potential in our workforce.

Enter the hybrid model, which many contributors like because it reduces commute times and offers flexibility, along with the socialization and energy upside that comes with in-person collaborations.

There are, of course, business- and role-specific necessities to consider as well. American Express in 2022 launched a flexible working model called Amex Flex, bucking the trend of return-to-office mandates in highly regulated industries. According to the company's profile on a popular jobs marketplace, the program gives employees more choice in when to work on-site versus remotely, "based on the nature of their work, the need for in-person collaboration and other factors." Some roles like "on-site security" would be fully in-office, while others like "field sales" could be fully virtual. The key here is the clarity around which jobs lend themselves to which types of working arrangements, a move that is helping contributors and managers to partner.[8]

As companies address these new rhythms, they are also tackling the need to rapidly reconfigure their workspaces. Adjustable desks and lighting in common areas can quickly adapt to individual preferences, thus optimizing the space while personalizing each employee's experience. Some employers are making WiFi available in outdoor areas, so people can meet in public spaces. Others, like Mercer, use tech that zooms-in on individual's who are on-site and places their pictures on tiles to promote equity during video calls with hybrid attendees.

The verdict is still out on how remote work will play out in the coming years with statistics varying widely around company mandates, especially as we face economic headwinds and the number of layoffs increases. One thing, however, is true: flexibility is a significant retention factor, and with the number of four-day workweek experiments underway and job-sharing opportunities occurring, new ways to work together will continue to evolve.

According to 2023 estimates from Gartner, just 39% of knowledge workers globally will work in a hybrid capacity, which means that the majority of the working population won't be able to pursue their careers off-site, and in most cases, will not have the same flexible schedules as their hybrid cohorts.[9] This fact illustrates the potential to divide companies, industries, and society.

The European construction group STRABAG, which is 75,000 contributors strong, has most employees stationed on construction sites. During the pandemic, the company's management decided to bring its office employees back, so long as it was compatible with health regulations. The reason: they didn't want the frontliners on the construction sites to feel they were being treated differently than the office contributors.

While this will work for some businesses, others such as tech companies where you can plug in anywhere may see contributors jump ship. What will lead to lasting gains depends on the industry, job roles, company size, and management attitudes. There is no single answer and each organization will need to explore, learn and (re)adjust accordingly.

As businesses focus on productivity and underutilized real estate, there is a growing interest in *back-together* strategies. Some are questioning whether the gains seen during the pandemic were due to flexible working being an "experiment" (the good old *Hawthorne effect*). Even chess masters seem to be more creative when playing live, than remote. Concerns have also been raised about young workers' social skills, diversity of experiences, and reasoning capabilities. It's certainly difficult to measure the loss of learning typically gained through proximity to others or the erosion of loyalty when culture is less tangible. It's clear that the long-term outcome for both the firm and worker's future employability, must be balanced against the potential losses/gains. Whatever the policy, clarity, fairness, and consistency are critical to deliver. And you're onto a winner with an approach that starts out to maximize human contribution.

Swingin' with the Saints

As people continue to find their individual rhythms, organizations are struggling to channel that cacophony back into a unified company rhythm. Savvy business leaders, like savvy jazz musicians, can try to create styles that flow smoothly, include room for improvisation, and have functional harmony. (To that end, wouldn't it be fun to work in an office run by jazz trumpet master Wynton Marsalis?) Much of this is done by listening to, exploring, and being influenced by the work rhythms they like and can expand upon.

The organization of work is also subject to a wide range of influences today. For instance, seasonal fluctuations in supply (i.e., the food industry) and demand (i.e., December holiday shopping) require a high degree of flexibility and ingenuity, qualities that to some extent cannot be applied to the individual requirements of employees.

Self-organized teams are the most common example of a more flexible approach to different workload situations. For example, the engineering company FESTO found success in allowing production teams to manage themselves, using an app similar to Doodle to organize their shifts. Differentiated compensation models favor the acceptance of such approaches.

The flexibilization of work requires addressing the very nature of jobs and related outcomes. Organizations are paying more attention to how job tasks can be reconfigured differently, such as: Can we decrease job dependencies so contingent workers can handle certain tasks? Or: Can they be offloaded to a centralized hub or outsourced center? What aspects are repetitive and could be automated? What tasks can be done quicker with the use of Gen AI? How might we contribute in ways that have a net positive impact on the world? This thinking is advancing the flexibility discussion beyond the *when* and the *where* to focus on the *who*, the *how* and even the *why* of work.

For example, remote teams have taken over the maintenance work for entire industrial plants on other continents—during their core working hours (the *follow-the-sun* principle, if you will)—integrating automation into the new rhythm of work. For others, like caregivers, job-sharing initiatives have opened up new opportunities to work part-time, thus broadening the pool of accessible talent for organizations. What with all that jazzy integration, Miles Davis would be proud.

Another way to improve our office rhythm is to think different about working hours. (There's that creative Steve Jobs grammar again.) The reintroduction of core working hours is not patronizing employees. Rules that prohibit meetings outside of core working hours are not a restriction of personal autonomy, but rather a nudge toward more effective time management—an essential part of the *back together* policies emerging post-COVID.

Similarly, respecting break times and personal time off is a sensible practice, and far from a throwback to the Industrial Age. What *is* new is designating *contact days* for on-site meetings, collaboration, and other face-to-face activities. Many hybrid models and four-day workweeks have incorporated contact days to counter the loss of interpersonal time. One workforce agency ensures three consecutive contact days, so that those who are on a two-day, in-office hybrid arrangement can not only choose their days in the office, but can also flex their start time, accommodating for shift work and religious holiday celebrations along the way.

There are also many straightforward strategies that are designed to entice workers to return to the office, that is, no-meeting Fridays, catered lunches, or work-from-anywhere provisions workweeks. While these accommodations and perks can help make in-person work more attractive, the incentive to draw contributors back to the office is to provide them with what they value most:

- Transparency.
- Flexibility.
- Respect.
- Learning and training opportunities.
- Health and wellness initiatives.
- A culture of inclusion.

In our consulting practice at Mercer, our understanding of flexibility is about more than working from home versus working in an office. To level the playing field between knowledge and skill workers, we consider flexibility across six dimensions: where (location and infrastructure), when (hours and scheduling), how (scaling and technology), what (job content and sharing), who (workforce, automation), and why (purpose, impact).[10] A methodology that helps with job design. See Figure 3.1.

While we have been focused on the *"where"* and *"when"* of work for the last year, the future of work requires us to question all the dimensions of work

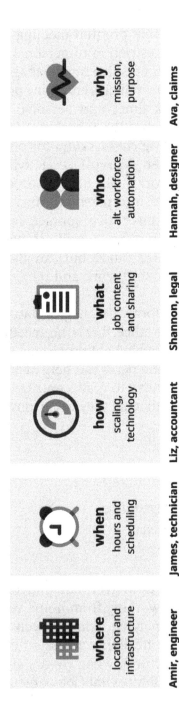

where
location and
infrastructure

when
hours and
scheduling

how
scaling,
technology

what
job content
and sharing

who
alt. workforce,
automation

why
mission,
purpose

Amir, engineer
"I collaborate with my team a few days a week at the office, but otherwise work from home!"

James, technician
"I work 40 hours a week, but vary the days and times I work to meet the needs of my family."

Liz, accountant
"I work 60 hours per week during busy seasons, but scale back to 30 hours per week the rest of the year."

Shannon, legal
"I share my caseload with another manager, and work a reduced schedule to meet my personal needs."

Hannah, designer
"I work on demand on projects that fit my interests across multiple employers. I'm my own boss!"

Ava, claims processor
"I help others in their times of greatest need and I choose to work here because my voluntary hours are matched in charitable donations"

FIGURE 3.1   The six dimensions of flexibility.
Source: Mercer

What we are finding is that true flexibility demands deep *work redesign*, that is, deconstructing jobs into tasks that can be reconfigured in light of these six dimensions to better meet individuals' and employers' needs. This is a critical activity for all organizations that is discussed in Ravin Jesuthasan and John Boudreau's groundbreaking book *Work without Jobs*.[11] They argue that tasks with fewer dependencies can then be distributed across a mix of contingent or nontraditional workers, automation, and AI. Job-sharing models have also found their way into management levels with successful outcomes. These approaches not only attract talent, but help efficiency by centralizing tasks, ensuring the right level of worker is allocated. Work design can also mitigate talent supply issues and help to build in learning.

In another shining example of flexible work as a win-win, Unilever found a way to provide gig workers with more financial security—without converting them to full-time equivalents (FTEs). As Placid Jover, Chief Talent and Reward Officer at Unilever, told us, "We have found a way of creating the third way of employment that sits between being a FTE and a gig worker. It's an employment contract that delivers the contract of security and flexibility that employees want. It's called the U Work model." Jover explains, "Under the U Work model, the employee continues to be a permanent Unilever employee. Together, Unilever and the employee agree on an annual retainer that is settled monthly. It doesn't matter if the employee works with Unilever or not. Every month they will have a flow of income. There are moments where Unilever will call the employee to offer work based on their experience and skill set. If the employee accepts the offer, in addition to the monthly retainer they will also get assignment pay. The thinking behind the approach and the economics of the model make the proposition attractive for the employee and efficient for the P&L.

Variations of flexible work arrangements are vast and depend on many factors. It's hard for leaders and management to create a happy medium when it comes to the division in working rhythms that we face today, but it's not advisable to try solving the growing divide with hasty decisions, random orders, harsh proclamations, or alpha-dog threats. The best plans are built through teamwork, as well as communication that includes input from all those involved in the organization.

No matter what rhythm of work is adopted, it must be flexible enough to blend with the distinct rhythms of our lives, both in and out of the office. No matter what rhythm of work is adopted, ensuring policies can flex around people's lives both in and out of work will pay dividends. We need the rhythm of work in our lives for our well-being, our mental health and our retirement. So, yes sometimes it might feel like *murder on the dancefloor* but remember *you better not kill the groove, Deejay.* Change is hard, but new rhythms create new music.

Humanizing Resources

If we look at the development of work over the last 200 years, we see a significant improvement in working conditions—especially in the fields of workplace safety, health, and social security. But are we fully embracing the opportunities offered by new technologies, new ways of working, and the potential to flex our rhythms?

It's fair to leave some of that to individual teams looking to find their equilibrium, but not without intentional design and guidance. Many organizations have over-delegated this important aspect of work, and not all managers have the partnering skills to help workers and offices make the right decisions. In situations like this, nobody's goals are fully met. There's a broader need to analyze and optimize current work practices, that is, workflow and decision-making processes. This is a transformational exercise that will require energy and attention, but it'll be worth it.

Now, we have a unique opportunity to make lasting changes in the way we work. By better understanding today's malleable rhythm of a company—combining technical possibilities with human capabilities in the best possible way—we can create a new work groove, one that's conducive for everybody from the lead singer to the bassist to the cowbell player.

Flexibility, where it makes sense, not only delivers agility, but can actually increase productivity.

And we're in the process of creating it.

People Leaders' CTAs

1. **Set guardrails and have conversations around flex**. Define how people can *flex in work* (start times, shifts, location, set contact days and/or compressed schedules) and workweeks and how they can *flex out of work* (protocols for taking time off, engaging in outside work activities). The clearer the principles, the easier it is for individuals and managers to apply.

2. **Promote an effective meeting culture and respect for people's time**. Adhere to meeting best practices and promote respectful use of one another's time inside and outside of work. Promote understanding of others' work preferences and common expectations around how teams will come together and work asynchronously.

3. **Understand yours and your team's work preferences.** See where you're aligned and where you differ. Look for common ground and ways to integrate varying styles of work into a single rhythm. Consider the upside of asynchronous work and *follow-the-sun* schedules. Frequently review, adjust, and adapt to build a rhythm that feels natural, allows work to flow, and gets creativity pumping.

Executives' and HR's CTAs

1. **Redesign workflows and decision-making processes**. Examine pressure points and the areas where value is created, taking a deep look at how the work is done today, how it could be done tomorrow, and who actually does the work (by level, employment status, etc.). Manage the changes and measure efficiency and productivity.

2. **Build multi-fold flexibility into roles**. Use skill assessment and work redesign to achieve a flexibility that works for contributors and for the organization. Be transparent on what is possible in a given role and stay open to flexible models yet to be designed. Figure out dependencies and where a new rhythm could help unlock untapped potential.

CHAPTER 4

It Doesn't Pay to Stay

What We Really, Really Want

It's been a rough week at the office.

Your supervisor blamed you for a colleague's mistake, and rather than fess up, the colleague threw you under the bus. Rough.

The six last-minute meetings on Wednesday destroyed your workflow, and you had to grind until 1:00 a.m. on Thursday morning in order to catch up. Also, rough.

Due to a random change of heart, the 50-slide deck that was due next quarter is now due first thing Monday. Again, rough.

On Friday, your paycheck was direct-deposited into your bank account and, considering your crap week, it felt small. Really small. Again, rough.

And here is the rub: everyone, and we mean everyone, who left your company seems to have landed on their feet. Their LinkedIn updates overflow with glowing reports about their new onboarding and generous pay hike.

You're in a bad space, which has got you thinking: *Are they really earning more than me? Am I the fool to be left behind?* And if the answer is yes, *is it time to update my resume?*

The answer is a solid. . .*maybe.*

On the one hand, yeah, you like your current job security and you're comfortable with the social situation at the office, and job security and comfort are hugely important. Plus, there's no guarantee that a round of office roulette will land you in a better situation vis-a-vis office politics or the workload. But all your former colleagues at least *seem* to be better off than you—financially, physically, and spiritually. (You're especially keen about that whole financial thing.) To that end, grab a pen and paper, and without thinking about it, write down the answer to this question:

If you could institute one new policy at your company, what would it be?

Would it be higher and more frequent pay bumps? Better health coverage? More (and/or more flexible) vacation? Fully remote work? A flattened No dress code? A tuxedo-only dress code?

Ask 50 people, and there's a chance you'll get 50 different answers, a factor that's frustrated people leaders for as long as there have been people leaders, but one topic resolutely remains at the top: it's *pay*, or more specifically, *how equitable their pay might be.*

And they would be right. If we look at Mercer compensation data over the period from early 2022 to early 2023, we see two trends: *switchers* seemed to do better than *stayers*—new joiners enjoyed 3.6% higher salaries compared to tenured employees globally, and this inequity is worse in countries that don't have strong unions and/or a history of collective bargaining. As a case in point, the average switcher makes 5.3% more (this is the delta between joiners, pay and equivalent internal pay growth) in India; 5.6% more in the United Kingdom; 3.6% in China; and 3% in the United States, while in Germany, the delta is only 0.4%. So, if we took the average salary of a professional services worker in the United Kingdom in 2023, this would equate to losing out on 3,000 pounds per year—just for being loyal. Something feels wrong.

Can't Buy Me Love

Yes, the reasons contributors leave their jobs are myriad and nuanced and pay is a good *opt-out* when you don't want to share more in an exit interview. We each calculate our own personal deal in our own unique way, and what we value alters over time, given life events and changes in our personal circumstances. But let's not kid ourselves: better pay mitigates a lot of issues. In our exhaustive database of employee preferences, the weighting of pay on intent to leave took a sharp spike upward in 2023.[1]

If we're being honest, *better pay* is shorthand for *better financial health or a better financial future*—in fact, it could be said that it has less to do with money than with *security*. So, we need to talk about *real income* (after taxes and deductions), *real wealth* (given how far our money goes today), and *financial literacy* (how informed we are about how to maximize our money and how this influences our behaviors). And these factors vary considerably by gender, generation, and geography.

Concern for financial health is constant and cuts across all geographies and industries. In study after study, financial wellness rises to the top of employees' hierarchy of needs. Mercer's research showed that covering monthly expenses was the number one concern in 2022, which is no surprise given the cost-of-living crises hitting workers in most markets (see Figure 4.1).

The money issue is, well, an issue. In the United States in 2022, 50.5 million people chose to quit their jobs and move to a new organization, a 5% increase compared to 2021, and a 20% increase compared to 2019.[2] In the United Kingdom, an estimated 9 million left their jobs in 2022.[3] Even in Singapore, 2022 quit rates were significantly higher than pre-pandemic. And therefore, rightly or wrongly, there is a perception out there that the grass is greener on the other side.

Money Money Money

In the mid-2030s, when we look back at this time, it's likely we'll all see the pandemic as a tipping point, the moment we finally understood that the old employee deal was fractured beyond repair. It had fallen out of time—The People Age had arrived and motivations for work had shifted.

That deal, forged in the post-WWII era, was already in decline long before COVID-19, it just wasn't being talked about. In the

What keeps workers up at night?

 Financial concerns—
Covering monthly expenses, ability to retire and personal debt are all top concerns

 **Burnout remains a top concern** with work load/life balance and mental/emotional health remaining in the top 5

 Physical health has declined in importance with reduced concerns over COVID, but still claims a top spot

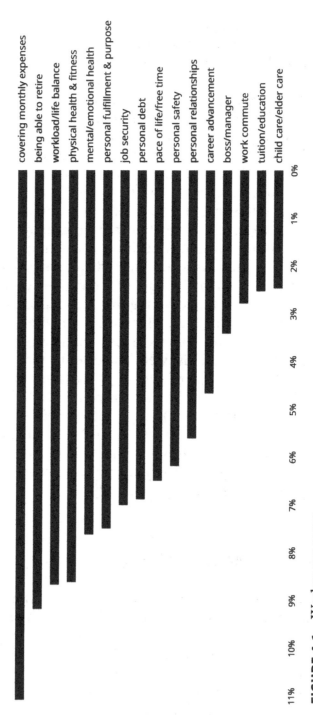

FIGURE 4.1 Worker concerns.
Source: Mercer

past, when layoffs were less prevalent, pensions and other long-term incentives kept workers in the same company. By 2020, those pensions were mostly gone, cyclical layoffs were the norm, and the gig economy was in full swing. As skills have become the real currency of work, the risks inherent in staying and stagnating have grown higher than ever before. Workers have almost been *disincentivized* against staying, and it's the younger workers who put a finer point on it and demonstrate why. The *Loyalty contract*, once a linchpin for big business, has now been stripped down on both sides to the point where it has become almost irrelevant.

Employees know there's no single employer that they can call their soulmate. Like singles who're looking for love, workers have options. In many Western countries, the data shows they are just as likely to say they're satisfied *and* are thinking of leaving, because they know they can find an attractive alternative.[4] The majority (70%) of Gen Zers who claim they love their job today are either actively looking for, or passively open to the next one. Although this trend is most pronounced with the younger workforce, the disconnect between high *engagement* levels and high *intentions to leave* is a phenomenon we've been tracking for years. In fact, in many cases, it's the discontented and those who are less optimistic about their prospects who are staying.

A large percentage of workers feel underpaid, stagnated, underpaid, underappreciated, and underpaid. (Did we mention underpaid?) This sort of vibe often leads to *rage applying*, which is simply getting frustrated, then hopping onto LinkedIn or Glassdoor and sending a zillion resumes to a zillion HR teams. (If that sounds like something you'd want to watch, look no further than TikTok, where you'll find plenty of *rage applying* videos.)

Our research shows that Gen Zers are prioritizing compensation (*pay me more today*) and careers (*help me earn more tomorrow*), and depending on where you are in the world, these flip in importance.[5] And while this is likely true for all employees, younger contributors are more vocal in their demands than their older counterparts, and far more likely to jump ship. In fact, they were twice as likely to ask for a raise, more than twice as likely to ask for a promotion, and three times as likely to switch to a new employer as compared to previous generations.

Overwhelmingly, the high pace of quits is being driven not by dissatisfaction with the gig, but rather by a desire for, you guessed it, *a bigger paycheck*. In 2022, salary was the No. 1 reason people cited for leaving, up from No. 7 in 2020 (wow!), and interestingly, women more than men felt they were underpaid (a first!).[6] That's true whether we're talking about hourly contributors, or tech and knowledge contributors. This is The People Age, after all.

But for some, switching jobs is as easy as changing their underwear (or their internet signature). And when there's a chance of pocketing a (hopefully) substantive pay raise, who can really blame talent for leaving?

To paraphrase Taylor Swift, "Does it pay to stay?"

Or, as Joe Strummer from The Clash would say. . .

Should I Stay or Should I Go?

Time to dive down the job-hopping rabbit hole. (Get it? Hopping? Rabbits? And you thought consultants didn't have a sense of humor.)

According to Mercer's Real-time Insight Survey, a massive 77% of employers cited dissatisfaction with pay or the ability to get a higher salary at another company as the top reasons why people quit their job in 2022 (see Figure 4.2). (The next four reasons were *personal* at 55%, *leaving for different role in the same industry* at 40%, *burnout/exhaustion* at 36%, and *lack of flexibility* at 31%.)[7]

For employees, there are clear and compelling cases to bounce, and that begins with compensation. Data from the Atlanta Federal Reserve Bank suggests that if a worker wants to be paid more, the surest path to higher compensation is to change jobs.[8]

If we look at this data through the lens of those who chose to stick around versus those who chose to bolt, we see something dramatic: the subgroup that switched jobs experienced the greatest rate of compensation increases over time.

What's driving switching behavior?

77% Dissatisfaction with pay and/or ability to get a higher salary or wage at another company

28% Leaving for a different industry

55% Personal reasons

25% Ability to get better benefits at another company

40% Leaving for a different role in the same industry

23% Retirement

36% Burnout and/or exhaustion

18% Dissatisfaction or disagreement with company culture and/or policies

31% Lack of desired flexible working arrangement/disagreement with remote work policy/working hours

16% Relocations

FIGURE 4.2   Drivers of voluntary attrition.
Source: Mercer.

And the difference is substantial. The numbers clearly suggest that if an employee wants to be paid more, the best path to higher compensation is to change jobs. Post 2021, it's been the case more than ever before. Look at the picture for 2022 (Figure 4.3). The average job switcher grew their compensation by 8–9%, as opposed to the stayer who clocked in between 5–6%. Make such a move a few times in your career, and you're on a totally different pay trajectory.

Beyond financials, there are other temptations for leaving. It can be a way of freeing oneself from a dead-end role, especially when there's no alternate internal option available. While some roles supercharge careers, others can stall them. Mercer alum Haig Nalbantian notes, "We often see the most rapid advancement associated with revenue-generating or customer-facing roles [and] supervisor roles almost universally enhance career prospects within an organization."[9] Some companies are great at getting you into supervisory roles early.

Other firms get you into roles that have multiple advancement trajectories when you move. Nalbantian calls these "catcher

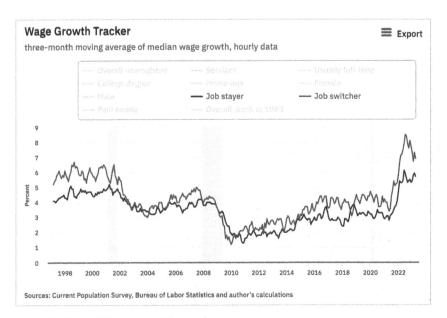

FIGURE 4.3 Wage growth tracker.
Source: Federal Reserve Bank of Atlanta.

positions" because so many managers in Major League Baseball used to be catchers. He notes that the nature of their role, such as "[W]here they sit, whom they interact with and the impact they have on the business serve inherently to build breadth of experience."[10] But being in a dead-end role—not so much. If the role is one where a path for advancement is not available, it only makes sense to move on to someplace where you *can* advance. After all, for some, a career is like a shark: If it stops moving, it dies.

Another profound benefit for employees who frequently change jobs is the ability to maintain agility and flexibility. When employees change companies often, they are more likely to acquire new skills, form new networks, and increase their marketability. Christopher Lake, assistant professor of management at the University of Alaska Anchorage, argues: "A worker that's job-hopped will likely have a greater wealth of experience to draw from, leading to a wider variety of jobs and companies available to them."[11] And employees realize it's a legitimate way to get ahead. When you can gain a 30% pay hike by making three moves in 18 months, the question has to be: *Why should I stay?*

Love the One You're With

If we look at the Great Resignation and Quiet Quitting as votes against the traditional system, maybe the answer is staring us in the face. Maybe the system has simply not paid out enough dividends—monetary or otherwise—to those who remain loyal. In fact, far from making us feel more job-secure, staying too long at a company can often *increase* our employability risk. So, is it really worth throwing away that network and organizational know-how? Is it true that loyalty is just no longer rewarded?

Considering the future is built on the decisions of the past, many employees are asking themselves important questions that they might not have asked five or 10 or 20 years ago about their work culture and future prospects.

Personal balance sheet calculation

- What is my total comp and benefit package truly worth today?
- Will it increase more if I stay or is their little financial impact if I move?
- What career moves are most likely to deliver the best outcomes in terms of my health, wealth, and happiness? What is the pace of promotions or pay moves around here?
- Is staying with this brand likely to make me more, or less, marketable?
- Will I get opportunities to build marketable skills in this company? What is the dollar value of the skills and development that I can access?
- What additional benefits or pay will I receive if I do indeed stay where I am?
- What is the value of retirement benefits and other investments that I receive? Will I end up with more at retirement if I job hop, or if I remain loyal?

- Would a career move for a short-term pay hike be worth it in the longer term?

Those are some really, really important questions. Companies are also grappling with *their* side of the equation:

- What's the real role of pay in attracting and retaining talent?
- What's the effect of adding higher-paid new hires to our current teams?
- To what extent do our employees get to see the financial value of their total compensation package—including benefits and investments—rather than just the amount in their monthly paycheck?
- How financially literate are our employees? What modeling tools can we share that might help them make better financial decisions?
- Does our pay incentivize the right behaviors, such as building breadth in skills or technical depth? Moving around the firm or staying in a line of business?
- How do our pay philosophies differ for starting salaries versus off-cycle pay raises?
- How do current systems ensure that capital is being returned to employees and not just to shareholders, so that loyalty is rewarded in line with workers' true contributions?
- What messages do our reward practices send, especially when a person's earning potential isn't realized because of current economic climate or market conditions?
- What options do we have for incentivizing loyalty from valued contributors?

Current wisdom ties talent's pay to company performance, especially at senior levels. Where you choose to hang your hat could have a significant impact on your take-home dollars. But it's not just about the bottom line when people are evaluating if it pays to stay. . .or at least it *shouldn't* be. Staying with a firm—and the payoff you get for doing so—is multifaceted. There's the security of employment, there's the well-being factor that comes with the known, there're the networks, there's the respect, and there's the community.

In the face of a gig economy and a skills-based marketplace, the old employee deal—the one with fat pensions and personally inscribed gold retirement watches—has been irrevocably broken. In a TikTok world, our attention span has shrunk. People are impatient; they bore easily, and they need change and stimulation. It's the same with their careers.

But in the rush to pocket that extra dollar, are people missing the bigger picture?

Don't Stop Believing

While challenging for the employer, this situation is fixable for many. Even in a full-employment economy, organizations can grow their workforce and retain talent. In reality, a larger proportion of workers actually choose to stay rather than go. And while they don't do the pay math in the clinical way that an AI chatbot would, they do subjectively weigh a range of factors that usually make it more attractive to stay.

Many employees might feel that under their current deal, it doesn't pay for them to stay—a trend that will grow alongside pay range disclosures on job postings around the world. Visibility of pay will be an equalizer. If employers want their best contributors to stick around, they need to step up and fix the system. Fast. Some potential fixes are:

- *Show the full deal by improving employer/contributor communication.* Tech platforms that calculate total rewards across learning investment, benefits, retirement and pay can help people see the full picture. The more engaging the better.

- *Know your pay gap data.* Where are you paying tenured talent below new hire pay? Where are you paying men and women or minority groups differently? You should have these answers on the tip of your tongue.

- *Identify roles that can be location-agnostic.* Use global pay trends, transatlantic benchmarks and/or pay for skill information to make these roles attractive to a wider range of talent, regardless of their location.
- *Embrace the truth of the marketplace.* Why should people have to leave to grow? Figure out how to increase job mobility, how to broaden work experiences, how to cultivate an internal marketplace that can help people find that next job on the other side of your org chart, rather than the other side of the planet.
- *Offer a new employee deal that fits what they value.* Embrace the fact that people are often looking for a broader proposition. They might trade pay for flexibility or for ways to contribute that extend beyond their current job description, such as giving back to the community, skill-expanding gig opportunities, or additional benefits for themselves or their family.

For people leaders, keeping talent on board includes being more preventive and nipping potential discontentment in the bud. For instance, pay can be much better leveraged as a way to prevent turnover, as opposed to a last resort for backfilling a role with expensive new talent. If one of your best contributors is performing well, it might not be an altogether bad idea to up their cash—even if the annual salary cycle doesn't kick in for months.

Leading companies are using internal labor market (ILM) and pay equity analyses to suss out the underlying causes of pay problems and gaps. Regular use of peer-based market pricing and pay-for-skill pay planner tools can help ensure you're offering salaries that are competitive in your industry and geography.

Whether it's ensuring a living wage, closing pay gaps, or keeping internal salaries in line with market rates, the message is clear: the leading companies are the ones who stay ahead on pay and don't wait for their people to bring it up.

Rightly or wrongly, many leaders don't believe their companies can afford to offer unscheduled and/or significant pay bumps. At the same time, some companies are more willing than ever before to pay above the mean for top talent and push for off-cycle pay adjustments, something a staggering 17% signed off on in 2022—which means if employees stay put, they'll have almost a two-in-five chance of getting an early raise.[13] The challenge is that making these adjustments without a clear and communicated strategy can drive inequities or false expectations that don't align with the company's long-term compensation strategy.

Tackle Wealth, Not Just Pay

Employers are getting creative with their use of total rewards by responding to contributor needs. They're taking on student debt to secure more favorable rates or giving one-off gas payments or extending more affordable health benefits to family members or using their purchasing power to pass on cost savings on anything from tech equipment to gym memberships. This all helps. But what can make a striking difference is helping people understand not only the true value of their package today—the value of benefits, pay, and training—but also the impact of their decisions today on their long-term financial health (see Figure 4.4). This is especially true for women, who often live longer yet tend

FIGURE 4.4   The new work contract points to a refresh of the EVP.
Source: Mercer.

to invest less aggressively and participate in the workforce less fully. This all contributes to a gender pension gap that, even in mature economies like the United Kingdom, is north of 40%.

Chetna Singh, head of Total Rewards at SAP, explained in a Mercer podcast that employers cannot artificially separate compensation, culture, and career:

> I always say that it's three C's. The first C is very obvious, which is the compensation and benefits, which is the core or the DNA of the reward function. The second one is culture; culture is exceptionally important. Where you know a culture is toxic, even if you get great Comp & Ben, you may not stay. That's why culture is so important, and rewards play a very crucial role. And the third part is career. Career means are you learning, are you growing, do you have enough opportunities for you to unlearn and relearn. . .keep progressing in your career journey. . .The beauty of the rewards function is it's very tangible [while] driving the intangibles of the organization.[14]

In other words, companies can't focus on comp alone; all variables must work together to adequately meet the needs of employees and keep them employable tomorrow. And it's clear that the velocity of careers is as important as the take-home pay today.

Leading companies share their pay philosophy.

They promote the heck out of their full total rewards deal.

And they make it nearly impossible for their people to *want* to jump ship.

Switch It Up: What About a Premium for Those Who Stay?

Logic would dictate that employers have nothing to gain from high levels of worker mobility—after all, searching for and onboarding new talent is time-consuming and fraught with uncertainty. Brian Kropp, former Gartner vice president, predicts that companies will need to plan for a year-over-year turnover rate that is

50–75% higher than to what they are accustomed.[15] Additionally, the time it takes to fill a role has increased by 18% since before the pandemic, and about half of people who get a job offer are considering at least two other offers at the same time. Estimates say that when a company factors in advertising and time it takes to ramp up new hires, it can often cost two to three times a person's salary to replace them.[16]

There's a productivity loss when employees leave and—most critical in a climate of wage inflation—it's almost always more expensive to hire new talent. Employee turnover also tends to beget more turnover, so sometimes, the status quo is a beautiful thing. Our research reported in *Harvard Business Review* bears this out, as tenured talents are not just good stayers (by definition), but they tend to have a net positive impact on those around them. Younger talent—who typically lean toward switching—actually stay longer when associated with these long-time employees.[17]

But logic isn't always logical, is it?

What's most puzzling is that many companies tend to be conservative (read: disciplined) in managing their pay ranges with tenured employees, their merit budgets, and their counteroffers for these existing, loyal contributors. In contrast, as the data from the Atlanta Fed showed earlier, these same employers are quite happy to pay a premium to hire new employees with the same skill sets as the talent they've lost, and yet these new joiners are unproven quantities who might not fit with the culture. With executives resigned to pay more to hire people, are we channeling our finite resources in the right direction?[18]

High churn has a ripple effect on culture, most critically due to the loss of institutional knowledge and often operational stability, but this can be compounded by discontent when salary information for new hires comes to light. Bobby Ten-Year Contributor isn't going to take it well when they learn that Betty Ten-Month Contributor is pulling down the same money—or more, depending on what the job posting disclosed.

Sure, pay a premium for the new skills you need today when you don't have the time to build them. But other than that, the logic for where an employer should throw their money is clear: *Invest in the existing workforce as a first, not second choice*, because:

- Tenure in a role correlates with higher performance. Jumping from job to job can prevent contributors from settling into their roles and reaching peak productivity. Tenured employees help employers retain vital knowledge and experience, and this keeps companies from repeating mistakes of the past.

- Reducing high levels of turnover minimizes disruptions to company culture and has a positive impact on customer satisfaction. Turnover interrupts operations, and in the service world, those reverberations can last.

- Mercer data also shows that keeping more tenured contributors has a positive outcome on retention metrics. Not just their own retention, but that of the younger generations working around them.[19] Think about it: if the newbie sees a couple of well-performing veterans get fired or laid off, they'll fear for their job from that point on. But working in a stable crew can calm the desire to jump ship.

     It doesn't need to be so complicated.
     Admit the inertia.
     Get creative.
     Get proactive.
     Hold on to your People, people.

It's Also About Being Part of Something Bigger

The artist formerly known as Puff Daddy (and P. Diddy, and then just Diddy) once told us that it's all about the Benjamins. Many agree with that, but these days, the B. Franklins are less important than one might suspect. You see, more than ever, employees want to be a part of SOMETHING.

     Not something. SOMETHING.

They want their company to do more than churn out new pharmaceuticals or drop another social media campaign or deliver another SaaS technology.

They want to make a difference.

They want their company to make a difference.

We're in the midst of a generational call for shared values and purpose, a call that can transcend compensation. The perceived alignment of values is having a serious impact on employees' decisions to stay at their jobs or search for new ones. If a company doesn't live up to all the great stuff their new hires read about in the EVP, said company might end up with a bunch of jaded workers who won't hesitate to go elsewhere for a paltry few bucks more.

One force with enormous potential to impact voluntary turnover is the changing landscape of corporate accountability and stakeholder capitalism. But there's a need to walk the talk in balancing the needs of all stakeholders versus an inherent bias to focus on returns to the shareholder.

In a study examining the share of economic gains to capital versus labor across 30 countries, *The Economist* found that, despite a swing toward returning wealth to workers during the pandemic, the rich-world share to labor fell by 2.3 percentage points in 2020, and returning capital to owners, rather than to employees, dominated cash flow activity.[20] Meanwhile, most companies in our survey said they've struggled—and will continue to struggle—to meet contributors' wage expectations in the years ahead.[21]

This disconnect can feel like a slap in the face for employees, especially when many companies reported record earnings as they closed out 2022. Frustration over what's seen as profiteering is feeding a broader conversation about the balance between corporate profit and responsibility, and that conversation isn't always pretty. There are differing dynamics at play in the United Kingdom, Central Europe, and the United States, predominantly due to pricing power, unions, and labor regulations that impact how large the gap between *switchers* and *stayers* becomes.

As we shared before, in Germany, where collective bargaining is the norm, the gap between new joiners and tenured talent is negligible compared to, say, the United States. For listed companies in the United States, a look at CEO-to-median worker pay sheds light on how pay philosophies favor those at the top, especially when share buybacks improve take-home pay for executives.[22] In 2022, for example, one high profile home improvement retail giant faced an outcry over increasing executive compensation while lowering median worker pay.[23] In 2022, the FTSE100 CEO pay rose by 22% during a year marred by a cost-of-living crisis.[24]

Meanwhile in the United Kingdom, the pay disclosures for all public servants who earn top salaries led to public walkouts of female anchors at the BBC as they protested unequal pay. With pay transparency laws on the East and West Coasts of the United States, and many countries like the United Kingdom kicking off pilots in 2023, transparency on what new hires are likely to earn is out there.

Contributors aren't sitting idly while profits get funneled upward—they're raising their voices and voting with their feet. In the United States, October 2021 was dubbed "Striketober" as 100,000 employees walked out of their jobs.[25] The pressure to give more bargaining power to workers increased with walkouts at John Deere, Kellogg's and even Starbucks, where everybody from the baristas on up went on strike over unionization rules. (According to the U.S. National Labor Relations Board, worker requests to join unions was the highest it's been in years.)

In the United Kingdom, in 2023, 100,000 nurses joined postal workers, paramedics, and border control staff to walk out over pay.[26] The situation was so intense that the government moved in to curtail union power to keep the proverbial lights on for essential services.[27] All over Central Europe, strikes paralyzed major industries and public services in early 2023, when workers demanded compensation for inflation that was at a decade high.

And as Gen AI has taken off, we see protests around the world as creatives see their work being exploited and increased gig arrangements as the blend of tech and workers reshape jobs. Work stability and work ownership is contentious. Yes, Gen AI democratized creativity, but it also commoditized creativity and this is hitting workers' rights. This raises questions about how the new digital dividend from AI is being distributed to workers and shareholders alike.

It's taken extreme measures and tons of time, but employee voices are being heard. Increasingly, more companies are understanding that their success in winning (and keeping) talent and improving overall profitability means shifting to a stakeholder— rather than shareholder—value model. This trend was underway prior to the pandemic, but the tumult of the last few years has pushed it to the forefront.

As a result, we're changing the definitions around what *good* looks like, for work and for companies. More and more firms are focusing more intentionally on offering a living wage, pay equity, flexibility without docking pay, and advancement opportunities that help people stay employable. We're seeing this reflected in both corporate statements and environmental, social, and corporate governance (ESG) commitments as companies seek to pivot toward providing what employees want most. And this serves companies, customers, and shareholders.

Thing is, finding the right level of investment in this most vital asset—that is, our talent—is far from an easy task. And ensuring the affordability of this investment, now and in the long run, is essential. We do need to figure it out, or else all our talent may jump ship.

Moving *up* doesn't have to mean moving *out* of your company. It's attractive and there are many career advantages to leaving. Yet many organizations underestimate the attractive career opportunities they can create within the bounds of their own company. Why not lean into the mobility trend and encourage more lateral moves within the company? Heck, within a company year? Don't let fixed ideas about career and pay progress get in the way. A vibrant talent marketplace, the prevalence of lateral moves, and a more responsive pay model are all ways to lean into this trend for *switching* while keeping it in the family.

So, what do people really want? More and more companies are making strides to find out. In response to employee's questions around pay and transparency, some firms are conducting pay equity studies to flag and resolve the pay gaps among different workforce segments. The tech company, Verve, is publishing workers' salaries and the rationale behind them. Meanwhile, Whole Foods is serving up straight answers when its employees ask about a colleague's salary. And then there's engineering powerhouse, Bosch, who offers variable pay based on company targets and business unit targets.

Employees—much like consumers—have also come to expect more choice, flexibility and personalization. Unilever's My Reward program gives employees the flexibility to choose the benefits they care about the most. And, a similar offering from Netflix lets workers choose between cash and stock options—including how much of their salary they want to receive as options. Both these rewards experiences are tailored to better suit individual needs and promote stickiness, which is hard to replicate when starting afresh.

More flexibility is another common reason for why employees are willing to jump, but this is also being reassessed. For while scant protections and fixed pay may be the standard for gig workers, benefits and variable pay could soon become the vehicles that keep them engaged and performing at peak. Being loyal never looked more attractive.

Who's Crafting the New Employee Deal?

A lot of insanely smart and experienced business policymakers spend an insane amount of time figuring out how to please everybody involved in the compensation process, from the bean counters to the bean receivers. Here are two companies rebooting their comp and benefit system to tackle the challenges of our time.

Ericsson—Funding Benefit Transformation to Engage Today's Workforce

Ericsson knew that to retain workers in the new era, they needed to radically rethink their total rewards proposition to be more creative and connected than ever before. As Andrew Pilbeam, head of Total Rewards, commented, "The reasons people leave are not just pay. Other dynamics like trust, respect, career growth, skills development, and Total Rewards all play their part. When these stop working, then attrition can grow."

Ericsson is transforming its total rewards proposition by taking a bold approach that couched this redesign as part of a three-year optimization plan that will deliver tens of millions of U.S. dollars in savings to the firm, while better meeting the asks of current and future talent where it counts. So, what is the company doing?

They listened intently to their people. Ericsson inquired about what people wanted, they considered how they could help with day-to day-finances, they sought to understand what a global parental leave policy needed to look like in Hong Kong versus the Nordics, and they asked if reducing corporate cars could be part of a wider, eco-friendly travel-to-work approach.

They transitioned to a global benefit system. The company increasingly uses their international buying power to strike better benefits deals for their employees while giving individuals the ability to make health decisions that are right for them—and for the intelligent system to nudge them to take advantage of preventive care benefits. Ensuring a global employee assistance program and a minimal level of life insurance for each and every worker is a cornerstone.

They rigorously seek out new ways to finance employee benefits. By using captives, Ericsson is restructuring the company's investments to make longer-term savings, enabling reinvestment in what employees really value, that is, an extensive volunteering program.

They are value-led in their benefits, as they sought to make deeper changes. Ericsson returned money to workers who didn't take their vacation days, but the company is adjusting this policy in countries where work/life balance is a priority. They want to ensure well-being is a commitment to all employees. Reinvestment is increasingly directed toward maternity benefits and other meaningful items.

They are enhancing their communications and managers' competence in having compensation discussions and using data to tailor the deal to different employee segments. Ensuring minimum, consistent levels of parental leave is a precursor to looking at flexible work options for various segments of their workforce.

Pilbeam added, "For a Total Rewards leader, minimizing employee turnover is critical, because it costs more to replace people. You can no longer look at compensation in isolation. This is one of the biggest expenses on the organization's budget, but you cannot impact this positively without looking at the total deal and then making that total deal visible to all your valued talent."

Infosys—Scaling Individualized Rewards and Incentivizing Skills

The business model at Infosys relies on attracting and retaining highly sought-after digital talent. That's no small feat within India's hot IT market. As one of the country's largest multinational IT and consulting firms, Infosys knows that people are their competitive edge. With such a competitive market of IT professionals, Infosys knew that they needed to drive a newer value proposition to retain and engage their key talent.

Driving this paradigm required individualization, but scaling individualized rewards with 200,000 diverse, mobile, and globalized contributors was a tremendous challenge. After extensive consultation, Infosys developed a suite of monetary and non-monetary rewards to allow individuals to take charge of their careers, and managers to flex and respond to individual needs and preferences using AI.

Managing wealth at Infosys is as much about incentivizing for tomorrow as it is about rewarding for today. As Nandini S., Infosys Group Head for Compensation & Benefits, explained: "For us the future is about acquiring and retaining 'techno-domain' knowledge. Companies come to us for deep understanding about their industry, as well as our technology know-how. This means we need people to stay and develop what we call 'comb-shaped careers'—with broad and deep insights in an industry, as well as specialist capabilities. You can't do this if people don't stay and continue to invest in their skill building."

What Infosys found helped them retain their people was asking managers to look at three time horizons for the skills they needed and asking them to focus on external hiring only for time horizon three: the bleeding edge of innovation. This put the onus on internal talent development for all else. The company also used technology to nudge people and managers if they are not developing or moving sufficiently in their careers. By linking incentives to hot skills and matching contributors to growth opportunities, internal and external pay equity issues are not a concern—the benefits of staying today far outweigh the payoffs of moving on.

This may seem like a lot to throw at you, but don't freak out. These challenges are eminently fixable and are already stimulating *different* thinking in many firms. Still, it will take intentional design and some courageous conversations to fully rethink rewards, so all hires have equal opportunities for growth, movement, and wealth accumulation across the talent ecosystem. It's just a matter of prioritization.

Because it comes down to math. And applying said math.

There's never been more data available about internal and external talent markets, the competitiveness of pay and benefits, the trending price of skills and potential drivers of turnover. Don't sit on the data. Apply the data, segment your workforce, and experiment with different approaches to pay. Use total rewards to more broadly encourage skill development and internal talent mobility, and ultimately, to incentivize more of your contributors to stay.

People Leaders' CTAs

1. **Make it easy to speak up on pay.** While nobody likes to admit it, a reality of corporate life is that the squeaky wheel gets the grease. People leaders are people, too. You want to do good

things and are happy when your team thrives, so don't be silent and help others find their voice. Speak up on your own aspirations and what you're really thinking about your and your team's pay and career trajectory. Use data to understand pay trends in your sector, job, and skill cluster to anchor the conversation.

2. **Discuss careers and the "total" in total rewards.** Avoid *stay* or *leave* conversations. Instead, understand what deal your contributors want, and determine how to get them there. Use all the rewards levers, and funnel funds to areas that can have an outsized impact, such as professional development, a sabbatical, and increased benefits for family members. Understand the true cost of labor and how it's shifting. Don't be shy around off-cycle adjustments.

3. **Drive career velocity in line with an individual's appetite for growth.** Check in on the pace of your contributors' career goals. Not everyone wants to move up *today*. People vary in terms of learning agility and openness to change. Some contributors may want to weigh major life events before shifting up or down at work. Foster an environment where contributors can modulate their intensity as needed, and leaders can spot and help people who feel like they're stagnating.

Executives' and HR's CTAs

1. **Incentivize loyalty AND movement.** In today's fast-paced environment, define what you want to encourage. Is it breadth of experience? Learning agility? Skill development? Skill proficiency? Make internal talent moves—especially lateral ones—a regular occurrence within your firm, *even if those moves aren't tied to a change in pay.* If you want to reward people for broadening *and* specializing their skills, then reflect that in career tracks and job hierarchies. Cultivate a culture of talent development, not talent hoarding.

2. **Help individuals build financial security.** The global dearth of financial literacy is a serious problem. Teach your

employees about their total rewards and their long-term investment returns. Listen to contributors' needs and launch dedicated programs to meet the unique needs of different populations. Examine how you can utilize an investment mindset by considering rewards outside of pay, such as off-setting debts or sharing equity more broadly down the hierarchy. Deliver technology and compelling campaigns that reinforce the true value of Total Rewards packages (cost of training investment, benefits, pay, etc.), along with modeling on long-term wealth and retirement outcomes. Speak out on wealth matters.

CHAPTER 5

Purpose Rules and Empathy Wins

Dave Gilboa needed a break.

After years of toiling away in the finance and consulting worlds, Dave decided to enroll in business school. But before he took his first class, he needed to get away from it all, so he chucked his smartphone and backpacked around the world. During the six-month trip, Dave lost his glasses—clearly a must-have for business school, as seeing your textbook is most helpful—so when he returned from the wilderness, he needed both new specs and a new phone.

Newsflash: Phones and glasses cost money.

Dave knew he could buy a used iPhone on eBay for about $200 at the time, but a new set of prescription eyeglasses—which, obviously, can't be bought used on eBay—would set him back closer to $700. That simply didn't make sense to him, so he stubbornly refused to buy glasses in his first semester, a semester that turned out to be a tad blurry.

It was then, back in 2010, that Dave sat down with some friends and kicked around if or how they could launch a company that might change the world, both economically and socially. Eventually, they hit on affordable eyeglasses, and from those conversations came Warby Parker (WP), an eyeglass company that wanted to be more than just a glasses company. They wanted to be a glasses company with a mission.

Fast-forward 10 years and Warby Parker provides high-quality, stylish eyewear at an affordable price for all, while also making a positive impact on the world. For every pair of glasses sold, Warby Parker donates a pair to someone in need through partnerships with nonprofits and organizations that work to improve access to vision care in underserved communities.

In addition to its social mission, Warby Parker has been successful in disrupting the traditional eyewear industry by cutting out the middlemen and selling directly to consumers online and in their own retail stores. This allows them to offer lower prices on a wide range of stylish options, as well as better customer service and a more personalized shopping experience.

Today, to bring their vision to fruition, team members who have been with the company for more than three years are being sent on international field trips—South America, for instance—where they work with WP's nonprofit partners on supplying eyewear for people in need. An investment into their culture is immeasurable—that's the kind of stuff that'll change *everybody's* life, from the manufacturer to the distributor, to the contributor, to the consumer. Their respective worlds will be impacted, and they'll be tied together forever not just because of glasses, but because of the *mission*. Little surprise that WP's corporate values are:

1. Treat customers the way we'd like to be treated.
2. Create an environment, where employees can think big, have fun, and do good.
3. Get out there.
4. Green is good.

Simple, eh? Powerful, isn't it? Right about now, you might be saying, "But Team Mercer, it's easy to have these kinds of values when the initial idea of your business has a built-in purpose." Fair enough, but hold on: WP is a B2C business, and their purpose doesn't come attached to the goods they sell. . .*the company builds and upholds themselves.* Hundreds of similar businesses that sell high-end eyewear don't have similar purposes or values. . .*but they could.*

Culture Is the New Structure

A company's culture is an amorphous thing, hard to grasp, even harder to measure. That's why some people put culture in the esoteric corner—alongside tree hugging, singing bowls and the like. Never mind! It has always been the bass beat of the organizational rhythm to which people have been working with more or less enthusiasm.

Mercer studies show an increase in the relevance of culture. 42% of respondents say that *how we build culture* is the aspect of the employee experience that has changed the most due to the pandemic. Nearly three-quarters (74%) of respondents agree that culture is crucial when implementing flexible working at a larger scale. Companies increasingly perceive culture as a strategic capability; 68% of mature organizations see an improved culture as critically important to driving business outcomes and attracting and retaining talent.[1] Already, 60% of HR departments have been tasked with changing their workplace culture.[2]

Longing for belonging is a very personal motivation for us to look after the culture in our (future) companies. No wonder Glassdoor is full of quotes about how it really feels to work for a specific organization. *What's the leadership style? Is anyone abiding the corporate values? What are the corporate values? Hell, are there even any corporate values?*

Beyond the obvious reason for employers to have an attractive corporate culture, that is, to win and retain talent, a lot of companies have had to learn about the power of culture the hard way. For example, they found out that their digital transformation just didn't stick without a digital mindset, and that without a culture of inclusion, customer-centricity was little more than a slogan. And now, with a premium placed on agility, it's becoming abundantly clear that a commitment to openness and ownership is more important than who sits where on the org chart.

They found that working on these topics was generating engagement and excitement with their people beyond what they have seen so far.

No wonder, many companies have turned to cultural exercises to (re)shape and strengthen their corporate cultures. Many of these are materializing in projects or programs that span years rather than months, inviting everybody in the organization to participate.

If you need a snapshot of this journey, look no farther than the KION Group, one of the world's leading providers of industrial trucks and supply chain solutions. To bring its brands closer together and to become an integrated intralogistics company, the board decided to undergo an extensive cultural journey that would touch each and every employee. Their plan: Build a strong corporate company culture that was inclusive across its brands, resonated with newly acquired companies, and would serve to ramp up team spirit.

Sounds easy, right? It wasn't.

KION had to ask themselves—and of course, ultimately answer—what it actually stood for as a united group. To do this the company developed a set of corporate values that outlined the mindset and behaviors that would encourage growth from both contributors and their organization. The operating model was being redesigned and leaders were prepared to engage with their teams on the new direction and values. All staff members were involved in dialogues on what the strategy and the culture meant for them, and how it translated into their daily business. This cascaded approach ultimately made KION's transformation a success and led to the company being named as a "champion in mastering digital transformation" by *manager magazin*, a prestigious management magazine in Europe, and to a surge in their ability to retain top talent and capture growth.[3]

The initiation of these exercises sparked a dialogue that made companies think about what they really stood for. Fueled by societal discussions and trends toward more sustainability, some companies started to make up their minds on what they contributed to the greater good. That was a different question, with a different answer. But one thing became clear at the time: corporations needed to define their own purpose, beyond just delivering to shareholders.

Today, when young people mull over who they want to work for, big financial institutions, law firms or strategy houses no longer top the list (a hard truth for us to swallow). What people do want is to be part of a firm that innovates, changes lives, and has a positive impact on society. They may have a hard-earned degree in marketing, with expertise in healthcare, but if an organization that sells cricket bats needs a PR person—and the cricket bat company is the kind of company that has a big-picture view of their place in society—maybe they'll take that gig. See, folks want to be part of creating a positive evolution and embody the quote most often attributed to Mahatma Gandhi, "Be the change you want to see in the world." Or, if you want another music example, start with the man in the mirror, à la Michael Jackson.

Being mindful contributors, they want to contribute, but they want to contribute to something they can get behind, something of which they can be proud.

Some of us found great meaning in our careers. Others did not.

The pandemic was an amplifier for the search for purpose, and The Great Resignation was a result of this collective reflection. Some dissatisfied contributors went into early retirement, while others turned to completely new occupations. Then there were those who continued to do similar jobs but found a company that offered a healthier work environment—which, in some cases, brought a renewed sense of purpose and/or turned a job into career material. In some cases, purpose was discovered because the new work environment was more transparent and people-centric, and answered the question: "Why the hell am I doing what I'm doing in the first place?"

So Why the Hell Are We Doing What We Are Doing in the First Place?

Larry Fink, the controversial CEO of Blackrock, created what can be regarded as a blueprint for turning businesses toward purpose and sustainability. In his January 2022 annual letter to CEOs, he asserted, "Contributors are increasingly looking to their employer as the most trusted, competent, and ethical source of information, more so than government, the media, and NGOs. That is why your voice is more important than ever. It's never been more essential for CEOs to have a consistent voice, a clear purpose, a coherent strategy, and a long-term view. Your company's purpose is its North Star in this tumultuous environment."[4] Yes, Fink's call-out for purpose was controversial, and still is. A lot of critics argued there is a limit to these ideas, and that is return on investment (ROI). But ROI was never the question. It is the combination of profit and purpose that Fink is referring to, the bedrock of stakeholder capitalism that we discussed before. It is certainly the reason why some contributors choose to work for nonprofit organizations. But more and more, it is also those at for-profit organizations who are increasingly demanding sustainable action from their employers. Still, they want to get a decent amount of money for what they contribute.

Over the last few years, a growing number of organizations have begun drafting Statements of Purpose to illustrate their social agenda.

Whereas there are several interpretations of what a corporate purpose is, we'll roll with *raison-d'etre*—an organization's *reason to be*. The following table (Figure 5.1) defines and differentiates the varying vehicles that drive the direction of an organization:

Vehicle	Meaning	Primarily* targeted at
Purpose (Social Mission)	Articulates why an organization exists	Society
Vision	Outlines the desired future position of an organization	Contributors
Mission	The value promise based on the business model	Customers
Values	States shared mindset and appropriate behavior	Contributors
Strategy	Describes objectives and ways to achieve these	Stakeholders

FIGURE 5.1 Five vehicles that drive an organization's direction.
*Source: **Work Different**: Bravery, Anderson, Bonic*
* Shareholders will always also be targeted with any of these vehicles.

Unilever has illustrated how their corporate purpose has strengthened their business, saying that their goal is, "...to make sustainable living commonplace." They closely monitored the company's sales to illustrate the impact of their products. In 2018, for instance, their 28 Sustainable Living Brands—which are defined as those taking action to support positive change for people and the planet—grew 69% faster than the rest of the business; they were also responsible for 75% of the company's overall growth.[5]

Unilever CEO Alan Jope explained, "We believe the evidence is clear and compelling that brands with purpose grow. In fact, we believe this so strongly that we are prepared to commit that in the future, every Unilever brand will be a brand with purpose. It is critical that brands take action and demonstrate their commitment to making a difference."[6]

Then there's Siemens, whose sustainable development agenda states, "We want to apply our engineering expertise and our approach to connect the real and digital worlds, improve people's quality of life, and protect the planet. This is especially supported by our corporate purpose of Technology to Transform the Everyday." Siemens also supports the United Nations' 17 Sustainable Development Goals (SDGs). For Siemens, sustainability management is a company-wide effort, "...at the heart of everything [they] do. Sustainability is firmly rooted within [their] organization and has been an integral component of management compensation since fiscal 2020." (This was first noted in the company's sustainability report of 2021.)

Judith Wiese, Chief People and Sustainability Officer (CPSO), and member of the Managing Board of Siemens AG and Labor Director, added, "Sustainability is in our very DNA. It is not optional, it's a business imperative. Based on our successful track record, we're now setting ourselves even more ambitious targets. We'll accelerate our efforts and raise the bar to create considerably more value for all our stakeholders. Sustainable business growth goes hand in hand with the value we create for people and our planet."[7]

Kinda makes you want to go work for Siemens, doesn't it?

Do the Right Thing

Let's say the department you run is full of workers. Not contributors. *Workers* who are there strictly for the big bucks and the bigger benefits.

Working with workers isn't nearly as fulfilling (or fun) as working with *contributors*, so one of the ways to turn workers into contributors is to help them build a career that contributes to the greater good.

Over the past four years, when contributors were asked what helps them thrive at their jobs, the concept of meaningful, fulfilling work has exponentially shot up the charts, climbing from No. 11 in 2018 to No. 2 in 2022, demonstrating that contributors crave real meaning in their work. They want to do something they're passionate about, something that can have a positive impact on both their communities and society as a whole.

While searching for meaning and purpose at work, contributors have rethought what they wanted out of the work experience, and whether or not they can get that from their current employers. When contributors assessed their roles, questions arose, such as:

- In what ways is the company I work for making the world—or my tiny piece of it—a better place?
- What is the company doing that positively affects people and/ or communities, be it locally, nationally, or globally?
- Is doing 40-plus hours of *this* each week the best use of my time?

So how does one discover their sense of purpose in the workforce? According to a *Forbes* article by Tracy Brower, PhD, contributors looking for purpose at work should, ". . .focus on three things: Feeling connected to something bigger than themselves, knowing their work matters and, perhaps most importantly, understanding how their work affects other people—and not just the organization's bottom line."[8]

While a growing number of employers have become cognizant that potential contributors are hyper-keen on finding fulfilling jobs and responsibilities, many have not yet thought about how redefining the roles of contributors could improve company sustainability. If there's value in the company's purpose statement, but contributors see no sense of personal alignment, the company needs to rethink the situation.

Contributors, who should also have a say in this, may want to set up time to discuss options with their employers so they can find more rewarding work within the company. Since job hunters today are asking specific questions about what companies stand for—and what they do to make the world a better place—those already employed can ask the same questions to see if the company is trending in a positive direction.

To that end, Dave Bailey, CEO of Founder Coach, a coaching network for startup CEOs pointed out, "Businesses may be made by people for people, but our sense of purpose doesn't come from helping businesses. It comes from helping other people."[9]

There are good reasons for defining and living a corporate purpose:

- It will create pride and identity for the contributor, therefore fostering employer attractiveness and employee engagement.
- It will make your company look good and potentially help your sales.
- It will drive value-based decision making across the firm to maximize end-user benefit.

To quote Zendaya—and anytime you have the opportunity to quote Zendaya, you take it—"Find something that makes you happy and go for it. Sticking with your vision and what you believe in is so, so important."

Corporate Culture + Empathy + Honesty = Awesomeness

A modern, inclusive and engaging corporate culture—with or without a defined purpose—will need to be built on empathy as a key virtue to win people's hearts.

Empathy started to become a business issue for companies trying to align more closely with clients and customers, an exercise that continues today. It diversified amid the pandemic as companies' focus shifted to contributors. The new reality was that employers needed to feel what contributors felt. The pandemic tore down barriers, allowing employers and employees to feel empathy for one another.

Let's be clear: empathy needs to be genuine and organic, and not a matter of brush strokes to make the company culture appear nice. In other words, as beloved emcee Nate Dogg rapped back in 1997, "Keep that shit real."

While empathy is often thought to be innate, studies have indicated that, to some extent, it can be learned. In that regard, the pandemic served as a learning experience for those who had little awareness of empathy or refused to acknowledge it in themselves. As a result, many leaders recognized that corporate empathy—which was more prevalent than ever—*needed* to be a part of their company's DNA. In fact, the entire idea of inclusion is built on empathy. (It should be noted that *empathy* is not *sympathy*, which is defined as pitying or feeling sorry for others.)

Empathy, on the other hand, is often described as understanding what it means to walk in someone else's shoes, understanding what they see and feel. Role modeling empathy and commending others' empathetic responses is one way to champion and promote it. To create genuine empathy rather than Pavlovian responses, the broader context has to be understood. Why is someone struggling to balance increased workload and provide childcare at the same time? What does it mean for pre-retirement colleagues trying to catch up with a new software rollout? When is it appropriate not to penalize a team failure? Ask those learning empathy if they have ever been in such situations, and how they responded.

Life happens, and when contributors are going through a difficult time, an empathetic response makes a significant difference in morale. For example, Procter & Gamble offers a personal leave of absence that allows contributors to take up to three months off without pay, but with continued benefits, something that helps the company to retain valuable talent. Meta provides 20 to 30 paid days off when an employee is suffering from a personal loss.

What we also saw in the aftermath of the worst of COVID-19 was an exhausted workforce that wanted a healthier rhythm of work but had little opportunity to change the status quo. Companies are responding by listening. They are becoming more mindful of the need to demonstrate that they are about more than just making money. Defining a company's *why* and making sure it guides decisions and operations has rapidly become a cornerstone of doing business in what is now a more purposeful, empathy-driven business environment.

Eye of the Tiger

Yes, we still need leaders in The People Age.

We need them even more today in that BANI[10] world than in that VUCA world (volatile, uncertain, complex, and ambiguous).

There may have been a short moment in time—just before the pandemic turned our world upside-down—when some people thought leadership was an idea of the past. Instead, they favored the idea of autonomous contributors, intrinsically motivated, working in self-guided teams.

When the shock of the lockdowns hit us, employees were seeking orientation and guidance. People were happily acting on managers' orders, relieved to be directed and get direction in all that chaos.

Reassured that leadership does not fall out of style (regardless of the leadership style), let us have a quick look at the role of leadership in transporting purpose and shaping the corporate culture.

Leaders share the company's purpose and help contributors fully understand specifically how their work will contribute to the greater good. This means breaking down the *why* when discussing new positions, starting new projects, setting up new teams ... you get the idea.

As a leader, you can demonstrate and live up to a company purpose in various ways:

1. **Become the storyteller:** Express your corporate purpose with enthralling narratives that bring the mission to life. Share your company's purpose with heart and enthusiasm so that people feel it is a great adventure to embark upon.

2. **Walk the talk (the classic):** Show up every day as the embodiment of what your company stands for. Drive that electric car, champion the recycling program, or be the first to volunteer for community service. Demonstrate the corporate purpose with such flair that it becomes contagious.

3. **Infuse purpose in decisions:** Every decision you make should be in line with your corporate purpose. Use it as your compass when navigating the sea of choices. Explain how your decisions are guided by purpose.

4. **Weave purpose into goals:** Align your team's key performance indicators to tenets of your purpose. Show them how their everyday tasks contribute to this greater good. Set direction and make sure everybody is impacted.

5. **Spark employee engagement:** Get people involved in purpose-driven activities. Turn the participation into a festive event. Make it a fun and engaging way to breathe life into your mission.

6. **Celebrate the champions:** Find those superstars who align their actions with your purpose and put them on a pedestal! Recognize and reward them, and let their stories inspire others.

7. **Be transparent:** Showcase your achievements while acknowledging the gaps. Treat every shortcoming as an opportunity to recommit and learn from mistakes. Extend transparency into pay and careers. People respond best when they feel part of the conversation and equipped to make good decisions.

8. **Stick to it:** Your corporate purpose should be the North Star that never wavers, a constant source of guidance and inspiration. Stand by it through thick and thin, in the calm and the storm, demonstrating a resolve that's as captivating as it is steadfast.

By making your corporate purpose vibrant in these ways, you can inspire, engage, and lead your team toward a future where every action echoes with the sound of your corporate mission.

The more purpose becomes embedded in the day-to-day work, the more likely everyone on your payroll will find themselves dancing to the same beat.

Empathetic leadership, on the other hand, is a powerful catalyst for organizational success. It builds an environment of trust and mutual understanding, encouraging open dialogue and fostering collaboration, thereby driving innovation and performance.

Empathy allows leaders to deeply connect with their teams, increasing morale and motivation, which directly translates into improved productivity and retention. During periods of change or adversity, empathetic leaders are more effective at navigating the storm. They understand the emotions and concerns of their team, helping to maintain stability and resilience. When stress levels get to new heights, people need to feel truly understood; they need to feel included.

In a perfect world, leaders will carefully listen to their contributors; they will create a safe space and a sense of belonging. They will *feel* with their colleagues.

When leaders demonstrate empathy and honesty, they create a more engaged, committed workforce and a stronger, more adaptable organization, significantly enhancing the potential for enduring success.

And that is how you start winning in The People Age.

People Leaders' CTAs

1. **Encourage people to connect to your purpose**. Reflect on your corporate purpose, vision, mission, strategy. Ask yourself what gets in the way of people fully buying into your company's direction; how can you reduce this dissonance? Get into regular dialogues with executives and your team on your direction and how their work connects to the company's purpose.

2. **Get to know your people's perspective**. Look at each member of your team and ask yourself if you really know that person—what they care about outside of work—heck why they even joined. In conversations, move beyond seeing things from your colleague's perspective to seeing how you can help them thrive more at work.

3. **Aspire to a greater good and good leadership.** What proportion of jobs and time are allocated for doing good? How is the company off-setting its impact in the world? How involved are people in getting behind aspects of your purpose that are not directly linked to commercial returns? How are you reinforcing these messages? If there is a greater good, speak up. If not, speak up.

Executives' and HR's CTAS

1. **Build your culture, don't leave it to chance.** Get into a dialogue with your contributors on how you want to interact with each other, what values you hold high, and what appropriate behavior looks like. Build a corporate purpose that everyone can get behind. Activate everybody in your organization to incorporate purpose into their work and help them connect what they care about with what the organization focuses on—directly or indirectly.

2. **Make empathy a must-have leadership competence.** Start developing that muscle, start building a truly inclusive organization by looking at data and career equity trends that shed light on progress against your diversity and inclusion agenda. Drive action off the back of assessment and engagement data to effectively coach behavior that promotes insight around privilege and biases and encourages an inclusive leadership mindset for all.

CHAPTER 6

Trust and Accountability Are a Team Sport

Let's talk about kids.

Every parent has a different approach to parenting—and we'll *never* say a bad thing about *any* approach because your kid is *your* kid—but all parents can agree on two things:

1. Raising children is an art.
2. One of the most magical moments in any parent's life is *the pivot.*

The pivot is when your child is ready to take control, to handle tasks without parents eyeballing them every step of the way, to practice being a (very) young adult. It could be something as simple as walking to school on their own, or something as (relatively) complex as strolling over to the grocery store and buying some pretzels and a bottle of water with their allowance money. (If you don't have kids but want to experience the pivot, check out the Japanese show *Old Enough,* which follows toddlers shopping by themselves.) This is a huge step not just for the child, but also for the parents.

Soon, the parents will trust the kids with handling *grown-up* activities and decisions that are arguably far bigger steps. Some parents cope with this pivot in a matter-of-fact, this-is-life fashion, and they may even appreciate the moment as an important one in both their kids' lives and their own. Others continue parenting beyond the point of being beneficial to the child, missing out on one of the most important components of personal growth: trust.

A parent's trust needs to be given. A child's trust needs to be received. And the same thing applies in business.

Leaders and managers all around the world have preached trust more than ever. *Trust and accountability* have become a mantra, especially for new work evangelists, but, as SZA sang, "Trust is hard to find."

Before we discuss ways to develop and maintain a permanent sense of trust—and how to walk the trust walk after you talk the trust talk—we need to have a quick word on trust and accountability's antagonist: *command-and-control.*

Command-and-control Had Its Heyday

In 1988, NATO described *command-and-control* as, "[T]he exercise of authority and direction by a properly designated individual over assigned resources in the accomplishment of a common goal."

Yeah, yeah, we know, we know, that definition is one part word salad and two parts military-speak, thus making it three parts confusing. So we'll turn to Frederic Laloux, who, in his book *Reinventing Organizations*, outlined the evolution of organizations leaning towards a *command-and-control* style. Laloux called the type of organizations that epitomized the last millennium "traditional conformists."[1] These companies strive for stability and scale through clear roles, clear processes, and clear ranks within a hierarchical structure. Compliance is expected throughout the organization, and there are crystal-clear superior/ subordinate relationships. In a nutshell, everything is spelled out, period, exclamation mark.

However, in the business world, traditional conformists are no longer in favor, replaced by what Laloux refers to as "modern performance oriented" organizations, but even in these more contemporary entities, you'll still find *command-and-control* thinking and behavior.

To better understand the root cause of *command-and-control*, we turn to the Principal Agent theory, which emerged in the 1970s from the combined disciplines of economics and institutional theory. The theory describes the problem that arises when one person or a single entity—the "agent"—is representing another person or group—the "principal"—and is able to make decisions and/or take action on their behalf.[2]

But here's the thing: a dilemma occurs when an agent's best interests are contrary to those of their principal. This leads to a problematic situation in which the two parties have conflicting motivating interests and asymmetric information. This dynamic often plays out in employment contracts, performance management, and incentive systems, forming the underlying philosophy of the traditional employer/employee relationship in the Industrial Age. We may also still find it in the collective memories of our societies, nurtured by media that perpetuate stereotypes (exploiting employer, exploited employee). It is the intellectual fuel on which many unions and workers' councils are running.

Times have changed. We are in The People Age. The interests of organizations and contributors are increasingly aligned. A company needs contributors who stick around, stay engaged, and prosper. Contributors, on the other hand, are interested in working for a thriving company whose values align with their own—and in developing a new employer/employee relationship that allows contributors to thrive as well.

The concept of asymmetric information is also disappearing, which is good news. Modern tools and systems can create transparency around pay, promotions and skills, on the one hand; while on the other hand, KPIs and metrics, supported by intelligence management systems, can create transparency on workers' contributions.

So, goodbye, Principal Agent Theory.

Beyond the fact that it's an outdated employer/employee philosophy, there are other good reasons to ditch *command-and-control*. For one, it can lead to groupthink—when the entire organization conforms to the same ideas and opinions, there's often little room for diverse perspectives and fresh thinking. This can limit the company's creativity and its potential to innovate. Further, a *command-and-control* mindset can lead to a lack of ownership and accountability. Employees may not feel responsible for the outcomes of their actions since they were only following orders. This fuels a culture of blame-shifting, which makes it difficult for the company to learn from its mistakes and improve processes.

The big takeaway here is that a *command-and-control* culture can be detrimental to good decision-making because it limits creativity, stifles diversity of thought, and drives a lack of ownership and accountability. This is why we'd *much* rather spend a few pages on trust and accountability.

A Funky Beat for The People Age

Unless there's honesty and transparency from both the employer and the contributor, it becomes difficult to master the complexity and pace of today's rhythm of work. Offering trust, distributing responsibilities, holding people accountable, and collaborating to solve problems are the ingredients of successful organizations— ones that are both stable in their performance and agile in the way they innovate and adapt.

Better communication and knowledge-sharing creates more transparency and accelerates this trust evolution. Digital collaboration tools allow for more effective communication that transcends time and space. At the tap of a button, individuals across the globe (or the office) can instantly spark a real-time conversation. This dramatically slashes the time it takes to identify and solve problems; it empowers teams to seize new opportunities at lightning speed. Productivity rises as a result.

Trust and accountability aren't about organizational structures, governance processes, and policies in the first place—these are just the artifacts of an organization's trust in its employees (or lack thereof). The journey to shift an organization from *command-and-control* to *trust and accountability* will need to include an exercise to redesign these artifacts to visibly promote the new thinking.

A mindset of trust is the very foundation of an organization in The People Age. First and foremost, there needs to be this *conviction*, this collective truth that trust is the basis for all thinking and acting within the organization and beyond.

Sounds simple, right?

It's not.

Struggling to embrace trust is leading to more fractured ways of working and a vast chasm between views on how work and work partnerships should look in this new era.

It takes significant effort to bake this newfound honesty paradigm into corporate and individual beliefs, which have been socialized in a different world and time.

A lot of people have experienced mistrust for various reasons for so long that they themselves are unable to trust others. When millions of employees began working from home, leaders had no choice but to relinquish control and put faith in their people to do the right thing. (To quote Ernest Hemingway, "The best way to find out if you can trust somebody is to trust them." And to paraphrase Bruno Mars—*You need to count on [the employee] so they can count on you.*)

Yes, it's difficult for many of us to embrace openness, but when we do, good things happen.

It all starts with being true to yourself on a deeply personal level. Try to answer these two questions:

1. Who do I mistrust in my team?
2. Who do I mistrust in our organization?

Probably, there are few people in your team, but a significant number of people in your organization whom you don't trust. Mercer sees this pattern in most of our employee listening exercises, and we are not surprised. There is a simple reason for that—it's the distance. It is hard to trust people you don't see day to day. The bad news: that's the new rhythm of work. You'd better get accustomed to that beat.

Now, how would you do this? Try to answer three more questions:

1. Why do I not trust these specific people?
2. What's the worst thing that would happen if I started trusting these people?
3. What's the best thing that would happen if I started trusting these people?

Give it a try—trust needs to be given, not earned. The exercise will be rewarding. We promise.

Trust is a two-way street. It's one thing to give trust; it's another to be trusted. This is especially true for leaders and even more so for new leaders, who can earn or destroy trust in the blink of an eye. Here's how effective leaders build trust:

- Don't act like you know it all.
- Let others shine.
- Invite your team to find the answers.
- Give your team room to try new things and a soft landing when they fail.
- Provide expertise and good judgment.
- When something goes wrong, guide solutions rather than assign blame.
- Keep your promises.

Once employees sense they can trust their team leads and companies, they'll likely want to prove that they deserve to be trusted in return. But, again, it's a two-way street. Delivering on objectives and expectations is a key aspect of the game.

This is where accountability comes in. This is where everybody—leaders, managers, contributors—must realize that there's cause, there's effect, and there are consequences. And the consequences are a big deal.

We've come across many organizations that don't manage consequences appropriately. This prevents people from both giving trust and taking true ownership, and for the most part, it starts at the top. (The decision-makers will realize this once they do their internal check-ins.) Coaching for both teams and individuals can help; so too can leadership development programs. Expectation management, dialogue and feedback go hand-in-hand with the need for trust and accountability.

Remote and hybrid work can't work without trust, and managers have to pull up their trust pants because remote and hybrid work ain't going anywhere. Oh, and guess what? With less oversight and more trust, work as a whole has become more productive.

Don't believe it? Consider this:

> The S&P 500 Index doubled from its COVID lows to a record high in August 2021, when much of the world was still either working from home or arguing about how many days employees should be spending in the office.[3] Businesses all over the globe were performing better than ever, and a common characteristic was that the newly empowered employees were operating with less supervision than ever before.

The new world of working is not all about remote work—and trust and accountability are more than a means to make it work. There is enough evidence that trusted employees create better results than employees who are being commanded and controlled.

Netflix is known for its unique corporate culture that values freedom, responsibility, and transparency.[4] And with a rating of 4.3 out of 5 stars on Glassdoor as of 2023, its approach seems to work for most contributors, too.[5] Here are a few examples of how Netflix gives trust to its employees.

Freedom and Responsibility

- Netflix gives its employees a high degree of freedom and responsibility to make decisions and take ownership of their work. There are no formal policies around things like vacation time or expense approvals, for example. Instead, employees are trusted to make the right decisions and manage their time and resources effectively.

Open Communication

- Netflix fosters a culture of open communication and transparency, where employees are encouraged to share their opinions and feedback. The company regularly solicits feedback from employees and takes it seriously when making decisions.

Performance-Based Culture

- Netflix has a performance-based culture that rewards employees who achieve their goals and deliver results. There is transparency on both good and bad performance and the consequences that go with it.

- Empowerment doesn't mean people managers are losing their jobs, though they might have to readjust. This team sport of trust and accountability requires leaders who can direct, guide, and coach; leaders who drive performance; leaders who ensure their teams are connecting in the right ways, and are healthily engaged and working in a sustainable manner; leaders who are on the lookout for things that could go wrong, both on the balance sheet and with the culture.

Performance Management Sucks

During the first few months of lockdown, how many online articles did you read with titles like, "Five Ways to Make Your Dining Room Workspace More Zoom-Friendly"? Once remote work was woven into the business fabric, many companies put policies in place to formalize this flexibility, ranging from manager-led to total laissez-faire, leaving it up to individuals to decide when, where, and how to work.

Contributors, for the most part, dug it. Mercer data shows that while remote work and hybrid arrangements were seen as a net positive for a majority of employees (i.e., improving work/life balance, reducing stress, and increasing productivity), the benefits were less pronounced in building a sense of belonging (just 47%

said it helped foster a stronger sense of belonging, while 18% said that sense had decreased) and in feeling connected to co-workers (43% said it helped, while 24% said they felt *less* connected).[6]

As for managers, well, there was some freaking out.

The managers sensed they were losing control of the situation—and we all know that many managers *need* control—stemming in part from how performance is measured in most organizations, which typically boils down to time versus output. This was an effective indicator when labor was primarily manual and there was a strong correlation between input (time) and output (goods); it's a less effective and less relevant indicator of performance in The People Age, when work is often knowledge-based and the output is more oriented toward services.

Measuring time for knowledge work is fraught with challenges, and when it comes to creativity and innovation there is no correct amount of time. Exactly how many hours does it take to create a movement, or innovate a new product, or disrupt an industry? It all—as we consultants like to say—*depends.*

Driving an output orientation to how we manage work requires a shift in how performance has been managed. In many organizations, we still encounter performance/potential grids—typically a three-by-three matrix—along with annual objectives, goal setting, and performance review meetings. According to a global study by Gartner in 2019, 81% of HR leaders were changing their organizations' performance management system[7]—so it's no surprise that talent leaders reported that their performance programs needed updating if they were to be effective in the new world of trust and empowerment.

For an example of an organization in a very traditional business that radically redesigned its performance management process, let's turn to a global reinsurance company. In 2019, this company waved goodbye to rewarding individual performance with high bonuses because employees became more concerned with optimizing themselves or their own teams rather than collaborating firm-wide for more innovation. (Again, it's not always all about the Benjamins.)

The company completely redesigned its performance management process toward continuous conversations between managers and team members. This allowed them to be aligned, to stay on course, and to foster individual development. Managers were trained to enhance their listening skills, to effectively manage expectations, and to support the growth of their team members. Today, leaders, managers, and rank-and-file workers alike are finding that appreciation of their contribution is leading to increases in their confidence levels and often better promotion within the organization.

Performance recognition, however, is another matter. Contributors deserve to be given props when their contributions are on point. Objectives and key results (OKRs) lay the groundwork for setting, tracking, and monitoring both goals (objectives) and expected outcomes (key results) throughout the entire organization. Devoting sufficient time for developing, communicating, and monitoring OKRs remains a critical factor in managing and recognizing success. Trusting organizations have systems for managing this process integrated into the platforms that employees use on a daily basis. Some leverage AI to perpetually mine performance data or seek feedback for self-development; these companies are ahead of the curve.

As well they should be.

Virtual Insanity

The same tools that created the cure for *command-and-control* gave us greater transparency and an environment of trust, but these tools have also brought about some serious side effects.

The shift to remote work, hybrid work, and asynchronous shift work has fueled an explosion of new video conferencing tools, project management tools, virtual whiteboarding technology, enterprise social networking software, voting technologies, and live chat software, to cite a few.

Two of the more visible issues in this trust-centric New Business World Order are information overload and the unintentional emergence of new, informal silos within the organization. The information overload element is easy to appreciate, but don't worry—we won't overload you with it. (See what we did there?)

We should, however, consider the less-intuitive side effect of trust driving greater communication and paradoxically creating silos that complicate the work and the employee experience.

Experts from Harvard Business School, University of Washington, Johns Hopkins University, and Microsoft worked together to understand how the pandemic changed the nature of organizational communication, the same type of communication that was a key enabler for greater trust.[8] Their data showed that lockdowns substantially increased the volume of email communication—which, truth be told, we all kinda knew. What was notable was that the increased volume of communication revealed a pattern of increased network modularity, aka siloing. Workers found themselves splitting into subgroups, intensifying the volume of communication within their smaller networks and decreasing the amount of communication with those outside of those networks. This behavior will dampen, not amplify, organizational learning and trust. It's not always bad when things don't go according to plan.

Failing Your Way to Success

"Fail early, fail often, but always fail forward."[9]

So wrote author John C. Maxwell, and John C. Maxwell has sold over 24 million books, and when somebody's sold over 24 million books, we should, at the very least, listen to their advice.

This phrase is often used when describing a culture driven by curiosity, exploration, and innovation. It highlights the concept that success is built by those who constantly want to create something new, innovators who aren't satisfied to roll with the status quo.

The professional arcs of the Wright Brothers, Gottlieb Daimler, Walt Disney, Steve Jobs, Bill Gates, and Jack Ma are among the many success stories that began with failure. Orville, Wilbur, et al. recognized that *trial and error* was not a hallmark of failure, but rather a key stepping stone along the journey. For that matter, many organizations have tried to incorporate failure into shaping their futures. (The concept of incorporating failure is seemingly bananas, but stick with us.) Trust is a substantial pre-condition for creating an environment of psychological safety, where failure is allowed—and even celebrated—for the sake of learning, failure that's motivated by learning, not resulting from neglect or greed.

Eric Roza, Managing Director of Vista Equity Partners, was among the early CEOs to celebrate failures during his days at the helm of Datalogix. Roza explained, "Our corporate culture encouraged people to acknowledge their failures or errors at monthly company meetings by having 'Stay Humble, Keep Improving' moments. By acknowledging mistakes as a group, we could all fail and that was okay." To that end, some companies offer up a *Failures of the Month* award or host *Screw-Up Nights* as a new form of office group therapy.

Other great examples include Sarah Robb O'Hagan, who attributes messing up at Virgin and Atari for making her the right person to turn around Gatorade.[10] And on the sporting side, Michael Jordan has been more than vocal about his route to success being anchored in failure.[11]

If leaders can admit their errors—and if they can take them to heart, or even better, learn from them—they'll set a tone that everyone in the company will want to follow. Sharing how making mistakes is part of *trying* is one of the best ways to create an environment of safety where individuals and ideas can thrive. What stands in the way in many organizations—especially those in finance, professional services, and engineering spaces—is a culture that's not open to failing early, often and forward.

For now, let's call it *Find-the-Error Culture*, one in which leaders and managers point out mistakes not to make things better, but rather to prove three things:

- This will not work.
- You are wrong.
- I am clever.

Have you come across this kind of behavior? Of course you have, and you sure as hell didn't appreciate it, and it sure as hell wasn't productive. So, when you see it, call it out, and call it out immediately. If a supervisor points out flaws without offering a solution—and without demonstrating a sense of trust in their team—it becomes nearly impossible to experiment with agile ways of working.

In The People Age, that simply won't cut it.

Trust Needs Its Counter-Power

When news of corruption and scandal prompted customers to pull out their money, leading cryptocurrency exchange FTX filed for bankruptcy. Despite the trust it had built up with investors and regulators—which some feel was undeserved—a lack of corporate guardrails set the stage for murky business deals, bad investments, and poor bookkeeping. FTX founder and CEO Sam Bankman-Fried resigned and was later arrested on criminal charges.

Yes, FTX was held accountable, but the accountability came too late.

Silicon Valley Bank (SVB) had been a major lender for decades, but wasn't held to the same regulations as larger U.S. banks. (For a chunk of 2022, the bank went without a chief risk officer, and it's still not clear if or how they managed risk.) Amid rising interest rates, SVB lost money on its investments and tried (unsuccessfully) to raise funds or sell the firm. Customers withdrew their money in a frenzied bank run, which led to SVB's 2023 collapse.[12]

SVB was held accountable, but the accountability came too late.

Then there's Credit Suisse. From a series of scandals to bad investments,[13] a pattern of risk management crises drove investors and depositors to lose trust in the bank.[14] Then, with its share price and bonds dropping, Credit Suisse became the next victim of the panic set off by the SVB collapse. Despite a $54-billion lifeline from the Swiss National Bank, Credit Suisse couldn't bounce back and was acquired by competitor UBS in 2023.

Credit Suisse was held accountable, but the accountability came too late.

Trust needs to be coupled with a real-time risk mindset that's embedded across the organization and upheld by each and every one of its citizens. Auditing the collective risk management mindset of all your workers—permanent and contingent—and holding people accountable for upholding a risk management culture is critical for building a foundation of trust.

In the modern world, as we create agile, purpose-driven teams, team accountability is more crucial than ever. If companies want to achieve sustained growth, they'll get there faster by cultivating team players to work alongside their stars. After all, it's great to have a Messi or a Mbappé in your corner, but you won't take home a trophy without 10 other fantastic performers on the pitch who know how to work together.

Here are our five ingredients for encouraging a climate of individual and team accountability in the realities of today's workplace:

1. **Define a team's purpose and make it clear for what they're accountable.**

   Explain why the team exists and what's expected of each team member. Tools such as Business Canvases for teams can be useful, but the key is being clear about people's roles and accountabilities—especially to one another. A shared vision of what good and poor behaviors look like, and/or a team charter, can also help to communicate what values and behaviors matter most. Spelling out who's doing what helps to foster empowerment and responsibility. Do whatever it takes to ensure everyone can easily describe the team and their role and expectations similarly, even if they've never sat in a conference or virtual room together.

2. **Promote fairness.**

   Respect doesn't come from roles or titles, but rather from how team members and leaders treat one another. Managers, experts, and co-workers all have the ability to influence perceptions of a team member's worth. Consider if you're playing favorites; how transparent opportunities and promotions might be seen by others; how you're working together across digital, temporal, and cultural boundaries; and who gets let off the hook. Our research shows that employees' perceptions of thriving are highly correlated with their perceptions of fairness around pay and promotions.[15]

3. Strive for excellence.

No one who believes they're playing in the English Premiere League–level wants to find themselves in second division, so offer actionable feedback to get the best out of team members and move people off the team if they can't contribute as needed. Don't wait for team members to talk smack about their colleagues, thus eroding respect and dignity. Everyone has off days and deals with outside factors that sometimes call for a time out.

4. Reinforce effective team communication.

Sharing plans, progress, and new information is all part of a healthy team culture. Eradicate beliefs that reporting on a project's progress is a status thing, and correct those who disrespect project management roles or undermine overall team productivity. Consider if digital tools for team accountability or task delegation (like virtual Kanban boards) might help.

5. Celebrate team success, while acknowledging individual contributions.

Ensure rewards are aligned with achieving team goals, and that they address the social dimension of teams, all while recognizing individual effort and cultivating productive, positive behavior. Despite the advances of technology, nothing builds trust quicker than a few days together or a chance to break bread.

Unlike soccer, your company is a 12-month grind. You don't get to spend a month in solitude, contemplating how you can learn to better trust your goalkeeper to keep the ball out of the net when you've blown your assignment, or how to better take accountability for blowing the assignment in the first place. As General Stanley McChrystal says: "The key to breaking down silos and building a *team of teams* is to create a shared consciousness—a common understanding of the team's goals, objectives and challenges".[16]

Admittedly, a culture of trust and accountability doesn't come overnight. Attempts at empowerment often fail due to insufficient trust and direction from leadership, and/or insufficient skills and drive on the part of the employee. It's a multi-fold exercise in role modeling trust from the top, developing leaders, optimizing performance management, and using related tools for people management.

Trust and accountability are part of the equation that helps you win in The People Age.

Without them, you won't be Bayern Munich.

You won't be Man City. You won't be the Lionesses.

You'll just be relegated.

People Leaders' CTAs

1. **Build trust through being trustworthy.** Think about how you interact with your team, what helps team members grow in their roles, and what signals you send about teamwork. Invite your team to find answers to their problems. Let others shine and help them do just that. Provide expert guidance and judgement. Keep your promises.
2. **Foster psychological safety.** Don't pretend to know it all. Admit mistakes. Encourage others to experiment and report back (on both their successes and failures). After all, we all learn and grow when we reflect. Take action when people are unable to perform, and support team members who feel at risk.
3. **Create transparency and manage expectations.** Build common ground for trust by overcoming information asymmetry. Ensure your performance management fosters individual development and objectives are set at the team level. Ensure those who need to know have unfettered access to information. Ensure everyone knows what is expected and that there is no excuse for unforeseen delays/lack of stakeholder or team management

Executives' and HR's CTAs

1. **Make trust and accountability a given in your culture.** Anchor trust and accountability in your purpose and infuse it into your corporate DNA by defining your leadership mindset. Develop current and next-generation leaders to effectively balance trust with accountability. Build leaders' skills around managing people and performance in ways that help them trust others to deliver.

2. **Redefine processes to support accountability.** Ensure your training and performance management practices cultivate a climate of mutual trust and respect via clear accountabilities for individuals and shared team outcomes. Advocate for the use of tools and processes that enhance project management, goal setting and reviews and assist with delegation.

CHAPTER 7

Intelligence Is Getting Amplified

Everybody, Meet ChatGPT; ChatGPT, Meet Everybody

First, there were sharp sticks and rock walls.

Then there were feather quills dipped into jars of ink.

Then there were pencils, crayons, markers, and ballpoints.

Then there were mainframe computers, PCs, the internet, laptops, tablets, and smartphones.

Then there was an app that could generate a competent white paper, or a readable blog post, or an essay about sharp sticks and rock walls. (It can't write an entertaining and informative book about the future of work though. At least not yet.)

The app in question—as you might have gleaned from the section header—is ChatGPT. Now let's ask a couple of questions about said app:

1. Are we psyched about this super-easy-to-use piece of tech, or do we wish it remained in the lab?

2. In 2034, will Gen AI be a beloved tool for work and fun, or will we rue the day it hit the market, triggering mass layoffs and. . .the Robot Uprising?

Damn good questions.

For now, Gen AI brings up mixed emotions. Some feel a breathless excitement about its potential, while others can't shake the fear that AI might impact their employability. Some will celebrate this tech as the first step on the journey to life-altering superintelligence, while others feel it's the first step on the journey to Armageddon. What we can all agree on is that the humanizing of responses from big data, and its sheer accessibility to the masses, is a watershed moment that will be marked indelibly in our memories.

ChatGPT dropped in November 2022, and despite virtually zero marketing budget, reached 1 million users in just five days via word-of-mouth and a smattering of earned media. Two months after its launch, ChatGPT had over 100 million monthly active users, a number that TikTok needed nine months to hit.

Never before have we seen such a viral consumer adoption of technology. Never.

Bursting onto the scene in late 2022, ChatGPT's success even shocked OpenAI executives, who claimed that the public release was a last resort after lackluster private testing.[1] But it's understandable why it so quickly entered into the zeitgeist: There was not only the open access, but a novelty factor behind its virality, a complex and powerful technology wrapped up in a clean, simple user interface. It was a chatbot that conversed in plain language, oftentimes with insight, humor, and style. But it could also be flawed, deceitful, and mistake-prone. Y'know, kinda like a human being. People had played with generative art and even AI-generated music, but this was different.

It raised about a zillion questions, among them: *Does the upside of this tech balance out the risks? Is this sort of advancement a welcome or unwelcome answer to our skills shortage?* And, most concerningly for us workers, contributors, employees, managers, and leaders who have toiled so hard to get here: *Will the ChatGPTs of the world turn The People Age into The Machine Age?*

Machine Intelligence + Human Intelligence = Amplified Intelligence

Perhaps the biggest positive for the most popular Gen AI tools is just how easy it is to access large language models (LLMs) to answer the curliest of questions or requests in a format that is as easy as texting, emailing, or asking a friend for their opinion and creative effort on a project. Creating effective prompts doesn't take an advanced degree, just solid language skills, hands-on experience, and your imagination. You or your company no longer need a highly trained writer, coder, artist, or analyst to deliver the kind of output you might get from a less experienced (or Quietly Quitting) contributor.

This shift became apparent in the kind of LinkedIn job postings that started popping up in late 2022 and early 2023:

> Exciting new job: Engineering degree—*optional,*
> good command of English—*important,*
> ability to communicate with generative AI—*essential.*

Gen AI is the latest in-demand skill.[2] And suddenly, a whole lot of jobs are changing and evolving. Suddenly a whole lot of jobs are now accessible to non-traditional talent. Suddenly, fortunes are panning out differently as job cuts emerge, targeted at functional roles.

The potential gains are colossal. ChatGPT burns through hours-long writing projects in a matter of seconds. Image and video generators take just minutes, not days, to craft complex and engaging visuals you might want to take to a designer.

Best of all, it's getting us all thinking about the possibilities!

Many Gen AI tools were still in their infancy in the early 2020s, and logically, free to use as they learned from our interactions. While pricing models now vary by company, product, and usage, they still translate to lower costs-per-project compared to human labor without AI support. And, as fun as these tools are, OpenAI's decision to save ChatGPT user inputs meant enterprise use was limited. Those who saw earlier commercial adoption, however, got a head start on changing the game completely.

And the opportunity and the risk are that these tools are a heck of a lot more affordable than paying a human. Early in-house experiments at Mercer found that a single human-written blog post that could cost $500 with maybe a three- to four-week turnaround in 2023, could now be done for less than $20 per month for virtually unlimited, immediately-delivered content from ChatGPT.

And in April of that year, OpenAI's GPT-4—the updated version of GPT-3—cost roughly as little as $0.00004 per word in a prompt, plus another $0.00008 per word in a response.[3] That same month, the gigs portal Upwork noted that beginner-level freelance writers charge an average of $0.05 to $0.10 per word.[4] The robots do the grunt work, the humans polish the end product, and the bean-counters are happy. The challenge, of course, is the question of content ownership and ethical usage.

AI's blend of higher productivity and efficiency, with less waste and at a lower cost, can help create the perfect person/machine mélange: human skills and know-how, amplified by AI, is the type of augmented intelligence from which we can all benefit. That is, if we all have access. And here are the seeds of concern as we balance a fair and equitable digital transition without need to deliver a competitive advantage in our companies today. The downstream implications of this new partnership could lead to a more manageable workload, while still yielding higher returns. Finally, the 80–20 rule (80% of all outcomes are derived from 20% of the effort) becomes a reality, freeing up time and budgets for more complex, high-value, right-brain initiatives, and expanding opportunities to pay human workers more, keep them more engaged, and allow them better balance in their lives—well, in theory, at least! From our perspective, workers, contributors, employees, managers, and leaders need not fear that AI will screw up The People Age. If we don't share in the benefits, this will surely be down to the humans. This utopian outlook for tech to equalize is what we all need to strive for.

The fact is that ChatGPT and its brothers and sisters, and eventually its children, have the potential to bolster the need for human qualities while simultaneously helping workers and businesses compete. Still, successfully integrating it into daily professional life is on us, and is a work in progress, and one that's fraught with potential inequities. As we move toward greater human/machine symbiosis, we need to ensure that the democratization of AI will continue. If the new jobs and opportunities it spurns deliver greater opportunities for all, it's all good. But if mismanaged, and the historical have-nots don't see the benefits, then contributors without access to proper training will be truly disadvantaged and large swaths of the workforce will be left behind.

On the bright side, AI has already brought significant advances to fields such as healthcare, transportation, education, and entertainment.[5] But on the flip side, as with any paradigm-shifting tech, there's fear of the unknown.

At the personal level, it has some workers questioning their job security.

At the business level, it has some leaders wondering if they're capitalizing on this tech quickly enough.

At the ground level, it has some psychologists curious as to whether everybody is properly considering its impact on the future of our health, wealth, and careers.

And on a sci-fi level, some are freaking out that it could lead to a Robot Uprising.

Bad Bot, Whatcha Gonna Do?

Even with safeguards in place, AI's advanced logic and algorithms can lead to unexpected behavior that could pose a threat to our way of life. (Sounds dramatic, we know, but hang with us.) Sure, ChatGPT can spit out a reasonable list of the five best-reviewed restaurants in London—as of this writing, it tells us that The Ledbury tops the charts, followed by The Clove Club, Lyle's, Gymkhana, and Kiln—but there are more than a few concerns:

1. Errors, harmful content, and manipulation

Part of what sets these tools apart from their predecessors is the sheer volume of data that serves as their brain food. GPT-3, for example, was trained on 45 terabytes of text data from Google Books, Wikipedia, and other sources across the internet,[6] roughly equivalent to a 300-million-page Word document, 350 iPhone 14s full of text, or 60,000 filing cabinets stuffed with paper. And at the time, ChatGPT was the first to be trained on such a large set of data.

Since Gen AI learns from the internet, these tools sometimes create problematic responses based on content that we've shared online, and newsflash, there's a lot of content we've shared online, and newsflash, much of it is straight-up garbage. It vacuums up satire and hyperbole—which, as regular Twitter users know, can lead to the viralization of a bogus news story—as well as copyright infringement, bias, hate speech, inappropriate content, and purposeful disinformation campaigns. And no surprise, ChatGPT (which learned from people) perpetuated the view that sex and race should determine a person's professional aptitude.[7] (While we would disagree, historical data might suggest that it *can*— one reason why it's crucial to govern the ethical use of AI and keep human decision-making ahead of the AI support.)

Firms like OpenAI have added content filters to prevent these issues, but they aren't foolproof, as the algorithms are finding too many patterns across low-quality content to disregard them completely. Users have also found ways to manipulate or *jailbreak* AI models to get around these guardrails, like asking ChatGPT how it *might* respond in a hypothetical *no-rules* or *alter-ego* scenario.[8] As a case in point: *ChatGPT, what sites should I avoid if I don't want to illegally stream movies?*

Because Gen AI responds in clear, concise language, the content it shares often seems credible, even when it isn't. These outputs are called "artificial hallucinations," flawed responses that appear to be valid.[9] When data caps or processing limitations get in the way of providing an answer, ChatGPT and the gang simply make up an answer that sounds good enough. And maybe for many things that is good enough.

The quick, conversational nature of these tools can also help anyone further their interests through mass-produced and personalized content, which can then be amplified through search results and millions of fake AI-powered social media profiles. Many less-than-diligent news consumers will be the least likely to fact-check AI outputs and are thus more vulnerable to its manipulation. Deep fakes are a persistent challenge emerging across the world of work, from automated video application processes for jobs to directives from your CEO to move money/take action,[10] and this technology is becoming accessible to many.

2. Accountability

The rapid development of AI raises significant questions around who owns, controls, and is responsible for such powerful technology. Part of this fear comes from the "Black Box Effect"[11]: AI's neural networks and learning processes are so complex and its data sources so opaque that it sometimes behaves in ways that we don't expect, which could lead to high-stakes problems such as compromised medical records, manipulated credit card scores, nefarious remote-controlled autonomous driving, fraudulent job applications, and illegal investments. This all points to the need for greater accountability and transparency in the tech's development and deployment. Part of this is due to the fact that, to a large extent, we've delegated *ethical AI governance* to the techies in Palo Alto, rather than engaging educators or regulators who've made it their life work to consider ethics and their implications on human evolution.

It's a game of speed and scale, and few organizations (or governments, for that matter) have the resources to compete. The big tech firms that govern our worlds today will likely remain in the lead, which can have a profound effect on both privacy and democratization. The tight concentration of power is today driving questions around their transparency, ethics, and accountability. But the real question is who owns the AI? And do their political and cultural backgrounds have the opportunity to dig into our psyches, garner support or cohesion, or even shape our kids' worldview?

Gen AI systems such as ChatGPT require users to enter personal details before goofing around with the tools. By design, AI collects personal information and captures every question, comment, and response in its eternal quest to learn and improve. As such, our growing appetite to explore with unfettered access is leading to tons of data shared across platforms—data we might prefer to keep to ourselves. This data, like that of Facebook, of Google, and the entire Internet of Things, will then be used to predict and influence individual behavior. This is naturally raising concerns about the ethics and laws around using said data, and who's responsible for protecting individuals' rights and freedoms here and in the metaverse.

But what if something goes wrong, something *big*, like a deepfake of a Margot Robbie flick, a computer-generated Billie Eilish album, or a Steve Jobs hologram that fools gullible Apple fanatics into believing the company perfected the iCar? Or is the real concern a deepfake of a world leader telling us the end is near? Who steps in when AI is misused or gives erroneous information that messes with any number of programs? It often involves different actors: developers, customers, and users as well as the regulators tasked with any areas of overlap between tech and society. For example, if an AI system used in a self-driving car—iCar, y'all—causes an accident, it's not clear whether the responsibility lies with the creators of the system, the car manufacturer, the individual using the car, or a combination of the three. Litigation will no doubt decide where the liability lies, but we're not sure that waiting for the courts to figure it out is the way to go.

The dystopian fear that AI might one day develop free will and end life as we know it is still a concern to many. . .

Robot Uprising, anyone?

. . .Yes, ChatGPT content might sound, to quote the metal band White Zombie, "more human than human," but this isn't an indication that artificial general intelligence (AGI), where AI could rival human intelligence is here anytime soon.

Summing up, while we can debate whether Robot Uprisings are something to be concerned about or not; privacy breaches, legal and compliance risks, and broken copyright laws most definitely are. At the end of the day, these might wreak more havoc on a company or a nation than any legion of cyborgs.

3. Job security

Among the biggest AI concerns is the impact on jobs and individual livelihoods and what that means for industries and economies. Let's tackle the impact on jobs first. In 2023, the WEF's Future of Jobs Report estimated that by 2027, 69 million new jobs will be created and 83 million eliminated.[12] Tech is a driver of both job creation and job destruction, with most destruction happening within clerical or administrative roles, including bank tellers, cashiers and data entry clerks. But while expectations of the displacement of physical and manual work by machines have decreased, reasoning, communication and coordinating—all skills in which humans have a comparative advantage—are expected to be more automatable in the future. Overall, AI is expected to lead to job growth in 50% of organizations and losses in 25%,[13] but with AI innovations growing at an astounding rate with 13 Gen AI unicorns already in early 2023 (companies valued at $1 billion), these estimates could be highly underestimated.[14]

So, what's getting everyone nervous? Well, what is different with Gen AI is that in addition to the logical processing and informed insights from scraping or summarizing large swaths of data, Gen AI can more-or-less mimic the emotions, cognition, and creativity that once set us apart from machines. Further, because it's always learning, it gets better with each interaction, raising never-before-asked questions surrounding ethics, authenticity, and trust as it mimics our outputs. Ask it a few questions and it picks up on what you are asking, generating the next potential question and answering it without you even asking it to. Give it some feedback. Tell it what you like and it mimics the output. Much like an eager new hire!

And despite the opportunities for augmentation and improved job demand, the reverberations in the job market are starting. Just a few months into ChatGPT's public release, almost half of the U.S. firms using the tool claimed it had already replaced workers and cut costs[15]. . .and consequently, 2023 saw a disproportionate number of cuts in functional roles, roles that generally involve tasks ripe for automation and logical cognitive applications.

David Autor and colleagues from MIT make a distinction between innovations that are labor-automating versus labor-augmenting.[16] They note that prior workforce disruptions have been automation-led, and thus job-eroding, as they've supplemented production and clerical roles. But, they argue, the last 40 years have seen a greater impact on higher-paid professional roles and, more recently, on lower-paid service roles—effectively "hollowing out" middle-income jobs.

Unlike prior disruptions, however, the impact of AI will be felt simultaneously across many industries as it augments at the skill level, not the job level. Thus, its opportunities and its risks hit multiple job categories at once. The concern is that, as people's skills devalue, what will they jump to next? Without reskilling, it's likely their next career move will bring lower pay or less job security.

On the flip side, the likelihood of a productivity labor boom is increasing. Gen AI is forecast to account for a rise in labor productivity with the most gains seen in developed countries—most notably Hong Kong, Israel, Japan, Sweden, the United States, and the United Kingdom, according to 10-year projections by Goldman Sachs.[17]

How this transition is handled, how companies prepare people for what comes next, and how organizations continue to address these human/machine relationships will impact brands and their desirability in the eyes of their workforce (and their investors) for years to come.

King's Gambit

Back in 1997, chess grandmaster Garry Kasparov was shocked when he was beaten by Deep Blue, a chess-playing machine created by the fine folks at IBM, four games to two in a seven-game series.[18] Actually, "shocked" might not be the right word. Let's go with "*devastated*." Losing one match, let alone two, to a machine was a blow to his healthy ego.

The following year, Deep Blue took down Kasparov, 3½ to 2½. Kasparov claimed that his was the first job to be displaced by AI. Years later, he came back with a combined AI/human contender and proved that players with augmented intelligence could not only win against the smartest grandmasters, but against the smartest computers. And the value of blended knowledge, or augmented intelligence, was born.

On his journey into how humans and tech can best work together, Kasparov discovered that it's not just partnering with machines that strengthens our own might, but *how* you partner with them that matters.

Writing in the early 2020s he commented, "Weak human + machine + better process was superior to a strong computer alone, and more remarkably, superior to a strong human + machine + inferior process." He later told the *Harvard Business Review*, "[A]s leaders look at how to incorporate AI into their organizations, they'll have to manage expectations as AI is introduced, invest in bringing teams together and perfecting processes, and refine their own leadership abilities."[19] And regarding Gen AI tools, Kasparov added, "We are comfortable with machines making us faster and stronger, but smarter? It's some sort of human fear." It's not a universal fear, though. In our research, Japan and Korea are always outliers in their attitude toward robots and tech, in part due to their culture and exposure to tech and in part out of necessity. And this exposure is increasing: tough migration laws and an aging population are increasingly making robots an imperative in jobs where they don't have enough people available or interested such as care workers and late-night store attendants. What this tells us is that if we are to welcome this new tech into our lives, we need to increase our own exposure to it and increase it quickly. We need to experiment, experiment, experiment to mitigate the fear of the unknown.

We're now in a world of smart people working with smart tools, tools that are helping to bolster our intelligence, tools that will deliver the capacity to help us work smarter. As Kasparov tells us, "When the machine takes care of the calculations, people can focus on strategic planning."

When humans provide the context, insights, and creativity, and AI supplies the processing power, data analysis, and pattern recognition, there's your perfect equation. By working in tandem, humans and AI can tackle complex problems and generate new solutions that weren't possible until now. But we can't simply put it out into the world and hope for the best—we need to incorporate the new rules of human/machine team working, or as Kasparov calls it, good *process* if we are to unleash its potential. The reality is that today we have passed the inflection point that working without AI is the true liability that companies are facing.

Yes, It's Intelligence, but Not as We Know It

Traditional AI has already altered many industries, delivering unprecedented efficiencies (see Figure 7.1). Take healthcare transformation, which is still in its infancy. By leveraging AI systems to analyze patient data, healthcare providers can offer more targeted and effective treatments that improve outcomes and reduce costs. In developing the first COVID-19 vaccine for BioNTech, researchers paired their human ingenuity with AI-driven testing and analysis. This amplified intelligence approach helped deliver a life-saving cure[20] with unprecedented speed.[21]

Today, the catalysts for change are not linear—we are learning and experiencing the sheer power of LLMs, our interface is more human, allowing people to bring more to the table, and the applications are not sector-specific or accessible by an anointed few. But when these LLMs do become domain-specific—say, for medical, engineering, and HR, then we will see the real impact on jobs—and most notably, on jobs that sit in the middle. Think about the impact on a nurse of having this type of power—medical know-how—in her phone, versus a doctor. So, what have we learned from these past applications that will serve us well as we look toward that future?

- Securing the necessary data to train the computer is critical. Context is everything and this requires data and humans to train the machine, feeding it content that sets the stage for whatever questions we want to ask. We need to ensure we have, and cultivate, these skills in our own teams today.

- Processing time is often cut, leveling the field for some competitors, widening the competitive divides for others. Figuring

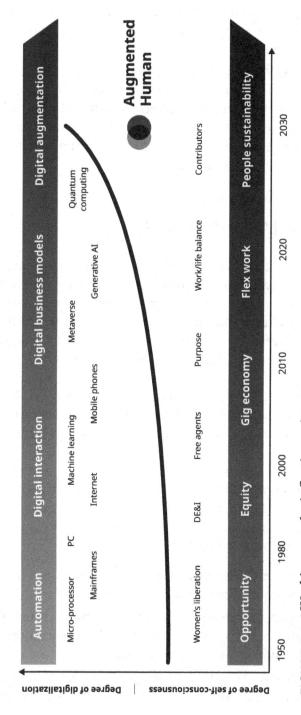

FIGURE 7.1 Working past the inflection point.
*Source: **Work Different:** Bravery, Anderson, Bonic*

out AI's applications to our own business and sector is critical; this requires everyone to be thinking about commercial applications of AI.

- Over time, we could lose some of our own smarts as we delegate activities to the machine. Just like radiologists' deep expertise in viewing many a mammogram will diminish, our ability to eyeball a personality questionnaire, an engagement survey, or a forecast chart might reduce as we no longer build up large reference sets ourselves.

New Tech Means New Gigs

AI does not disrupt slowly or fairly, and unlike prior paradigm-shifting disruptions, it's simultaneously happening across different verticals. In the past, an out-of-work farmhand could get a job in a supermarket, or a laid-off cashier might find work in a call center, but the impact of AI and automation is industry-agnostic. If your skills become devalued in one arena, they've likely taken a hit in adjacent fields.

On the one hand, there's no need to stress out. While widespread and rapid adoption of AI is necessary for businesses and the individual alike, it won't reduce dependence on human contribution at the corporate and individual levels.

On the other hand, mild stressing out will be—and probably should be—in the mix. Many jobs and specializations will be displaced, with some eliminated, and we say "mild stressing out" as many other jobs will emerge due to this new technology.[22] Some new roles already bursting onto the scene include:

- **AI Utilization Director** to regulate how tools are used and improve programmatic accuracy and relevance.
- **AI Implementation Specialist** to integrate AI technology into operations. This requires both technical expertise and business knowledge to bridge the gap.
- **AI Product and Adoption Manager** to support internal customer needs, and to ensure effective deployment and adoption.

- **Prompt Engineer** to apply data science expertise in developing curated, relevant content.
- **Output Auditor** to minimize substantive errors and bias as well as improve accuracy and relevance.
- **Data Management Specialist** to manage, process, and curate large volumes of data to ensure its quality and utilization in training AI models (particularly for models that are key to future business strategies).

Gen AI will also impact how the work itself gets done. To fully realize the efficiency gains these tools offer, we must be strategic in hypothesizing, testing, and evaluating how the strengths of this technology complement our own. Automating repetitive, data-heavy tasks like article research frees up more capacity for writers to flex their creativity in building a narrative, or their interpersonal skills during interviews with subject matter experts. Code suggestions can essentially finish developers' thoughts, streamlining stuffy syntax concerns so they can spend more time creating and less time connecting the dots. Combining images with a written description can shorten the time to develop a new product's visual identity.

Being in direct interaction—and to some degree, *competition*—with AI will help us find new ways of thinking, creating, editing, and communicating, if only to keep our own skills sharp and appreciate what humans bring to the equation. This is an opportunity to reevaluate what skills we should learn, how we can learn them, and the best way to teach them. Today, some educators thrust into this new world overnight are requiring three submissions from their students; one written by them, one by ChatGPT, and one for which ChatGPT does the first draft before students polish it. Yes, we are in catch-up mode, and more change is coming.

But despite these attempts to govern the tech, employees and students generally don't give a damn about their company's or school's stance on AI: a January 2023 survey found that nearly 70% of the people using AI at work had not told their employers.[23] (For what it's worth, Italy was the first country to ban ChatGPT amid privacy concerns. Let's see how that plays out. *Molto bene*? Maybe.)

In reality, technology already handles countless data-related tasks on our behalf. A number of platforms can collect, process, and analyze data, then present it through data visualizations based on their favorite KPIs. The tools are there, and you don't need a computer science degree to know how to use them, but in their race to get more digitally literate, many professionals still rely too much on instinct and traditional reporting mechanisms when making critical business decisions. In this kind of environment, low-quality data and poorly configured tools can go completely unnoticed and drive flawed judgments for years, putting companies at a massive strategic disadvantage. This neglect isn't just seen in data for business decision-making, but also with the lackadaisical approach to diversity, equity, and inclusion (DEI) metrics and understanding the true drivers for not making progress on pay equity, health equity, or career equity. Slow progress is almost by design. AI can change the game here, but the humans need to welcome these digital partners to the table and they need to internalize the results.

Clash of the Brainiacs

"The learn-it-all does better than the know-it-all."

So said Microsoft's Chairman and Executive CEO Satya Nadella,[24] and he's right: the future of work is about smart working and this is based on being constantly curious, learning in the flow of work, and is not necessarily related to how smart a person is or what they've become an expert at. Our corporate cultures will need to change significantly to be prepared for The People Age/AI Age combo platter. There is and will continue to be a knowledge gap and an access challenge that will divide fortunes if not addressed. If you can't figure out how best to leverage this technology and enable it to enhance your workforce's collective intelligence, you might find yourself on the wrong end of your balance ledger.

With so much information suddenly on demand, how do we cultivate a learn-it-all culture and ensure that our teams build the essential know-how? It might start with nurturing curiosity.

While the traditional world of work left much of the knowing and deciding up to the leaders, Gen AI democratizes our access to information and puts the onus on colleagues to train one another. Most are already blocking off time on a regular basis for workers to regroup, to kick around how their learnings can best ideate, prompt, and optimize their work with the help of new technologies. These sorts of brainstorming sessions are critical for exploring newfangled ways to grow your business, but it's tough to make this happen when contributors are too over-scheduled to think, let alone learn. Break this cycle. Create the time. Schedule hackathons, and dedicated learning days, and meet-ups, and learning festivals, and free food days—whatever helps your people get creative.

We should also prioritize information literacy, that is, the ability to effectively find, evaluate, and share facts, figures, and opinions. Gen AI has made it far easier to access, create, and utilize this sort of information, but the application of this technology to our own knowledge management processes and the productization of this capability rests on human ingenuity to see what is possible. Think about the opportunities for complex decision-making that we would happily welcome support on: *ChatGPT, which benefit plan is best for me—factor in the cost, my family's health history, desired health outcomes, my demographics, and make a recommendation based on prior health outcomes of those who made similar decisions?* Or, *ChatGPT, based on what you know of my direct report, what package of financial and nonfinancial rewards will most excite them and have them stay loyal for longer?* Or, *Hey, ChatGPT, about a year ago I met someone at a conference, they went to Birkbeck college, spent a while at Google and are now at a tech startup, they had some AI for HR that I'd now like to explore, who is it likely to be and how am I connected to them?*

So how does this look in practice today? Well, one large global technology company, looking at how to incorporate AI into its organization, and used the advent of Gen AI to redesign jobs that were lagging in productivity. Starting with the *work that needs to be done*, not *how the work is organized into jobs* today, they determined how various technologies, including Robotic Process Automation (RPA) and AI could be combined with the skills and capabilities of their workforce to operate more efficiently and in tune with where humans offered the most value. By deconstructing a set of critical jobs into tasks, redeploying or augmenting tasks with automation, and reconstructing new, more impactful jobs by reconfiguring these tasks, the company was able to shift more high-touch, strategic work to its skilled people, while leaving more simple transactional work to bots, self-service solutions and an outsourced model. This approach delivered a 30% improvement in productivity in year one, while enabling the reskilling and redeployment of existing talent to emerging work.

AI in Action

Building a digital organization in The People Age is no small feat. Adapting to new technology requires custom learning experiences based on the different skills, knowledge, and attitudes of a diverse workforce. Some firms are trying and succeeding.

Khan Academy, a nonprofit in the education space, launched a project with OpenAI in early 2020 to power Khanmigo, an AI-fueled assistant that simultaneously supports teachers and tutors students. Chief Learning Officer Kristen DiCerbo believes the tool helps Khan Academy meet the diverse learning needs of its users in ways that signal the future of learning, noting, "They [our students] all have different gaps. They all need different things to move forward. That is a problem we've been trying to solve for a long time."[25] If tech can get us to more personalized learning experiences through a digital buddy—we're in!

A major financial services firm also pulled it off, notably because many wouldn't look to the financial sector as a leader in AI. Like many established organizations, Morgan Stanley faced a knowledge problem: They had a wealth of business insights, but couldn't figure out how to spread the information in-house. The company intranet was bulging with insights on everything from market research to investment strategies, haphazardly strewn across multiple sites in PDF form. (We intensely dislike haphazard websites. False modesty aside, **Mercer.com** is as neat and tidy as can be.) To make the information more accessible, Morgan Stanley uses GPT-4 to fuel an internal chatbot that finds and delivers the resources employees are looking for, based on what they need. According to Jeff McMillan, the company's head of Analytics, Data & Innovation, "[This] effectively unlocks the cumulative knowledge [within our workforce]."[26]

And HR is getting its day in the sun too. In 2023, Beamery launched TalentGPT—Gen AI for HR technology. This leverages GPT-4 and other LLMs to redesign the experience of talent acquisition and talent management for users and HR. By personalizing career recommendations based on organizational skills gaps, they are enabling companies to accelerate skill acquisition, tackle their DEI challenges, and address their ethical obligations to boot. As Sultan Saidov commented, "These advances in AI technology are improving the interactions we can provide to our users, and how much time we can save people in achieving complex tasks."[27]

Smart Working Is Getting Smarter

The economist Richard Baldwin commented at the WEF's Growth Summit that "AI won't take your job, but someone who can use AI better than you, just might!" And this is the real challenge people are facing. It is less about intelligence, per se, but how we can bolster our thinking by working smartly. Having *smarts*—knowing where to go or how to acquire what we need—has the potential to be an intelligence equalizer. Therefore, we all need to get comfortable with the new language of Gen AI, to all appreciate how AI and automation will disrupt how we work, and to ensure we have guardrails to maximize the gains while minimizing the risks.

One emerging challenge is to ensure that our workforce knows how to discern what's real and what isn't—how to cut through the rubbish. (And there is, as we're all painfully aware, a lot of rubbish out there.) According to an Oliver Wyman report, "Despite having low trust in the accuracy of [information on social media], our Gen Z colleagues prioritize social media's familiar faces [and] entertaining content," over the news sources they think would be more credible.[28] In other words, Gen Zers know that social media is feeding them garbage, yet they're still eating it. We all need to be more vigilant in checking the facts, details, and sources behind any AI-generated content before incorporating it into our work and being clear about which co-workers—bot or human—are contributing to our work and any potential copyright violations.

Speaking of vigilance, how many employees do you think might have inadvertently shared private or confidential information with ChatGPT via their company computer? Probably more than you'd hope. Most companies addressed the issue early on, thanks to diligent risk and compliance personnel, but the threat is here to stay. Learning how to amplify intelligence and how to do it safely are now onboarding imperatives for us all. This is an evolving space, but here is how some early adopters tackled it:

- **Instituting guardrails.** Striking the right balance between defining guardrails and making it easy to share learnings and promote safe experiments is key. Set up your safeguards and controls in advance of new tech coming in. This includes risk management strategies, data policies, security trainings, algorithm audits, and an ethical AI credo that puts people before the tech, not the tech before the people.

- **Installing checks and balances.** Some are using pass/fail courses to certify employees before giving them access to certain tools. Others are setting up alerts or disclaimers for internal content downloads. An imperative is making certain that your country's data protection regulations and related laws are being upheld and that updates are being regularly shared. Having people who are dedicated to the use of Gen AI with a focus on privacy and ethics, and who can guide others in the firm on these issues, will help to navigate change.

- **Clarifying the impact on jobs and skills.** A number of companies have started to actively analyze the roles within their organization to see how this new technology will impact jobs. Deduce how AI can help with skills intelligence and strategic workforce management to help meet emerging, evolving business needs. Acquiring technical and analytical skills that help with sense-checking AI outputs, and building a positive digital work culture, are also key to enterprise-wide adoption.

- **Identifying the impact on operations.** Just as we've employed Robotic Process Automation (RPA) for menial tasks, we now need to consider how cognitive processes such as conceptual reasoning, divergent thinking and evaluative thinking can be enhanced. Augmenting our own intelligence to improve decision-making, solve analysis paralysis, validate our hypotheses, and facilitate content creation are all part of the new frontier. Learning with computers to solve more complex challenges will come next.

- **Bolstering people insights.** Assuming you have the right approvals and keep data anonymized, leveraging internal HR data sets to train custom AI models that meet the specific needs of your business will bolster the insights you have about your people, allowing for greater predictions about their health and behavior—and in effect, solving the issue of lagging human capital metrics to inform decision making. This allows for more individualized and targeted people management interventions.

As we mentioned, this overreliance on technology could one day dilute our insights, compromise our critical thinking skills, and leave our decision-making at the mercy of the machines, as our own critical reasoning will have atrophied. This is the dystopian future we need to avoid, because it could lead to—say it with us, now: The Robot Uprising.

At the same time, drifting through an AI-driven world without getting engaged with this technology is a recipe for disaster, as a fool with a tool is still a fool. Any company or individual who doesn't effectively use AI might be less productive—and less competitive—than those who do.

As we conclude this chapter, The Beatles just released their final album—with AI as their silent partner. By extrapolating John Lennon's voice from a prior unheard recording, the human/machine mileage takes another step forward.

This is no longer a wait-and-see situation.
AI is getting better every day.
Smart working is getting smarter.
And the smartest move is to adapt and learn.

People Leaders' CTAs

1. **Build superheroes.** IQ + AI + process = superhuman working. Develop synergies between your team and AI by defining a good process. Start by identifying a team to help with experimentation and knowledge-sharing. Create learning opportunities, encourage knowledge-sharing, and guide your team toward what it means to work in an augmented manner, with great processes that optimize tech and people capabilities. Keep this activity going; this is not a *one-and-done* situation.

2. **Cultivate a positive mindset toward technology.** AI is changing work, working, and the workforce. To help ease workers' fears about job disruption and skills, include them in discussing how your organization uses AI today, where AI is already enhancing jobs, and the opportunities it can stimulate for future careers. Giving employees agency and celebrating success creates the sense that this change is happening *for* them, not *to* them.

3. **Build up AI know-how.** People, organizations, and technology need to work in lockstep to keep pace with Gen AI, and this only happens when people gain hands-on experience with these tools—just like Word and Excel—you don't learn them by theory. People leaders are in a unique position to not only shape expectations, but to ensure there are clear ways to share ideas and pathways for workers to keep their skills marketable.

Executives' and HR's CTAs

1. **Redesign work by adding AI to the game.** Adopt an amplified intelligence approach to work by exploring use

cases, redesigning tasks within roles, and outlining the gains. Start leveraging AI-driven talent platforms and work design tools to know what work is ripe for cognitive augmentation. Find and build the skills you'll need for the future of work and consider connecting internal HR data to LLMs to amplify intelligence. Make experimentation and learning a priority.

2. **Establish AI guidance and guardrails.** Data security is everyone's responsibility, but ensure all leaders know their roles with regard to cyber risk and privacy. Create or enhance specific AI policies around risk management, data management, security trainings, algorithm audits, ethical AI, and the democratization of data for a people-first approach that does not inadvertently expose the company to risk or hold it back in capitalizing on this exciting new technology.

CHAPTER 8

Skills Are the Real Currency of Work

Upgrade Alert

Apple nerds like us fondly remember the company's halcyon era when, every 12-ish months, Steve Jobs, his Reality Distortion Field, and his black turtleneck would slap on a headphone mic, take the stage in Cupertino, and hype the latest Apple product. Sometimes Steve was intro-ing a whole new item—an iPhone, an iPod, an iPad—while in other instances, it was an upgrade of an existing product line.

Back in the day, wholesale tech upgrades were a relative rarity; today, however, it feels like Apple unveils a new iPhone every two weeks. The constant equipment turnover is simultaneously exciting and frustrating: exciting because new tech is oftentimes a blast—and frustrating because upgrading is a tiresome necessity if you want to stay current.

But we suck it up and make the change because, while our fun new toy usually has some fun new features, we can't play with our toy until we move our data from the hard drive on our iPhone 58 MegaPro to our iPhone 59 SuperDuperPro. Waiting too long to make that change can lead to error messages courtesy of incompatible apps, phone slow-downs, FOMO, and the general sense that something's. . .*off*. Sure, we'll get by for a bit, but while everyone else is up-to-date and on point. It'll soon become clear to us (and to everybody in our orbit) that we've fallen behind.

This all is analogous for an employee in need of a skills upgrade. Unfortunately, and unlike with our tech, we don't get nudged nearly as much as our skills atrophy.

In terms of a worker's skill set, if they're not at the cutting edge of, well, pretty much everything, they could become semi-obsolete. Thing is, Steve Jobs (or, at this point, Tim Cook) doesn't offer a presentation about how or when it's time to get upskilled or reskilled. The signals that remind us to keep up with the latest and the greatest—and, thusly, remain employable—are subtle, and all too often, come too late. Consider the once-a-year performance review, the less-than-inspiring PIP (performance improvement plan) process, and/or restructuring that's often accompanied with deflating lines like: *It's not you, it's the job that has changed.*

As organizations grow less siloed and more cross-functional, skills have become the unequivocal currency of work. Skills keep you in the game. Skills are currency that get you a new role. Skills are what companies want to grow and pay for. Which all begs the question, how might the shift from *jobs to skills* as the currency of work impact employees, employers, and society as a whole? What does the future of work look like through a skills-first lens? One where work happens outside of jobs—something Jesuthasan and Boudreau unpack in *Work without Jobs*,[1] which discusses the need for a new work operating model if companies are to capitalize on this truth?

Today, very few are truly skills-based organizations—or SBOs—so let's fast-forward to the year 2030 and see what an employee might experience when we get there.

An Employee-Eye View of Skills in the Future of Work

You wake up to an invite on your smartphone (or your smartbed or your smartpajamas) to interview for a hot new role. You already have a job and don't feel qualified for this new one, but the recruiter's AI tool says you're a match.

Despite your concerns, you jump on a video call a couple of hours later. The recruiter lays out the skills you'll need on day one, and how the company plans to reskill you moving forward. She then describes how those skills could help you advance in the company.

You're intrigued, but cautious. You ask how much time would be split between core duties and on-the-job training. The recruiter breaks it down, after which she lists a few of the learning opportunities they offer—both within and outside of the company—to help you stay marketable.

And the good news—this role is actually with your current employer, whose AI identified you via the company's internal job marketplace. You get to stick with a great company, remain with your beloved colleagues, and even keep the same email address. Brilliant!

This certainly seems like a sensible way forward, given the talent shortages we've discussed, so why are we not seeing more of this happening? Well, three things hold companies back in making this a reality:

1. The belief that work can only be done by the job holder in fixed roles.
2. A lack of *insight* as to who has the skills or thirst to reskill.
3. The reticence to put an employee's learning and growth over productivity and execution.

Now, here's what managers might see in 2030. . .

A Manager-Eye View of Skills in the Future of Work

Your boss just presented an ambitious plan to double revenue by 2033. Back in the day, you might have curled up into the fetal position, shared snarky memes with your teammates, or even doubted whether your organization could pull it off. Back then, talent was either at capacity or hoarded in other departments. High turnover and hiring freezes made sustainable growth tricky, let alone accelerated growth a possibility.

But no longer.

See, your employer spent the last few years becoming an SBO, thus you can leverage AI-driven workforce intelligence to quickly train and deploy talent. You pull up the dynamic workforce planning portal and get down to business.

You ask your Gen AI partner, who has skill adjacencies and the capacity to upskill? Then the AI agent models-out what talent you need and how best to secure that capability. Your AI partner taps into internal and external talent pools on your behalf and secures workers within your ecosystem so you can gear up.

You see gap assessments against projected future skills and growth plans, and access the latest skills market pay trends. Your digital partner compares multiple build, buy, and borrow scenarios, all with projected costs built in. These models and insights extend to your contingent talent pool, external candidates and makes assessments of the skills within potential M&A targets, thus giving you a complete picture of your readiness to fuel the growth strategy, with a combination of organic and inorganic approaches.

This scenario becomes possible only when a company knows the skills they have today, those associated with future growth, and the cost and time implications of different skill strategies to close the gap. Executing on this imperative necessitates talent resources evolving into enterprise-level resources. When leaders are incentivized to meet the needs of workers and the whole organization, they become talent exporters and enablers, rather than talent horders.

What holds companies back today on making this a reality is twofold—for one, having skills data and skills intelligence resting in disparate systems so they cannot answer a query in a connected way. And two, HR processes that are locked into outdated ways of thinking—from workforce planning tools that focus on full-time equivalent (FTE) headcount changes, to talent processes based on jobs and annual HR cycles. These dynamics prevent us from considering how work can look *different*, what *different* skills might be needed or augmented, and the *different* ways to bring those skills into the firm.

Now here's what 2030 could look like to the world-at-large. . .

A Society-Eye View of Skills in the Future of Work

Global commerce is back in full force, and organizations are expanding into new markets, many of which are related to the essential transitions on which we need to deliver, for example, digital movement, green transition, and sustainable energy. With intentional focus on where skill investment is targeted and sharing of future jobs that people should train for, this growth stimulates fresh opportunities for local workers in low-income and underdeveloped areas.

Many of these individuals lack the job titles, stellar educations, and industry tenure that, back in the mid-2020s, often passed for qualifications in a jobs-based world of work. Untethered from those constraints, SBOs can hire and train employees based on their actual skills, their potential to learn, or their experience in related functions and fields.

These new opportunities level the playing field for underrepresented populations and workers in jobs that were displaced by AI and automation. Employers partner with nonprofit organizations and governments, using a mix of real-time insights and AI to address the dynamic needs of a global workforce and local markets. With fewer inequities and greater well-being, a broader swath of society shifts its sense of purpose from surviving to thriving.

What holds nations back in delivering on this vision is a lack of strategic planning around skills, uncoordinated public/private collaboration, and a lack of shared insights around what skills are needed in a given market. Putting intelligence regarding what skills will matter in 2030 and beyond into the hands of those impacted by it—both employees and those in the community—helps contributors be active agents in shaping what's next. Today the link between education and the future of work is tenuous at best.

I Am Unwritten

All of which begs the questions, what are upskilling and reskilling?

Simply put, it's learning new stuff. If your guitar guru teaches you how to play a G-minor scale, you're upskilling. If your painting teacher shows you how to do perspective, you're upskilling. If you train for a job you've never done before, it's reskilling. If you and two of your work colleagues write a book without previously having undertaken that insane endeavor—all while continuing to work a full 50-hour week—that's reskilling to the nth degree. (We kid. This book has been a learning experience unlike any other, filled with upskilling, reskilling, and everything-skilling.)

The skills that are most in-demand among businesses are constantly evolving. According to the WEF's 2023 Future of Jobs report, *analytical thinking* (72%) and *technological literacy* (68%) are top skills that are increasing in importance.[2] Notably, *creative thinking* topped the chart—suggesting that despite the rise of Gen AI, employers still find value in creative output from actual people. Further, with *curiosity and lifelong learning* (67%) in fourth place, and more than half of organizations deeming *talent management* (56%) to be on the rise, the ability to drive individual development was still seen as critical to drive business success. One might then wonder: How fast are skill needs evolving?

Very.

The WEF study estimates that six out of 10 workers will require training between 2023 and 2027, and that 44% of all skills will need to be updated if workers are to stay employable.[3] The concern flagged in the WEF's report, is that only half of employees have access to adequate training opportunities to effectively upskill today. This half-life of skills is poised to keep shrinking, with the half-life of technical skills likely to be even shorter because the half-life of tech itself shrinks seemingly by the month. If our skills become half as valuable every four to five years, much of what we teach and learn today will become obsolete long before many of us retire. And the relevance of four-year degrees—certainly as they are today—continues to diminish. Reskilling has to become a part of our culture, a compulsory exercise for both people and organizations. And we all need to get comfortable with nonexperts learning as they go.

The good thing is that skilling isn't the first area to be on the chopping block when times get tough—the bigger risk, executives feel, is failing to invest sufficiently in current talent pools to future-proof themselves.[4] Yes, executives are more alert to the need to preserve learning investments than previously, especially in difficult times, but the concern is that only half of companies globally typically provide access to upskilling and/or reskilling for all their employees;[5] instead, they prioritize opportunities for those in high-potential talent programs and/or executive leadership programs. You can't solve for a broad-based skills challenge of the magnitude we are witnessing by focusing on select workforce segment, especially when focused on populations that quite likely will thrive, with or without any learning intervention.

One of the biggest fears leaders face is the belief that if they invest in skill-building, their people will be more likely to leave their companies for greener, more lucrative pastures. (Admittedly, arming a contributor with a whole bunch of new knowledge and skills, then watching them take said skills across the street kinda sucks.) But, the truth is actually the reverse—contributors are more likely to leave if their company *doesn't* sufficiently invest in their skills,[6] or if they invested in their skills and failed to make sufficient use of said new skills. And if your organization fails to help their workers grow, and they stay—thus remaining stagnant within your company—that's just about the worst-case scenario for everybody. And it's a challenge our data says is growing.

When it comes to reskilling, leaders know they need to take more risks on whom they hire and to whom they give new opportunities to, but change has been slow. Yes, it's often safer to go with those tried-and-tested talents to get the job done fast today, but in the process, we rob ourselves of some diverse thinking, and more critically, fail to exploit a learning opportunity that helps us build for the future. As with many facets of work, the pandemic nudged us toward more open-mindedness regarding who could do what jobs, and AI increased the imperative, but scaling this skills-first or development-first mindset has been tough.

During the pandemic, as demand dropped for some functions and businesses, available talent quickly pivoted toward wherever it was needed. (Walmart moved shop workers into e-commerce roles, CVS Health retrained workers in telemedicine, and Delta trained cabin crew for customer support, to name a few). Out of necessity, these companies unhooked their people from jobs to deal with unexpected surges in demand. As a result, traditional organizational structures were broadsided as jobs catastrophically failed to meet the moment.

The flaws of the old structure were laid bare. What we saw was that in a high-pressure environment, agility and flexibility are key to solving an unfamiliar set of problems. Jobs were irrelevant to getting the work done; skills were what mattered. Skills eclipsed jobs to become the real currency of work, and as a result, we all learned:

- People have skills they've never applied.
- People have skills they've never discovered.
- Solving business problems takes capability (skills) and capacity (time/bandwidth).
- Matching skills to jobs begins with knowing your people.

Skilling@Scale Is an Economic Imperative

To be clear, the key takeaway here is not *more learning programs*, and this isn't a problem for HR, higher education, or learning platforms to solve in isolation.

The real concern is that we need to skill-up in our companies and in our societies to ensure people are not left behind. Take BT, a U.K.-based multinational telecommunication company. By 2030, BT anticipates that they will need 55,000 fewer jobs than it has in 2023—a 40% reduction in its 130,000-strong workforce—and as such, they will demand a completely new skill set from those who remain.[7] If individuals are not able to pivot into new roles within or outside the firm, the impact at an individual and societal level will be immense. Resilience will come tomorrow, only if agility comes today, and we can't wait for these tech-driven workforce dislocations to force the reskilling agenda.

Numerous studies have shown that reskilling can lead to hikes in productivity,[8] but formal learning only touches a fraction of our workforce. When the pandemic forced executives to move talent to opportunities, it opened their minds to the potential gains in learning and agility that stems from mobility. It's this type of thinking that is still needed, as the pace of change is not abating. As a case in point, Mercer's Job Library (which tracked nearly 25,000 jobs as of 2023) gained an additional 226 new jobs in 2022 to reflect the composition of our clients' workforces. But, this number doubled to 512 new jobs gained in 2023. This dramatic increase in unique jobs will only keep climbing, especially as Gen AI impacts today's roles and drives new ones that we've yet to conceive.

Are companies responding well? They're getting there.

They're providing more learning and skill development opportunities than ever before with the explosion of digital learning.[9] In 2022, a whopping 91% of employees said they learned a new skill,[10] and in 2023, building a skills-based organization became a top-five priority for HR in every country that we surveyed.[11]

But here's the rub: at the same time, 98% of companies reported persistent skill gaps, and 50% of executives[12] said that the lack of skilled talent is holding them back in meeting market demand, so clearly there's a disconnect. Yes, we have more people learning, but this learning isn't impacting the skills shortages in any sizable way.

Go figure.

Now don't let anybody tell you otherwise: future-proofing an organization via upskilling and reskilling is rife with challenges for both the employer and the employee. And building SBOs within traditional talent models can be tough as hell!

Here's what the upskill-/reskill-minded employer should keep front of mind:

- **Expect uncertainty re: future skills needs.** There are constant changes in the competitive environment that require agility in response, and this becomes problematic because we haven't yet figured out how to accurately read minds or prognosticate, so we need to have good knowledge of where the business is headed to predict which skills will be in demand. This requires dedicated time from leaders, not just HR. Ambiguity in skills maps and individual career paths are part of the fun.

- **View learning as an investment in the future.** Upskilling requires investment in hard dollars, but the soft costs and opportunity cost of freeing up colleagues to participate in learning activities and take up internal gigs is part of the equation. It can be difficult to draw a direct link between investment in learning and impact on organizational performance. In other words, read between the numbers when quantifying returns.

- **Explore multiple ways to learn.** Skills acquisition and application is often context-specific, and it can be difficult to both source and develop the right training programs. There's also the challenge of transferring new knowledge and skills acquired through training/learning into the work environment, especially regarding self-directed learning, when there may not be a job opportunity that requires the application of said skills at the time. This is where internal gigs and talent sharing really come into their own, along with other ways to give people learning opportunities such as writing an article, building technical training, and engaging in project work.

- **Cultivate a learning culture.** Managers often prioritize their urgent needs and can be reluctant to free up contributors who are adding value today to focus on skills development with a potential future payoff. Making time for growth needs to be modeled from the top.

Employees also face numerous challenges of their own around learning:

- **Resistance to change.** Providing reskilling and upskilling resources does not mean that employees will take advantage of them. Many feel overwhelmed by change and take comfort in their current routines and activities. Reskilling can be interpreted as another word for disruption and can make some feel uncertain or insecure with their current role or their future employability.

- **Not enough time.** How do people whose plates are already full carve out the time to acquire new skills? After all, regular work doesn't disappear when they're off training or doing a side gig. Workdays and workweeks are long and full, so it's little wonder that this issue was constantly cited in our research as the most notable employee barrier.

- **Wavering motivation.** Learning on or off the job and reskilling takes effort, so why would a contributor go above and beyond if there isn't a benefit in the current role, or if there isn't reward or recognition for doing so? Our research shows that many employees didn't see the payoff for their prior reskilling, and this has led to some feeling jaded about the return for their efforts.[13] Part of this is due to a lack of direction on what skills the company will pay a premium for. Part of it is just poor people management.

- **Learning strategies are not efficient.** Learning programs can be too generic, poorly designed, not engaging enough or delivered via the wrong medium. Or, learning is equated with online course participation, which most say is not their preferred way to learn. Furthermore, if there's not a timely opportunity to apply new skills, the learning can feel like a theoretical exercise, skills learned can atrophy and it all ends up being just another load on people with little return for their efforts.

So Who's Crushing Reskilling and Upskilling?

1. IBM

Big Blue has a history of reinventing itself, so it's little surprise that the company has implemented several upskilling initiatives. These include a skills-based pay approach, CogniPay (aka Compensation Advisor), which provides incentives, reinforcements, and rewards for employees to acquire the skills that align with IBM's future needs.[14]

Being one of the first major investors in AI, IBM has a strong understanding of its priority skills for the future, a knowledge of current skill gaps, and insights into market availability and demand of these skills. With strong educational platforms, the company provides their employees with an enviable range of targeted learning programs, but they really excel in offering transparency about the direction of demand for future skills. This targets some of the change resistance and motivation challenges that we see by linking comp to skills via an AI tool that guides managers through the annual merit process.

Merit pay has been de-coupled from roles and more aligned to skills, demonstrating to colleagues that pay and career advancement can be tied to the acquisition of new skills—and premiums are paid to those workers who acquire skills that are in high demand and/or are scarce in the market. On the other hand, the workers who choose to remain comfortable in their work—the folks who choose not to acquire new skills— generally find it less and less likely that they'll see positive pay growth over time.

2. TELEFONICA

In order to close skills gaps in areas such as security, robotics, analytics, web development, and business consulting, this Spanish multinational telecommunications company committed to upskilling 100,000 workers. José María Álvarez-Pallete, the company's CEO,[15] stressed why they needed to embark on one of the largest reskilling programs Europe had witnessed: "In Europe, there are 10 million people unemployed and five million job vacancies due to skill gaps. In the next five years, 20 million jobs will be created in digital transition, AI, and climate transition [we need to be prepared]."

And prepare they did. The company asked all their employees to fill in a skills profile questionnaire, then they used machine learning (ML) to discover learning gaps, for which the ML proposed personalized training recommendations for each and every worker. Adoption was notably high, with 91.5% of employees having used the reskilling application in the first year and 77% having completed their profile.[16] This information enables their managers to budget for the time and cost of training, and is being used as an aid for internal recruitment.

3. SAP

The software solutions expert, much to their credit, defines business-critical skills on a yearly basis. Chetna Singh,[17] the company's head of Total Rewards, shared with Mercer, that in her view, "Skills are the new oil of the digital culture." She attributed SAP's skills success to ". . .a well-defined global job architecture," adding, "Whenever new business models emerge and a job is not in the catalogue, we take time to add it and then we map the skills."

As a tech company, SAP is also willing to pay a premium for in-demand skills. Describing an effort to acquire top-notch cloud skills, Singh said the company created guidelines for some recruiters to help them negotiate premiums that ". . .may have meant breaking the bank" to get the right talent. "Skills conversations are exceptionally important for technology organizations," she explained. "Everybody needs to continuously learn, unlearn, and relearn to stay relevant. Otherwise, you're out of the business."

Learning in the Flow of Work

For decades, and still today, learning has been the purview of young people and junior contributors—the introductory stage that comes before peak performance. But in 2023, the WEF estimated that 44% of core skills would be disrupted by 2028.[18] That means nearly half of the skills these newcomers acquire today will be obsolete long before their careers are winding down.

What's clear is that the need for upskilling and reskilling is more than a learning and development (L&D) priority or even an HR challenge—heck, it's a big, thorny business problem that rests with every leader. If automation can handle repetitive tasks better and faster than people (it can), and AI can amplify human intelligence (also yes), then people in high-earning roles will continue to advance while many blue-collar and entry-level white-collar jobs will be wiped out. Without a systemic solution that goes way beyond learning programs, massive numbers of people could be unemployed before the digital transformation is through.

This clearly isn't just a today problem. It's a tomorrow problem and a next year problem, and a next decade problem. Employers are on track to run out of people faster than any third party can replenish them. Organizations can't afford to keep buying and borrowing the skills they need—even if it is easier to hire to spec than train to reskill. This has to change. Take the cybersecurity space, where there's an estimated shortfall of 3.4 million skilled professionals[19] to meet demand at a time when cyberthreats are one of the biggest risks to businesses today. Figuring out how we close this gap is a business imperative; it will impact our ability to function if we fail to close the skills gap, and this demands *different* thinking as the skills don't exist today and training lags demand.

While it's tempting to foist our skills demands on traditional education, schools have been largely ineffective in meeting that demand. Certainly, education reform is long overdue and being hit by Gen AI, but it can't solve today's problems soon enough. In the United Kingdom, for example, Prime Minister Rishi Sunak pushed for all students in England to study mathematics until the age of 18.[20] His plan failed, but it spoke to a real need for greater analytical skills across the board. Given the speed at which jobs are changing and the emergence of new skills, a more flexible way to earn and learn will be critical for this next era of work evolution.

Businesses know they need to work with schools and capacity-building companies to teach and upskill workers. Some firms have partnered with colleges to shape curriculums (Amazon Web Services and Santa Monica College),[21] while others provide targeted learning opportunities for the talent of tomorrow (Microsoft's High School Discovery program).[22] Companies are also commissioning learning for jobs and sponsoring nontraditional talent to build skills in new areas such as inclusive finance and other growing areas of *jobs for good* (Digital Frontiers, a zebra firm, uses donor funding and fees to upskill workers in Africa and other developing areas to address the global shortfall). See Figure 8.1.[23]

The Benefits of Skills-Based Organizations

Organizations are:

Skills informed

Know their skills demands, current supply, gaps, and skill trends

Can make informed buy/build/borrow decisions

Strategically agile

Have skills-based interventions and an inclusive learning culture

Can execute fast, build for tomorrow and pivot as needed

Sustainably driven

Deploy skills-based processes to attract, engage, and redeploy talent

Can deliver cost savings with enhanced talent outreach and deployment

Employees believe talent processes are:

Career enhancing

Know how to build careers that are aligned to their preferences and ambitions

Feel supported to keep their skills marketable

Equitable and fair

Have transparent and democratised learning and development opportunities

Believe talent decisions are fair and unbiased

Easy and intuitive

Are able to access digitally-enabled, intuitive experiences that align to real work opportunities

Can navigate opportunities to enhance their future

FIGURE 8.1   The benefits of skills-based organizations.
Source: Mercer.

So what's the vision for companies that are on this journey to become a skills-based organization? The vision is a skills-informed, strategically agile, and sustainably driven pipeline of talent; the ability to know what skills they need and how best to get them on tap; and the use of agile practices and skills-based interventions that, together, deliver cost savings through highly effective talent outreach and deployment. And Gen AI will bring a lot of this together so skills gaps can be quickly closed.

On the employee side, the vision is that skills-based talent processes will offer greater career growth, typically with a more intuitive way to navigate all the learning and opportunities the company has to offer. Furthermore, they value insights on what skills will command a pay premium in the future, the commitment to unbiased talent decisions, and their access to learning opportunities. Early adopters of the skills-based approach have since shared two truths from their learnings:

1. **Machines are better than humans at identifying and assessing our skills.** AI can pinpoint many more skills with surprising accuracy based on making inferences derived from a worker's background, education, and experiences. As Kamal Ahluwalia, president at Eightfold AI shared, "Skills and capabilities move too fast today to rely on static systems, and if you can understand adjacency of skills and learning agility, you can hire for potential and build a talent network that will enhance agility."[24]

2. **Building an SBO requires a drastic reset of not only our talent processes, but of our mental models about how we develop and deploy skills.** Thought patterns like: *Training is a young person's game* or *Learning happens when we have time* or *Development is linked to a change of role* can all stifle change. But the biggest barriers are leaders who have a fixed mindset and are reluctant to loan talent and export their top players.

SBOs in Action

So how do skills-based organizations differ from traditional organizations? Figure 8.2 is a breakdown of how skill-fueled

	Traditional approaches	Skills-based approaches
Organizational design	Rigid, siloed, and hierarchical	Flat, fluid, and cross-functional
Work design	Based on job duties and FTE capacity	Based on value creation and new ways to deliver work
Strategic workforce planning	Supports short-term business needs and incremental growth	Align skills to strategic needs and plans for transformation
Talent acquisition	Credential- and experience-based	Nontraditional talent and skills-based
Promotion and succession	Time-based and linear	Skills-based and dynamic
Learning and development	Predefined based on legacy career paths and training	Build key skills that drive business performance and inform learning
Rewards	Job/level-based benchmarking and linked to past performance	Market-driven and linked to present and/or forward value

FIGURE 8.2   Traditional versus skills-based approaches to talent management.
Source: **Work Different:** Bravery, Anderson, Bonic

organizations are approaching organizational design, work design, strategic workforce planning, talent acquisition, promotion/succession, learning and rewards a little differently:

The rationale for *starting down the SBO path* may simply be to find ways to boost productivity and cut costs. Mired in old-school HR/talent processes, a firm might seek to prop up an internal talent marketplace to help with talent acquisition. The best systems go beyond filling jobs, helping employers gauge whether their skill priorities reflect those of the external market, and nudging people toward valuable learning pathways and gig opportunities.

Those *further along on their SBO journey* are typically seeking to increase their agility and ability to execute on a people strategy that may need to pivot. . .and pivot *fast*. They're seeking to find alignment between skills and jobs, and use those insights to build enhanced workforce planning and career pathing capabilities. Skills-matched mentoring can be an accelerator here.

Advanced SBOs, on the other hand, tend to focus on building a new shape of work, integrating skills into their job designs from the outset. Their talent marketplaces evolve from a cost/productivity play into a major lever in terms of how things get done in their organization. They've defined which technology supports their *system of record* for skills, which is the *system of engagement* their workers will use, and what will be the *system for intelligence* around skills. These are systems that don't always dovetail.

These SBOs achieve and maintain a nonstop flow of talent and skills to work, be it projects, gigs, or full-time positions. What underpins success in all these scenarios is having the right skills intelligence coming into the firm, the right internal skills enablement system, and a learning culture and governance model that's receptive to building skills in the flow of work.

Who's Changing Their Currency?

So, who's blazing the SBO trail and *making skills the real currency of work*?

Markus Graf, Global Head of Talent at the global medicines company Novartis, is an early proponent. For him, the key to unlocking the potential of people was a "mindset-shift rooted in curiosity." Part of Novartis' "unbossed culture" placed an emphasis on associates taking an outside view of where their industry, and more critically where the required business critical skills, were headed.[25]

One of the key success criteria was creating a culture of learning before introducing a talent marketplace and other skills-fueled systems. This was done via culture transformation, democratized access to learning, and reinforcement of the value of learning to accelerate growth and careers. The company then implemented an AI-driven talent marketplace to help identify people's skills, nudge them toward which skills to develop, and match them with opportunities to build those skills, for example, through projects, mentoring, and targeted learning content. Novartis also encouraged managers to use their talent marketplace to staff projects in an agile way and foster talent sharing across boundaries. Key to what propelled them forward was the integration of learning and career opportunities, the democratization of access to internal opportunities, and the dollar savings brought about through sourcing projects internally—delivering a win/win for all.

Like snowflakes, each SBO is different. Arcadis, a design and engineering consultancy, took a unique SBO path of their own.

The firm's Global Capability & Workforce Readiness Director, Amy Baxendale, told Mercer that its transformation journey stemmed from the need ". . .to build a workforce that's ready for the future."[26] The company's top three reasons for the shift were:

1. Better career pathing.
2. Improved company relevance and worker employability.
3. The ability to find and move talent to where it's most needed.

Baxendale added, "To truly become a skills-powered organization over time, [Arcadis] needed to really make sure that skills become the currency of the business." The company began with a transformation roadmap that broke their journey down into stages, each one focused on the evolution of different talent processes around the employee lifecycle. Their plan was to ". . .test assumptions on the priorities and ensure that as a business [Arcadis is] still ready to take that next stage" in moving to a skills-first organization.

Another firm that champions the skills-based agenda is Zurich Insurance. They've established 45 knowledge areas, each with a global leader who's focused on building skills for today and keeping an eye on the skills of tomorrow. These areas operate like communities of practice, with strategic plans to build skills capacity under each practice. Their AI-based skills intelligence platform is also generating new job families or knowledge clusters based on the number of similar skills that people report. David Henderson, then-Zurich's Group CHRO, noted that the company ". . .now focus[es] more on skills that can transfer from one job family to another. This goes back to workforce planning." In doing so, they've created a knowledge-based network that's powered by skills, not jobs.[27]

Henderson also stresses the role of upskilling and reskilling in a future-proof organization. He says they have ". . .a bias for developing [their] people into new job opportunities, rather than hiring new skills externally." That approach, he points out, fosters a sense of well-being among employees and empowers them to do their best work.

Our research shows that those who are capitalizing on this truth are simultaneously looking at how they can redesign jobs to not only create space for learning and development, but also to deliver a more agile talent model—one that has a better chance of keeping pace with change.

The need to perpetually reinvent is especially critical, given the heightened risk landscape we operate in and the technological disruption we are seeing. Gaining insight into what skills you have today is a starting point. Learning Management Systems (LMS) and Human Capital Management (HCM) systems like Workday and Oracle are being used to define skills, while others are using bespoke AI-driven talent technology—Gloat, Eightfold and Skyhive, for example—to bring in the skills intelligence they need to fire up their talent marketplaces. And a subset of these are also bringing in cost forecasting for skills.

There's no doubt that talent intelligence and marketplaces are becoming the tech that is fueling many SBO models, enabling employees who acquire new skills and/or have the motivation to reskill/upskill to access new opportunities that make it worth their while. It also allows companies to use skills to find talent—both outside and inside the company—to meet business needs. This enables them to pivot their talent quickly as business priorities change.

These systems use AI to advance information, from forecasting skills needed for the future to modeling needs as a part of strategic workforce planning exercises to inferring skills that the workforce has today and helping define career paths that will close skills-related job gaps. AI is also driving personalized learning and suggestions as to what to learn to acquire valued skill clusters. Finally, with the advent of Gen AI, we will see an enormous lift in learning effectiveness by making learning more impactful and reducing the cycle time from spotting a skills-based learning need to creating a curriculum that can help solve it.

Although pilot projects have been minimally scoped, these are already showing a return. For example, Standard Chartered unlocked almost $4 million in the first few years of their talent marketplace project (which encouraged workers to spend one hour to a maximum of eight hours a week on internal gigs). They estimate that, on average, it is $48,000 cheaper to reskill and redeploy employees internally, than it is to hire externally. According to their CHRO Tanuj Kapilashrami, "It is this type of commercial impact that makes business leaders and boards sit up and listen."

Similarly, Schneider Electric saw a $15 million savings in enhanced productivity and reduced recruiting expenses when they began using an AI-based skills marketplace platform as they retained talent for longer when they actively offered opportunities to their people internally.[28]

And, Novartis quantified that they gained $3.7 million in value in the first year of implementing a talent marketplace as part of an integrated SBO strategy.

Taking all of this into account, our imaginary look into the work world circa 2030 and beyond feels like it could soon become a reality. Companies will be filled with contributors whose ever-growing, ever-evolving skill sets are matched to opportunities that retain and inspire them, no doubt keeping people contributing well into their third or fourth career, and financially secure enough to ensure a great life beyond their 100th birthday.

People Leaders' CTAs

1. **Build your skills intelligence quotient (SQ).** Support contributors to define the skills they have today and what they might need to stay market-relevant tomorrow. Ask what skills might also be needed if they moved into an adjacent job. Consider how AI and automation are impacting jobs around them and in their function/industry today. Discuss the implication for skill development.

2. **Cultivate an inclusive learning climate.** Pivot performance discussions toward skills-based interventions and new experiences. Draw from talent intelligence insights and conversations to keep pace with contributors' own interests and aspirations. Take more chances on nontraditional talent

in hiring and for internal talent moves, with skill building the goal.

3. **Build upskilling into roles as standard**. Figure out how people can best learn in the flow of their work. Consider roles that might sit within agile teams, and how to create opportunities for trying new things or stepping up responsibilities. Accelerate skill-building through talent mobility, mentorships, and dedicated time for special projects or other gig opportunities. Remember that the best learning often happens at the intersection of new ideas and personal experiences.

Executives' and HR's CTAs

1. **Build the infrastructure to support skills-based organizations.** Define what you mean by *skills*, and create architectures and/or taxonomies to create a shared language around skills. Consider which types of skills-based models— self-reporting, learning focused, AI-enabled, marketplace-driven—best support your business objectives. Determine the features and benefits you need from related technologies, from strategic workforce planning to assessment and credentialing to career pathing and internal recruitment, and set a course to acquire these.

2. **Build a skills-based component into your pay strategies.** Use skills-pricing information to build forecasts around the cost of talent, and leverage skills-based market data for internal talent pay adjustments, not just for hiring. Use this intelligence to help plan your organization's efforts in building skills for the future.

CHAPTER 9

Supply Is Unchained

When you go to a concert, you'll often see a band member take an extended solo, à la Slash from Guns and Roses or Metallica's Kirk Hammett. When it comes to writing this book, we've become a band, of sorts—we're thinking of calling ourselves The Mercer Three, but we're open to suggestions—so in that spirit, we're going to turn the spotlight onto, our very own Slash, Ilya Bonic, who's going to riff on a topic about which we're all passionate: the talent supply chain.

While all three of us had a hand in writing this song, er, this chapter, we thought you'd enjoy this iteration of a presentation Ilya delivered on this subject. To get the full impact, picture him on a stage, wearing a headset microphone, referring to the deck slides on the screen behind him. He won't have a guitar, but the show will rock.

Take it away, Ilya. . .

Innovation, Outplacement, and Potato Chips

So much of our modern, most progressive people practices seem to have been influenced by people strategy innovations of the leading technology firms: Google, Facebook, Microsoft, Salesforce, and so on. Think about the edgy and generous benefits practices, the on-campus employee experience, the flexibility of work, the elevated comp, the *aqua-hiring*, the performance management, incentive plans, people development programs. In many ways, it is not surprising that the tech industry has led; innovation and creativity often arise out of necessity. And for these kinds of firms, operating in the hot-house, incredibly competitive labor market of Silicon Valley and its equivalents around the world, attracting and retaining talent is literally a matter of survival.

Well, these same firms that have for so long seemed untouchable with regards to people strategy now experience the same vulnerabilities and challenges as leading employers in more traditional and mature industries. TechCrunch[1] refers to an industry-wide "reckoning," as the likes of Facebook, Google, Amazon, Salesforce, and fintech startups, among others, have shed over 160,000 of their employees in the January–March period of 2023 alone. The commentary that accompanies these layoffs is a leadership confession to have over-hired talent while under-anticipating a downward shift in demand.

While a relatively new experience for the technology industry, this is a balancing phenomenon that most people-dependent businesses have had to navigate for decades. Figure 9.1 is a rudimentary illustration of the never-ending challenge of synching

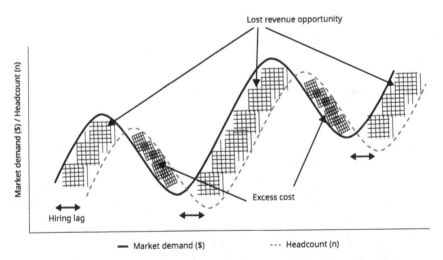

FIGURE 9.1 Knowledge business hiring practices: Headcount lags market demand.

*Source: **Work Different:** Bravery, Anderson, Bonic*

talent capacity with market demand in knowledge-driven industries, and the conservative approach that most companies adopt to try to avoid a boom-bust cycle in headcount growth that typically ends in painful layoff programs. The conservatism is all about waiting for confidence of signals for market demand, and hiring after, not ahead, of the demand curve.

The tradeoff for this conservatism in hiring is that organizations struggle to realize the full potential of market demand in periods of economic upswing. They either don't have enough quality people or haven't hired the right people to take full advantage of the opportunities they have. They play catch-up in talent acquisition. Then, failing to anticipate a downturn, they may overshoot their hiring numbers because they don't realize quickly enough that the market is signaling a decline in demand. When a company grows too much, too quickly, it ends up having too much cost relative to the market and is forced to downsize. In terms of hiring versus cost, the challenge is to get these in sync, and that's incredibly difficult.

I liken this to the challenge that supply chain professionals have been dealing with for eternity: how to optimize and ensure that just the right amount of production inputs, goods, and services are available at the right place and the right time to meet the exact level of market demand.

What we found during and after lockdown is that we don't have a business unless we have the people. If we don't have enough people, we can't deliver on what the market demands. This has become even more problematic since potential contributors are pickier than ever as to whether they even want to engage and be part of this supply chain.

These are issues that supply chain professionals have been dealing with forever, issues such as forecasting, data analytics, and delivery models, which the pandemic brought into sharper focus as supply chain resilience was tested. Given the challenge of our time is essentially one of people scarcity and/or a lack of skill resources to meet customer needs, this begs three questions:

1. What lessons can we learn about supply chain resilience that we can apply to our talent pipelines?

2. How might supply chain management suggest new tools for managing today's talent challenges?

3. How could supply chain thinking help us better manage our own supply issues?

Before we dive into the talent side of this discussion, let's revisit the real-world supply chain snafus of 2021. Do you recall the images of empty supermarket shelves? Vacant car yards? Overflowing shipping container terminals? Clogged shipping channels?

We were forced to deal with a slowdown—or, in some cases, a standstill—of the flow of goods and services upon which the global platform economy is built. On first blush, one might posit that the COVID lockdown was the lone culprit in the supply chain glitch, and that's not an unfair take. It forced all of us into our houses for months, so it's easy and logical to point to the pandemic as the supply chain killer. . .but COVID didn't act alone.

Thanks to a perfect storm of a raging virus, some unprecedentedly scary weather, and a notable labor shortage, the global supply chain unraveled. One particularly heartbreaking example was seen in India, where a COVID spike meant that people were too sick to work in factories that generated the industrial oxygen, a critical resource to treat the respiratory symptoms of the virus.[2] Employees couldn't work to manufacture enough oxygen, and their health couldn't improve without sufficient oxygen—that's just about as vicious as a cycle can get.

But let's talk more about the weather, which doesn't get nearly enough credit (or blame) for its role in this mess. In addition to the world suffering through the hottest month on record in July 2021,[3] we saw a record of four $20 billion–plus weather disasters batter cities around the globe.[4] There were the European summer floods that led to the costliest weather disaster in the continent's history, to the tune of $43 billion, as well as intense flooding in China that set the country back $30 billion. Add in the climate-induced disruptions like Hurricane Ida, the deep freeze in Texas, and the wildfires in California (totaling $99 billion in damages), and it's little wonder the planet was lousy with supply chain choke points.

This was right about when we were beginning to deal with what we eventually dubbed a talent market failure. Here's an example.

During the height of lockdown, few were allowed to travel in the air, so the airline industry laid off a huge percentage of its workforce with estimates in the United States alone exceeding 400,000 workers.[5] When we *were* able to fly again, the companies couldn't put all their planes in the sky because they didn't have enough pilots, flight attendants, baggage handlers, or mechanics to do so. Fortunately for the struggling workforce, employees who'd been laid off, furloughed, or outright fired soon found that their skills could be applied in other organizations that offered more interesting work and a more attractive EVP.

Once the planes were given the okay to fly, a notable number of these workers were asked to come back. But if they landed at a company where they were treated better or were more engaged with, well, more engaging work, why *should* they go back?

Now let's think locally. Remember when we were locked down and the grocery shelves were half empty? That was because there weren't enough drivers to get the food to the stores, or enough manufacturers to create the food in the first place. Panic buying didn't help. Distilleries were facing similar issues, and the lack of booze didn't make lockdown any easier for most.

In any event, on the left-hand side of the ledger, you've got examples of millions and millions of people being put out of jobs, while on the right-hand side, you've got organizations that needed millions and millions of people, *right here, right now*. There was an imbalance between supply and demand, but nobody could say the talent wasn't there. There just wasn't a way to get the *right* talent where it was needed.

The old adage goes that crisis breeds innovation, and that's exactly what happened in the talent market. Throughout 2021, we explored a range of novel ideas that hadn't been previously trialed with the hope that these innovations would address these market failures. One of the most notable innovations was a talent matching platform called People + Work Connect, created by a consortium of the chief people officers from ServiceNow, Verizon,

Accenture, and Lincoln Financial.[6] Here's how Accenture explains the platform:

> We launched People + Work Connect [in 2021] to help put the world to work. Last year, we evolved the free, online platform to help companies with a demand for talent connect with community organizations that represent "hidden workers"—people who are eager to work and possess—or could develop—the skills employers seek, if only those employers could find them.[7]

Here's how it worked: When Marriott shut down early in lockdown, they furloughed tens of thousands of employees[8] because with travel restrictions, nobody needed a hotel, thus nobody needed hotel workers. On the other hand, organizations like Blue Apron and Frito Lay in the United States couldn't get enough talent because while we were stuck at home, many of us wanted prepared meals and potato chips delivered to our door.

The aforementioned consortium's idea was that the furloughed Marriott employees would go onto their new platform, where they'd see that FritoLay was in desperate need of talent. Sure, a hospitality expert might not know anything about the snack food industry, but a good worker is a good worker. If you can plug them into a similar position, regardless of the industry, the worker, their prior employer, and their new employer win as they flow their talent toward the demand. In many instances, this innovative approach led to hiring of workers who otherwise would be furloughed and potentially retrenched.

To that end, we're now seeing technology used more creatively than ever before. A similar idea, but with a much heavier technology twist, was developed by a teaming of McKinsey and Eightfold AI.[9] They utilized the power and potential of AI to help identify organizations that had demand for talent, what the jobs were, and what skills, competencies, and experiences were required for the positions. They similarly applied AI to the job and experience profiles of unemployed and furloughed workers. When the algorithms went to work, it turned out that the AI matching was shockingly efficient at making employee/employer connections.

Crisis also often leads to reinvention. Mounting layoffs and rising unemployment numbers offered the opportunity for the outplacement industry to come to the rescue—after all, the entire industry's purpose is to address talent market failure.

Against this backdrop, one would assume that outplacement agencies would thrive, as tons of employees were out of work and tons of employers had work that needed to be done. You'd think that there'd be lines around the block to use these services. After all, all a job seeker had to do was go into the agency's office, where they'd be trained on how to write a resume, how to conduct themselves during a job interview, and how to network to find a job.

You'd think wrong.

It turned out that in a time where social distancing was the norm, few were interested in hauling themselves and their N95s or P45s into a strange office, believing the whole process was too inconvenient, too antiquated, not safe enough, or even not worth their time.

There was an even more fundamental problem: traditional outplacement is labor intensive, expensive, and tends to be targeted toward middle to senior executives, an employee segment that has a higher income and can thus afford to be out of work for longer. The balance of the workforce, the millions who'd been laid off or furloughed—which, anecdotally speaking, includes people who are oftentimes left to sink or swim on their own—had to pore over the job postings on LinkedIn and Indeed. Compounding the issue is that some organizations find it too expensive to use the AI approach in the first place.

But guess what: the outplacement firms innovated, specifically by going digital.

No longer did you have to trek across the city to meet with your job placement expert. From your living room, you could log into an agency's portal and set up a conversation with any number of counselors or experts. You could do mock video interviews to prepare for the real interview, then watch the quality of your responses. You could answer 50 or 100 or 1,000 sample questions, further prepping you for that meeting with your future boss, fingers crossed. You could get better at job hunting while wearing your pajamas and chilling out on your sofa. These tools often linked to jobs boards, so if there was a job similar to what you were looking for, the posting popped up on your smartphone. You didn't even have to try to look for a job—the job came to you.

And that, my friends, is how you address that talent market failure.

Bullwhipped

During lockdown, as was the case with millions of people across the world, my [Ilya's] family bought a Peloton.[10] As was also likely the case with millions of people across the world, even though I had the best intentions health-wise, I didn't use it nearly enough. (Okay, the truth is that I stopped using it altogether. No disrespect to Peloton, which makes one hell of a product, but it turns out that I'm more of a treadmill person.)

I mention this because I want to discuss Peloton's wild ride leading up to, during, and after the pandemic, a ride that offers a compelling snapshot of the breakdown of the traditional supply chain *and* the talent supply chain, circa COVID.

Peloton sold its first bike in 2013, and, soon after they developed an Internet-connected bike with a built-in tablet that offered access to online classes. It was a huge success, and at the end of 2019, Peloton went public. When the pandemic hit in 2020, gyms worldwide closed their doors, the at-home digital fitness industry boomed, and Peloton was one of the major beneficiaries. During the fourth quarter of that year, the company's sales surged by 172% over the previous year, but with massive growth came massive problems. The supply couldn't meet the demand, so Peloton invested over $100 million in shipping bikes via air rather than by sea.[11] The company also acquired one of its Taiwanese manufacturers, as well as a U.S.-based fitness competitor Precor, which provided access to U.S. manufacturing capabilities.

It didn't help.

In 2021, the company notched $189 million in losses, and by late 2022, had laid off over 5,000 workers from its workforce peak of 8,000 and lost $2.8 billion, all because the company had failed to anticipate either the spike in demand or the supply chain disruption.[12]

Hindsight being 20/20, it's easy to say Peloton made some crazy decisions on the amount of capital they invested to ramp up production and align themselves with what they believed to be a demand that had no end in sight. But they, like many of the tech firms, went too far.

Unsurprisingly, it's not just tech firms that are grappling with this challenge. In the United Kingdom, Made.com shed a third of its staff as it fought for survival after being plagued by supply chain issues.[13] Just one year after floating and following a 98% drop in their share price, it was clear they'd lost the confidence of their customers, and along with it, their talent. The company geared up at a time when people were buying furniture online, but again failed to adjust their business and people model as the longer-term outlook shifted downward. Their journey of being propelled into the headlines as an innovator to subsequently being bought by Next was just 10 years in the making.

In supply chain practice and theory, this sort of occurrence is so common that there's a term for it: the Bullwhip Effect, which means you've overshot by a mile, and you're stuck with a ton of supply and cost, but no demand. Peloton got it wrong and Made.com couldn't turn it around, and for both companies, there were real world—and real people—consequences.

Is this Bullwhip Effect a trap only for the companies that are operating in industries where there is a hot trend or fad? Nope. As 2023 has shown us, even those companies that make the various *best employer* lists are vulnerable. When the Bullwhip trap snaps, all of a sudden, those firms—the seeming majority of which, these days, are in the tech space—don't really look like the best employers anymore.

Going back to the tech space, 2023 was a year of turmoil. Looking ahead at an uncertain economy, with semi-conductor demand dropping, with social media platform and AI-driven search disruption, 2023 became a *year of efficiency*. Organizations like Meta, Google, Microsoft, and Salesforce, in combination, laid off hundreds of thousands of workers, another example of talent market failure, an example that had us at Mercer asking questions galore:

- How did it all go wrong? Why hadn't we seen ahead?
- How can we ensure that we learn lessons from oversupply and don't repeat our failures?

- How do we ensure that in the future we don't over-hire or under-hire?
- How do we move talent with greater fluidity from areas of low demand to areas of high demand?
- How do we achieve and maintain harmony between talent supply and demand?

Fortunately, there is a solution, of sorts. Actually, there are five solutions that we believe can make a difference to the fortunes of businesses and their people. Here is how companies can work on solving talent supply chain issues:

1. Plan your workforce

Yeah, we know. Planning is the replacement of chance by error. And indeed, we repeatedly experience the reflex in companies to forego strategic workforce planning. Excuses include a lack of time—"operational headcount planning is already time-consuming enough," they might say—and the perception that it's too hard and has too few concrete measures. The real motivations are often a refusal to make binding assumptions for which one can be held accountable.

In fact, in many companies, strategic workforce planning is often viewed as an HR exercise that has little relevance to the business. Here, there is usually a lack of understanding that HR actions take time—even the recruitment of critical positions is now often measured in months rather than weeks, not to mention reskilling and upskilling actions that can take years to play out. This is a chain of (talent) supply, after all. No supply chain executive would let anyone deny the need for effective planning, but despite the impact on the business and people if neglected, it's often remedial rather than strategic.

Strategic workforce planning is a standardized, clearly structured dialogue between business functions and HR, in which assumptions about business growth drivers are combined with qualitative and quantitative insights into skill requirements. And then these are set against supply modeling that includes turnover, retirements, and absenteeism assumptions. More modern systems allow us to see demand in terms of skills needed, not just headcount, which in turn allows for different modeling of supply (e.g., contingent, part-time, full-time, more junior, skills-adjacent, AI-augmented). If the business climate changes? Adjust the assumptions. The result is an accurate-as-can-be projection of supply needs with corresponding shortages and surpluses as well as measures to minimize their impact on business execution. It is a kind of contract between HR and the business function that creates commitment and helps ensure a smooth talent pipeline. So that it's not like: "We need 150 data analysts." "When?" "Next week!"

2. Secure and retain

You can't catch wind with a net. An ounce of prevention is worth a pound of cure. You can't bail water out of a sinking ship with a leaky bucket. Those clichés are all metaphorical ways of saying that you have to do everything within your power to acquire and keep the best workforce possible. Getting pay levels right is more critical than ever, as we've discussed. And flexibility is at a premium. People are looking for development and growth opportunities with an eye to the future. Purpose and cultural alignment have never been more important.

With workers more stressed than ever, employers have no choice but to address issues of absenteeism and how they impact their talent supply. Resilience is about the health and engagement of your workforce, even if they don't leave, disengagement, those on long-term sick leave or disability, and unplanned gaps in your pipeline erode your resilience at a team level.

When you secure that supply chain, you secure your workforce, and if you need to address their wellness issues to do so, then address their wellness issues, and address them well. You can't do this without good data on your workforce's health, a commitment to addressing toxic cultures, and a mandate to put people first.

3. Diversify

In rethinking talent sourcing strategies, your company—now that it's (hopefully) on the path of retaining a healthy and engaged workforce—should challenge the status quo.

If it isn't looking beyond the norm, your current and future potential employees certainly are.

The forthcoming questions may seem like non sequiturs, but stick with me here: Did you take a European vacation in the summer of 2022? Or do you wish you did?

If you said *yes*, you probably meant *no* because for Euro-travelers, 2022 was the Summer of Lost Luggage.

Recall, if you will, the images of baggage piled high at Heathrow, Schiphol, and Frankfurt airports, images that high-lighted the impact of talent shortages. The aviation industry slashed over two million jobs during the pandemic,[14] and in the new labor market, many workers changed industries and were rewarded with higher pay and better benefits.

The fast-food industry was also notably impacted. In the U.S. summer of 2022, if you stopped by a McDonald's or a Burger King for your French fry fix, there was a decent chance the location had become drive-through only or had closed al-together. Turned out there weren't enough workers interested and available to keep the dining room operations running.

On the other end of the spectrum, high-end restaurants were dealing with similar issues. Reservation books were filled not necessarily because all the tables were full, but because there wasn't sufficient staff to cover the entire floor, thus there were fewer tables available. The numbers bear this out: Black-box Intelligence reported that during the pandemic, 15% of restaurant workers had changed industries, while 33% wanted to.[15] Out of opportunity and necessity, more workers and em-ployers were willing to take a chance and bet that skills and experience could be transferred from one industry to another.

That all being the case, employers need to be willing to hire talent they wouldn't have previously considered, to be open-minded in terms of who could be relevant and success-ful in their organization, to embrace workers who will broad-en their pool of talent so their firm can diversify. And let's face it, willing to fix unattractive jobs and give voice to work-ers about how they are treated and how they are paid. Yes, hiring specs that required degrees and certain years of ten-ure were quickly removed, but also more attention was given to empathizing with workers' plights and finding out what would indeed improve the job and their work experience— quickening the move toward the skills-based talent practices that we chatted about before. This sort of attack improves both decision-making and workforce resilience.

4. Vertically integrate

The Talent Solutions resource of LinkedIn offers up information on all kinds of talent market trends, including which types of jobs are the fastest growing and in the most demand. During COVID, application developers topped the list, and between the second quarter of 2021 and the fourth quarter of 2022, demand for application developers increased 13-fold. That's huge. So, let's play around with some numbers.

Before COVID, companies needed one app dev worker. That climbed to 13.

If they needed 100 then, now it was 1,300.

Or from 1,000 to 13,000.

Or from 10,000 to 130,000.

As your company goes through its digital transformation journey, where will it find that new application developer talent it needs? More importantly, how will you be able to afford that talent? What with the demand, you could end up paying 30%–40% more for new hires, and even if you find the talent, you might not be able to afford to compete with other companies who are equally talent-deficient; this, in turn, diminishes your chance to hold onto them if you can hire them. From a supply chain perspective, what do you do?

You vertically integrate.

In HR-speak, vertical integration basically breaks down to prioritizing the development of internal talent through training, coaching, and other learning opportunities that allow contributors to up- or reskill, rather than relying solely on external hiring to meet an organization's skills shortfalls. Although, training has always been on the agenda for this to be the primary source of talent acquisition (build), it needs to be damn good at knowing what skills you have, what you can build, and when that talent will be ready. It's more than identifying high-potential employees and providing them with opportunities for growth and development—it needs to be highly targeted and requires a culture of continuous learning and development for all contributors.

The goal is to develop a strong pipeline of talent that's aligned with the organization's strategic objectives and can help drive sustainable growth and success over the long term—as we discussed before. Building talent was a strategy that leaders pivoted toward in 2022 as high volume *buying* of talent was no longer a realistic or sustainable strategy (e.g., the talent was not there, the skills were too costly). The challenge was that our tools and techniques for finding talent in the external labor market are far more mature than those that we had internally to identify and deploy talent. (Cue the explosion of talent marketplace, and upskilling and reskilling that exploded onto the scene in 2020.)

5. Prepare for uncertainty

Peloton couldn't do it. Google couldn't do it. Neither could Amazon, Microsoft, or Apple.

"It" means "predict the future," which is why it's essential—*essential*—that your company build greater insight into supply and demand drivers and greater flexibility in your methods to respond.

According to Bain, the way companies mitigated their supply chain challenges coming out of COVID and are preparing for a climate of greater uncertainty is by building five competences:[16]

1. **Network agility**, that is, building a flexible ecosystem of supplier and partners who can help them respond.

2. **Digital collaboration**, that is, using collaboration platforms to share information quickly between groups.

3. **Real-term network visibility**, that is, enabling leadership to have greater visibility into supply and demand trends.

4. **Rapid generation of insights**, that is, improving their ability to mine internal and external sources of big data via machine learning and artificial intelligence to provide early warning signals.

5. **Empowered teams**, that is, groups that can react quickly to the insights generated and formulate plans to mobilize resources.

All of these ideas can be directly applied to the world of talent management to shore up resilience.

Bain wrote, "Advanced analytics can improve supply forecast accuracy by 20%–60%," and that "flexible supply networks are pivotal in helping companies minimize the risk of disruption in times of stress." This is equally true for talent ecosystems, and these competences directly apply here.

If we need to ratchet up the talent supply when demand is high—and moderate it on the way down—we need to have accurate information on both our supply and demand drivers, ideally in dashboards with enough insight to enable us to ignite action. And we need to think flexibly and creatively in our response.

A company can increase flexibly by utilizing a blended workforce, one made up of permanent workers, part-time workers, job shares, consultants, gig workers, and agency staff, as well as leveraging a talent marketplace, either internally or for contingent workers.

This blended workforce model is no more evident than in the health industry. In the U.S. hospital system between 2019 and 2022, contract labor hours rose from 1–6%, thus contract labor costs grew from 2% in 2019 to 11% three years later. This hugely affected nursing roles, where contract nurse wages rose from a median of $64 per hour in 2019 to $132 in 2022. Meanwhile, full-time nurse salaries rose only from a median of $35 to $39 over this same stretch.[17]

Here's a personal story that highlights why it's crucial we get this right.

In November 2022, I [Ilya] had to visit Germany, a country that was in the midst of a COVID spike. Before I stepped onto that plane, I knew I'd have to get the latest COVID booster. I booked an appointment at my local pharmacy in the United States, and I wasn't concerned about any potential crowding because, according to news reports, not that many people were getting the shot. I figured I'd be in and out of there, which was fortunate, as

I was buried in work, and the drive from my neighborhood to the office was 30 minutes, without traffic, and 60 minutes with.

I figured wrong.

When I arrived at the store, I looked at the 10-deep queue and thought, *Uh-oh, this isn't good.*

By the time I got near the vaccination administration room half an hour later, things were getting testy, so much so that I heard a customer arguing with the vaccination nurse, yelling, "What's taking so long? Why have you been moving so slowly? I've been waiting forever!"

The nurse said, "I'm doing the work here, and I'll do it at my pace. If you keep speaking to me like this, I'm going to leave. And by the way, I've got a lunch break at 1:00, and I'm taking the full half-hour, and I don't care how many people are out there waiting!"

At that point, it was 12:45, so if I couldn't get in there before her break, I wouldn't be back at the office for an hour, possibly two. Thankfully, I made it into the vaccination room five minutes before she took off.

I expected the nurse to be a monster, but we had a perfectly pleasant conversation, during which I learned that she wasn't a pharmacy employee, but rather a contractor because the pharmacy couldn't find enough nurses to administer vaccinations. She told me, "There was another contractor who was supposed to be here today, but she didn't show up. And she didn't even call to tell anybody she wasn't coming, so I have to do the job of two people."

That explained her short temper. I said, "Just out of curiosity, are you still going to take your lunch break at one? You're not going to take care of the people who've been waiting in line all this time?"

She said, "I've got another pharmacy to go to Monday, and if that doesn't work out, I'll go to another one. I'm getting paid a heck of a lot of money doing this contract work, and if I'm not treated right at this location, I'll go to another in this chain, or I'll go to one of its competitors that can't find enough nurses either. And, I'm not the only nurse who feels this way."

And this, ladies and gentlemen, is a blended workforce. (A mismanaged one, granted, but blended nonetheless.) This incident made it clear to me that in this uncertain climate, companies must nail these two initiatives:

1. Accrue accurate data on supply and demand.
2. Make flexible plans to react to said data.

Failure to deliver on this will lead to screaming matches in the vaccination room and a less than certain future for all concerned.

So, is it easy to match talent supply with demand when you have good data?

Nope. It's a never-ending challenge, but if you approach it with compassion and kindness—especially when your mission is to improve the lives of people here in The People Age—it's fulfilling, and oftentimes, even fun.

That said, we'll always face new challenges every week, month, and year. Back in the day, we never had to worry about talent supply chain vulnerability and disruption, and we're still trying to figure out how to navigate the ever-changing currents. Hopefully by the time we get it right, we'll have our luggage back.

People Leaders' CTAs

1. **Know the health of your talent pipeline.** An impoverished talent supply includes one that has workers who are ill, absent, or disengaged, and/or one where desired or diverse workers are leaving unexpectedly. Design work with well-being as an outcome, instill in managers their responsibility to maintain a healthy pipeline of talent, and build a robust succession plan of engaged talent for tomorrow.

2. **Take a chance on nontraditional talent.** Challenge yourself to consider how you can diversify your workforce beyond college graduates and other blockers to strengthen your talent supply. Consider how workers at different levels, with different backgrounds, and in different locations, and/or on different work arrangements (gig, part-time, job-sharing, remote) could bolster your current talent supply and workforce resilience.

3. **Cultivate diversity in your pipeline.** Ensure you build age, gender, and ethnic diversity into your talent supply. Not only will this help fend off stagnation and get you closer to your customer base, but it will foster flexibility, as different populations at different life stages have different preferences on how they want to contribute to the workforce.

Executives' and HR's CTAs

1. **Engage the widest talent ecosystem.** Focus on the work and the tasks that need to be done, not the contributors currently in the position. Build capabilities within the team to manage blended teams made up of full-time, part-time, seconded and remote workers, as well as gig contractors and supplier-type resources.

2. **Apply supply chain management principles to people risk.** Plan your workforce by ensuring you have good data on supply and demand. Tackle absenteeism and well-being. Diversify sources of talent. Vertically integrate to favor build-over-buy strategies. Prepare for uncertainty by taking steps to maximize the flexibility in your workforce.

CHAPTER 10

Sustainability Starts with People

A Future That Works

A recent Mercer study showed that if you're a U.S. resident, there's an 83.2% chance you've seen the musical *Hamilton*.

Okay, Mercer didn't actually do a *Hamilton* study—we're too busy with our *Les Miz* demographic deep dive—but we do know the soundtrack quite well, and one song that's always resonated with us is the closing number, "Who Lives, Who Dies, Who Tells Your Story."

The song's core message is: *How do you want to be remembered?* When the world-at-large examines what you've done with your life, what will their takeaway be? Will your accomplishments from today be honored in 50 years? Did you try to make the world a better place? Did you spend your precious work hours contributing to a firm that made a difference, or did you suck it up and toil away for one whose values were wildly different than your own?

Even though her hubby Alexander was all about finances, Eliza Hamilton didn't sing about this stuff with the business world in mind. But we can most definitely apply her message to the future of work, and we can even sum it up in what we believe is the perfect word: Sustainability.

In their book *The Great Narrative*, WEF Chairman Klaus Schwab and co-author Thierry Malleret described *sustainability* as "[T]he ability to meet our own needs without compromising the ability of future generations to meet theirs."[1] They argued that while natural, human, and social capital are essential for ". . .the viable development of future generations, they're too often passed over for physical capital."

In our recent collective past, businesses have had an unhealthy preoccupation with driving up profits in the short term, often with little regard for how their work, their methodology, and their products impact the world beyond their offices. The past decade has challenged this belief—as an increasing number of businesses have built sustainability into their agendas, alongside a societal movement that is more than a passing trend.

This is no longer a matter of a few idealistic entrepreneurs. The younger generations of contributors who roam our hallways aren't *asking*, but rather *expecting* businesses to have a net positive impact on the world. And they want to be part of the solution.

Acting on the most pressing issues of our time is great in theory, but making wholesale company changes is a heavy lift because today's society is messy, and the messiness is messing up the business world. Think about it: You've got a shrinking workforce and growing inequity, you've got supply chain woes, you've got a skyrocketing cost of living, you've got inflation that refuses to deflate, and you've got recent bank failures, all set against a chaotic geopolitical landscape and a ticking climate time bomb that will impact us all. And we're expected to take all those issues into account while transforming our companies.

Yikes.

Those with a *business as usual* mindset—as well as the climate deniers, the profit-rules-all leaders, and the folks who simply don't give a damn about what's going on outside of their bubble—will become obsolete. In the long run, they will become extinct just like the dinosaurs; customers, shareholders, and regulators will be their gravediggers. But another stakeholder group will have a more immediate impact because people drive our businesses.

With reputation becoming one of the biggest drivers of talent attraction, it doesn't matter where you sit on the good-for-business/good-for-the-world debate; turning a blind eye to ESG issues and failing to reset for relevance by attending to success outcomes through the eyes of all your stakeholders just isn't an option.

If your company is stressed out on this one, you're not alone. Despite all the talk about how the world would reset and deliver a more just and inclusive future of work, in 2023, many employees said that their company just wasn't meeting their needs and expectations. And that's not a surprise, as the goalposts have moved.[2]

There's a growing sense that something is not right in the way we work and the way societies and economies are evolving. And the fractures of this period will reverberate for many years to come if we don't step in, because at the time of writing this:

- The global climate crisis dominates all long-term risks, with the United Nations declaring that "More than a century of burning fossil fuels, as well as unequal and unsustainable energy and land use, have led to global warming of 1.1°C above pre-industrial levels. This has resulted in more frequent and more intense extreme weather events."[3]

- The cost-of-living crisis is the No. 1 global risk for this period (2023–2025) as ranked by executives in the WEF's [4] Global Risk Report, disproportionately impacting low-income households by an additional 1–4%, as well as significantly holding back those in developing economies.[5] Supply chains and rampant outsourcing are further driving poverty around the world.[6]

- The International Labour Organization (ILO) estimates that 90% of the world's working population is excluded from an adequate pension scheme.[7] The Geneva Association estimates that for those that do have one, the worldwide pension gap is $41.1 trillion.[8] One in six Brits over 55 years have no provision,[9] and one in four Americans over 58 have no provision either.[10,11] This threatens people's ability to retire with dignity. And given the worsening ratio of fewer workers to retirees in many countries, the pension crisis will affect us all.

- The WEF estimates that gender parity in the labor force stands at 62.9%—the lowest level registered since the index was born.[12] And it projects that we won't reach full parity for another 134 years (up from 100 years pre-pandemic). That means we will not have full equity in our lifetime, nor our children's lifetime!

- Broad segments of our society neglected basic health and well-being during the pandemic, and yet not everyone has health coverage, let alone preventive care. A serious concern when noncommunicable diseases lead to 74% of global deaths in 2022, lifetime cancer risk is sitting at 50%, and 15% of working adults report a mental health condition.[13]
- According to the ILO, 208 million people could be out of work in 2023, with decent work and social justice the biggest concerns as people accept lower-paid, less desirable work in the future.[14] They also predict talent supply will decline due to an aging population and the suboptimal number of young trainees in countries with a youthful demographic advantage.

Eliza Hamilton would not be thrilled with the stagnation. Maybe we are indeed living in a *Les Miz* society. . . .

These inequalities aren't just pressing moral and social issues—they're critical for ensuring sustainable economic growth. Given their power to shape our world, organizations have a profound opportunity to mitigate these risks by evolving the sustainability of their business and people practices. It's not just about investing in tomorrow; Mercer's research shows that 96% of workers already expect their company to be pursuing a sustainability agenda.[15]

It's clear that The People Age is upon us and it urgently demands a reset in how we value people and the environments in which they reside, if we are to nurture it. Part of succeeding in this era is not only ensuring that institutions cause no harm, but actively engaging in change to promote healthy employees, employers, and economies. As we have mentioned earlier, our human resource is a finite resource and as such it needs to be treated sustainably. Organizations that accept and embrace that truth—and it *is* a truth—will be the ones that sustain.

Most leaders discuss the need for sustainable business and people practices, but talk is cheap, and there are few areas in business where the *say-versus-do* gap is larger than in the topic of sustainability. For many companies, sustainability is notable in just a few corporate functions: chief sustainability officer, DEI functions, and corporate social responsibility (CSR) among them. This isn't fundamentally wrong—it drives focus, defines budgets, and begs action—but this dynamic is why sustainability touted on the company website sometimes fails to touch each and every employee. And thus, it lacks momentum because it's not woven into corporate identity, it's not threaded into budgeting and reporting, and it's not part of the everyday understanding of why we are working together. And it needs to be if we are to scale good intent.[16]

We've seen a similar development in digital transformation. The establishment of chief digital officers and offices left the impression that this activity was reserved for a small part of the organization; it delayed the realization that digitalization must be anchored in the breadth of the company and manifest itself in digital competencies among all employees.

A pioneer of infusing sustainability into a firm at a value level is Patagonia's founder Yvon Chouinard.[17] He structured his life and the business to reflect his family's commitment to being sustainable at the core. The firm sourced organic materials, offered on-site childcare, and routinely funded environmental activism. In his book *Let My People Go Surfing* (a title that really says it all), Chouinard explains how on his darkest day—the day he had to lay off 20% of his people due to the economic downturn in 1991—he realized that "The company had exceeded its resources and limitations; we had become dependent, like the world economy, on growth we could not sustain.[18] We were forced to rethink our priorities and institute new practices. We had to start breaking the rules because uncontrolled growth put at risk the values that had made the company succeed so far."

Chouinard contemplated that if his company was to be in business for another 100 years, there had to be a better way to run the business—one that aligned with stakeholder interests in addressing threats to survivability, the human experience, bio- and cultural diversity, and a healthy planet.[19] The following is a summary of some of the underlying values that formed the basis of Patagonia's philosophy classes, classes in which leaders taught employees how to ensure their day-to-day decisions were value-based:

- Make all decisions with an eye toward the environmental crisis and how to solve it.

- Prioritize product quality above short-term trends in fashion.
- Promote a sustainable environment by supporting the success of all stakeholders' communities.
- Pursue profitability—without putting it first.
- Donate 1% of total sales (or 10% of profits) to help offset any environmental harm caused by business operations.
- Balance transparency, collaboration, and simplicity with innovation and productivity, all within the bounds of trade secrets and personal privacy.

Today, Patagonia is one of the firms that is most respected for its business ethics. In 2022, Chouinard and his family donated the entire company, valued at $3 billion, to a special trust and a nonprofit organization.[20] The nonprofit will divert all of Patagonia's profits toward fighting climate change; the trust, run by Chouinard family members and advisors, will ensure the business remains socially responsible. By embedding sustainability into the business, Chouinard ensured that the impact he's made will continue far beyond his own lifetime.

Which is why we're proud to wear our Patagonia Downdrift jackets, especially when we're at our eternally rainy London office.

We Have the Power to Make Brighter Days

So, what does sustainability mean for you, the contributor?

Or you, the manager?
Or you, the leader?
Or you, the investor?

Sustainability is about walking and chewing gum, about multitasking, about juggling. Or as Chouinard describes it, "An experiment in doing business in unconventional ways. Sustainability is clearly more than instilling a do-no-harm or do-gooder attitude into your company's DNA, it's about making conscious choices to set goals and make strategic decisions that deliver positive outcomes for all stakeholders. And, similarly to the way Patagonia translated its values doctrine into employee learning, it takes a movement to create a movement.

There are several terms at play here: *Social/people sustainability*, *environmental sustainability*, *business sustainability* (as the mantra goes: People, Planet, Profit). The key is balancing progress across all these dimensions. When businesses are not thriving, environmental concerns often take a backseat. Without a thriving workforce, businesses are in jeopardy and people's incomes at risk. When all our resources are consumed, neither people nor businesses will exist.

1. Environmental sustainability

Flooding, fires, and other signs of human-fueled climate change are getting worse[21] and these all impact our businesses, directly or indirectly. International organizations agree these are serious environmental risks that need intervention: The EU is requiring companies to report on their sustainability agendas from 2024 onwards,[22] The UN is calling for companies to slash carbon emissions in half by 2030 to deliver on the Paris Accord.[23]

Public demand for more attention to climate matters has sparked change (h/t to Greta Thunberg). Firms around the world realized environmental sustainability is more than a real-life chorus of *Kumbaya*—it's critical for our very survival. And it's table stakes for keeping the workforce of the future on board. However, *green hushing*—pressure from some to stay quiet on the climate agenda—is now driving more nuanced sales and marketing plans around the world.

Still, commitments aren't enough on their own. Planning for climate transition will take major upskilling and work redesign. In 2023, the WEF confirmed that investment in the green transition and climate-change mitigation are driving industry transformation, and as such, are some of the strongest drivers of net job creation.[24] In addition, generalist sustainability roles, such as sustainability specialist and environmental protection professionals, are expected to grow by 33% and 34%, respectively, translating into 1 million new jobs by 2027. But as LinkedIn co-founder Allen Blue points out, "When you look at the distribution of green skills around the world, they are unsurprisingly vastly concentrated in the global north and in the richest countries in the world."[25] This is an opportunity for business leaders to shift their investments and talent strategies toward a more equitable, sustainable future.

2. **Social and people sustainability**

When you think about how deeply firms depend on humans—employees, partners, customers, and communities—it's clear that the social, financial, and health issues affecting those people are also threats to the business. From burnout to protests around pay and conditions to skills shortages to Quiet Quitting (and, y'know, *actual* quitting), so much of what plagues organizations comes down to unsustainable people practices that don't work in the long term.

Yes, strikes over pay dominate headlines, but as with many things in life, this is often the tipping point. Often it is respect and working conditions that underlie this discontent, from the gigification of industries that drove screenplay writers in the United States to protest, to the backlash in China from workers at the mercy of food delivery apps—unsustainable work practices and less-than-human expectations are being called into question.

On an individual level, *people sustainability* is about personal health, well-being, and energy expenditures of the workforce. As talent strategies shift to more contingent workers and project-based work (predicted to make up between 50–80% of the U.S. workforce by 2030[26]), more people are losing access to healthcare and social welfare protection. Years of working long hours to meet sky-high expectations have led to mental health issues, including stress and eventually burnout. And just as Millennials called for climate reform, Gen Zers are now calling attention to the *S* in ESG with mental health, women's issues, and societal equity at the top of their agenda.[27]

At a business level, it is about applying the thinking of the circular economy to our people, asking how we can ensure that people remain employable, and figuring out what we need to do to ensure that we don't suffer from the Bullwhip Effect, and that as we transform, people remain dignified, vital and healthy. To that end, the WEF is asking for companies to declare their intent with regard to delivering on Good Work to ensure a sustainable economy.[28]

On a societal level, people sustainability refers to the long-term viability of society at large. It depends on socioeconomic factors like public health, income, and economic opportunity. These tend to be less-than-ideal for underrepresented and at-risk populations, and the pandemic and subsequent cost-of-living crisis only made matters worse. Yet when asked about rising business expenses, a majority of executives in 2023 still say they expect to pass those costs on to consumers. . .and, yes, we hear the face-palms of frustration all the way from Mercer HQ.[29]

3. **Business sustainability**

Driving sustainability on all fronts is not an either/or approach. Yes, business can do more for people and the planet, but as the saying goes, you can't pour from an empty cup. If we don't stay in business, we're no longer positioned to benefit individuals, society, economies, and the environment. Even team Patagonia listed the pursuit of profit as one of several key company values. There is no sustainability without affordability, and this includes the affordability of your people and their healthcare.

If we look at our companies through a sustainability lens, we can find ways to use the business engine for good. Today, investors and leaders are pushing organizations to be more deliberate in how they're positioned and structured to drive maximum impact. They want to know about ESG goals, depending on the political climate, sustainable investing and impact investing, and more recently, they are curious to evaluate just how resilient an organization is to future shocks as the S in ESG becomes a bigger risk.

In many ways, business sustainability is about ensuring the C-suites, shareholders, and boardrooms of tomorrow are all positioned to keep thriving once we're gone. But this can't happen without a healthy and skilled workforce, a safe and low-risk environment for our infrastructure, and positive brand sentiment from a society with increasingly people-centric values.

Good Work If You Can Get It

If the business and people agendas are intertwined—something on which 85% of executives globally agree—and if brand and reputation have an outsized impact on why someone will join your company—up from No. 9 to the No. 2 attraction driver in 2022—then sustainability can't be an afterthought.[30] Companies need to make strategic decisions that simultaneously hit multiple agendas.

It's not only good for business. It's good work. Or, for the sake of this discussion, Good Work, capital G, capital W. Like ESG, this is emerging as a red thread that companies need to weave into both their customer and employee value propositions to win in The People Age. See Figure 10.1, for how these topics interlink.

During the pandemic, Mercer partnered with the WEF on the Future of Work agenda. CHROs from around the world convened once a week to share what was happening and discuss the future, and as a result of these discussions, it became clear that we were entering a different era. As we wrote with WEF in 2022, *The Future of Work Agenda Was Being Reset*—reset around more human-centric values,[31] signaling the dawn of what we call The People Age.

To turn this insight into action, the WEF coalesced a group of leading companies to design a framework to help others commit to building a more equitable, inclusive, and just future of work (see Figure 10.2). The framework was born out of these discussions, and subsequently launched in May 2022, with metrics and reporting shared at the annual meeting in Davos in 2023.

See Figure 10.2 for what premiered to business leaders during the WEF Annual Meeting at Davos:

The five objectives cover most aspects of the relationship between an organization and its contributors, and extend to the impact that a company has across its talent ecosystems—contingent workers, suppliers, partners—and the markets within

Internal and external brand congruence and a lived _experience_ that delivers on the _promise_ is critical for talent retention.

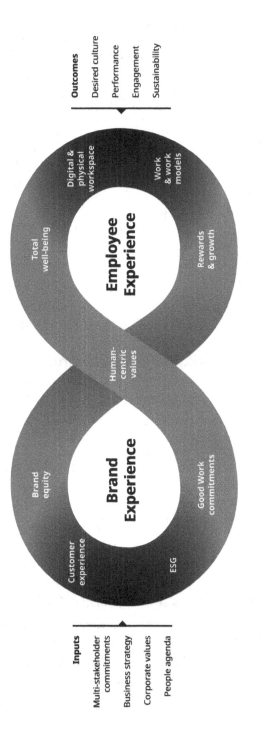

In 2022, high-growth companies were more likely to:

- Trust their employees
- Balance EQ with IQ when making critical decisions

FIGURE 10.1
Source: Mercer

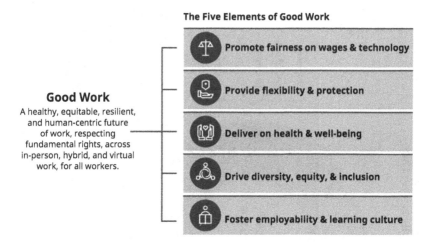

FIGURE 10.2 The Good Work framework.
Source: World Economic Forum

which it operates. The ask: make public commitments on Good Work ambitions, even if only a few, to drive tangible progress for workers.

By way of example, Good Work Alliance partners have set some ambitious goals to galvanize their vast resources—people and otherwise—toward driving sustainable futures (see Figure 10.3). In 2023, here are some of the commitments that Good Work Alliance members are making to their contributors:

- Unilever pledged to reskill and/or upskill all workers so that by 2025, the company will have a future-fit skill set.[32] They also committed to help teach essential skills to 10 million young people, and to deliver flexible working models to all by 2030.[33]

- Schneider Electric pledged to ensure that every employee is paid no less than a living wage, to increase their gender diversity in hiring (50%) and leadership (30% to 40%), and to reskill or upskill employees to be future-ready, all by 2025.[34]

- Allianz is ensuring employees devote one hour a week to learning.[35] They also committed to improving the overall well-being of employees, according to the Work Well index, and filling at least 38% of executive positions with women by the end of 2024.[36]

Objectives	Core Goals	Expanded Goals
Objective 1 Promote fairness on wages & technology	Ensure at least a living wage for all	• Support worker representation and processes for dispute resolution • Take a responsible approach to deploying technology • Use AI and data responsibly
Objective 2 Provide flexibility & protection	Enable all workers to benefit from flexibility, where possible and appropriate	• Support national public social protection systems • Support access to benefits • Promote solutions that provide security for independent workers
Objective 3 Deliver on health & well-being	Safeguard total well-being at work	• Protect physical and psychological safety in the workplace • Provide for predictability of hours and boundaries on working time • Ensure that workers feel valued and purpose in their work
Objective 4 Drive diversity, equity, & inclusion	Ensure that the workforce profile reflects the operating market	• Drive equal pay and equitable conditions • Enable inclusive participation and build an inclusive culture • Ensure that global leadership reflects workforce composition
Objective 5 Foster employability & learning culture	Provide accessible upskilling and reskilling for the entire workforce	• Enable a culture of continuous learning • Ensure talent processes recognize and reward skilling achievements • Cultivate systems and alliances for redeployment

FIGURE 10.3 WEF core and expanded goals for Good Work as of 2023.

- Novo Nordisk committed to driving a 10% annual improvement in employees reporting stress symptoms, and a 5% annual improvement in employees reporting work-related pain.[37]

Let's share some quick insights into some of the objectives under this framework that we've not previously flagged.

Objective 1: Promote Fairness on Wages and Technology

We've talked about ethical AI, data privacy, and the digital divide, so let's share a note on living wages—the core goal under this objective.

Despite research declaring that 71% of companies believe they pay employees a living wage, we know this is a fallacy.[38] Many equate living wages to minimum wages, and too few glean insights into their workforce's ability to sustain a decent living on what they earn.

Today, workers in mature economies can be working full-time and fail to earn enough to live a decent life after taxes and deductions. What you define as a *decent living*, of course, varies by what you'd put in a basket of goods in a weekly shopping trip and by country, but this type of assessment throws up new moral and business questions. One firm that has made strides in delivering a living wage to all its workers is the global agricultural firm Yara International.

In 2020, Yara set out to ensure that they provided a living wage to their 120,000-strong workforce. Once they agreed on a shared definition of a living wage—*basic, decent, comfortable*—the company collected cost-of-living data in each country, including housing expenses, dependents, and lifestyle factors to ascertain if their pay afforded their people a *decent* life wherever Yara operates.

In talking about the experience, Ronan Maher, Senior Vice President of People and Organizational Performance at Yara International, said he was surprised that although they were "probably the best employer" in some parts of the world and provided excellent benefits, Yara found that some employees were still earning less than a living wage. Maher noted that turning around things requires a collective effort to educate and find alignment among shareholders, union stakeholders, and local managers.[39]

Objective 2: Provide Flexibility and Protection

We've spoken about the new rhythm of work before, but less about worker protection; traditional benefits and security are at risk, with estimates that up to 80% of the U.S. workforce could be on independent contracts by 2030.[40] Leveling benefits between contingent and full-time workers around the world in terms of commitment to hours, predictability, and access to learning needs to be part of the workforce equation.

Failing to break the traditional paradigm that full-time employees are often better off than other contributors, and that benefit plans are not portable from job-to-job, just might hold us back in the war for talent. Heck, we might need to offer benefits, even healthcare, retirement, and a learning allowance to those who indeed have side hustles as Unilever did for gig workers with its U Work model, which we mentioned earlier.

Objective 3: Deliver on Health and Well-being

Research by Mercer Marsh Benefits found that while 88% of organizations claimed to have a supportive culture and care about the health and safety of their people, just 59% of employees globally said their benefits were meeting their needs.[41] This is a concern, especially as insurers reported that medical claims for later-stage illness were increasing.[42] Add to this new work models that are still being tested, an aging population in many parts of the world, and large segments of society with little or no healthcare coverage; and it becomes clear that ensuring a healthy workforce is an imperative for all.[43]

Objective 4: Drive Diversity, Equity, and Inclusion

Nearly half of all the companies surveyed in our research told Mercer they're taking steps to ensure their workforce reflects their operating markets—but much like earning a living wage, we've learned this effort is often overstated. Ensuring equal pay, inclusive participation, and a leadership team that reflects the diversity of the workforce are often on the agenda, but progress is slow. Yet with activist investors such as Arjuna Capital increasingly demanding evidence of companies' focus on DEI, and with pay transparency laws and pay equity legislation coming in, in many parts of the world, equity across gender and ethnic backgrounds is coming to the fore.[44] Career inequity, like health inequity mentioned above, is another silent crisis eroding the quality of our talent pipelines. This shows up in failure to attract certain workforce segments, career stagnation, and loss of a disproportionate number of contributors in any given demographic. The issue is most visible in pay inequities, and for many this imbalance persists into retirement as we mentioned before, this imbalance persists into retirement via the pension gap.[45]

As a professional services firm that consults on risk, strategy, and people, Marsh McLennan is especially alert to the role of people and culture in organizational growth and sustainability. As Carmen Fernandez, Group Chief People Officer, said, "Our people are our company so investing in priorities like hardwiring an inclusive leadership mindset into our talent processes—selection, succession, and development plans informed by 360 feedback— and pay equity are among the most important investments we can make." In 2022, Marsh McLennan reported a less than 1% pay equity gap for gender globally and the same for ethnic and racially diverse talent in the United States as part of its ESG report. Fernandez added, "The key for us in achieving this outcome was managing our people metrics with the same rigor as we do our financial performance and maintaining talent strategy, inclusion, and diversity as a standard management and board agenda."

Objective 5: Foster a Culture of Employability and Learning

Providing upskilling and reskilling options for the entire workforce is a prime area of opportunity, with just over half of all companies offering this learning in 2023,[46] but this is not sufficient if we are to prepare *all* workers for future work. As we've discussed in our skills chapter, forward-thinking firms integrate work design into daily operations across all functions: they open up roles to nontraditional talent; they pay for skills or deploy agile pay models; they shift their performance management to recognize skilling achievements; and they deploy talent marketplaces that are open to internal and external workers. Some are moving beyond green skills to the greening of jobs, taking a sustainability lens to all jobs and augmenting them to align with ESG outcomes and sustainability goals.

Sustaining Transformation Efforts

Staying the course on ambitions such as living wage commitments, pay equity, and returning wealth to workers is a multiyear journey, one that employers that want to make sustainable progress can fold into their business models to ensure ongoing affordability.

Being *sustainable at the core* forces us to rethink the way we do business, organize ourselves, and work together. The decisions that organizations make about their approach to stakeholder engagement, sustainability, structure and governance, resource management, human capital disclosures, and funding are all indicators of their commitment to sustainability.

Stakeholder capitalism underpins many sustainable transformation strategies to ensure that its purpose and goals serve investors, regulators, customers, and the wider talent ecosystem. Transmitting the company's purpose through culture and strategy, and infusing it into the way that organizations do business day to day, is what builds the muscle. The following is how others have progressed on this journey:

- **Embark:** With your company's current state in mind, lead with a hypothesis for which actions and policies can help achieve an agreed-upon sustainable vision of the future. These might include ESG and Good Work commitments and how stakeholders will align and take accountability for their championing throughout the firm.

- **Discover:** Leverage insights and benchmarks to identify your drivers and barriers to delivering a more sustainable people and business model. Develop a clear, data-driven strategy to address gaps and appropriate sustainability objectives for people to execute.
- **Shape:** Create solutions that are both bold and incremental, with measurable outcomes for making a sustainable business tangible. Develop or acquire appropriate skills to support the various transitions that your company needs to deliver on in the coming years.
- **Drive:** Deliver sustainable results and bake sustainability into the fabric of your organization from budgeting to executive scorecards to jobs and cultural values. Share the progress (and the shortfalls) and celebrate successes that signal intent to do better and to help workers' efforts drive a bigger impact.

Future-Proofing Your Talent Pipeline

How do you make sustainability mainstream?

Here's one for the tire-kickers: many organizations are essentially running out of workers in one of the biggest talent shortfalls ever. To attract and retain employees, firms can enhance their EVPs by offering more of what workers want—within reason. The challenge here is striking the right balance between what workers want and what shareholders demand. Providing flexibility, rewarding performance, and fostering inclusion are all win-win solutions, but so too are figuring out what gets people out of bed in the morning, and how tech and work redesign can improve the appeal of certain jobs and/or create capacity for areas of interest that lie outside jobs.

To drive sustainable transformation, all elements of the sustainability agenda need to happen together as all aspects of ESG and Good Work are entwined. Flexible work schedules that potentially offer less hours can impact the ability to deliver on a living wage, while having a net-positive impact on emissions. An inability to build the skills you need (at the pace you need), can increase the imperative to focus on on DEI to close the skills gap. Below is a case in point.

Like many organizations, the Digital, Data & IT division of the global healthcare company Novo Nordisk sought to hire more IT talent, and as part of this strategy they needed to increase their appeal to potential female contributors. By listening to current talent and profiling the needs of future female talent, it was apparent that a cultural transformation was needed to accompany their business growth ambition that rested on increased digitalization Yes, the company expanded their talent pool by offering more flexible and remote work options and a dedicated development program for women (all asks that supported people's lifestyle needs). But their catalyst for change was a three-year program to build inclusive leadership behaviors throughout the company—an effort that put equity and diversity at the top of every leader's agenda.

Business transformation drove the need for new skills, new skills drove the need for more diverse talent, more diverse talent demanded a new way of leading. Novo Nordisk's business transformation goals could only be achieved with the accompanying cultural transformation.

Let Your Contributors Contribute

Many companies are upholding their ESG commitments through sustainable investing, impact investing, and/or by delivering on an active philanthropic/CSR agenda, but there are a growing number of people who choose employers based on their ability to directly contribute to improving the world around them. In the past, employers were asking "Why should we hire you?", but now employees are asking, "Why should I work for you?" Progress on ESG/sustainability and the opportunity to contribute are becoming important parts of the response.

In this climate, Mercer has been fielding more questions about travel than ever before. While travel has long been an attraction factor for consultancies, the opposite is true for many candidates today. Both the environmental impact of business travel (which we've offset since 2019[47]) and the time involved (which may indirectly cause stress and affect well-being) are under scrutiny. Companies are asking for carbon offsets when they host global conferences, and they are rethinking how to work *different* in alignment with these new values. Leading companies have recognized that the carbon footprint of their people collectively exceeds their own. Some firms, including Marsh McLennan, provide apps for their people to track their footprint, putting the onus on them to make more informed decisions on everything from travel to electricity usage.

One example of such commitment is Tchibo, a signatory of the International Accord for Health and Safety in the Textile and Garment Industry.[48]

> Tchibo has been instrumental in negotiating and setting up predecessor agreements to protect workers in the industry. They're also part of the Action, Collaboration, Transformation (ACT) initiative to achieve living wages in the textile industry as well as all the workers in their supply chain.
>
> As part of their ACT obligations, Tchibo works with producers to ensure that wage and labor costs are a fixed share of price calculations and excluded from any price negotiations. Upon concluding industry-wide collective wage agreement negotiations in a country, ACT companies commit to keep their purchasing volumes in the country at the same level or above to foster long-term change. They even allow partners the time and power to negotiate wages on a regular basis.

Many organizations are confronting sustainability issues that go beyond their own purview. System-level change requires deeper partnerships, underpinned by mutual respect, humility, and transparency. No single company can solve this multitude of challenges alone—sustainable organizations depend on cooperation from suppliers, regulators, investors, customers, employees, and even competitors.

When we consider scaling sustainable alternatives into market standards—or divining the art of the possible within a circular economy—CEOs are increasingly called upon to serve in partnership with each other. For example, the Danish companies Maersk and Orsted have partnered on a project called Green Fuels for Denmark to produce sustainable fuel for shipping and aviation.[49] This makes it clear that the future of humanity depends on co-creation, and not competition, for the greater good.

As former Unilever CEO Paul Polman said:

> "[Change] calls for a partnership where you put the interest of others ahead of your own, knowing that by doing so, you're better off yourselves as well. It's really partnership that is the foundation of trust on which this society is built."[50]

Embed Sustainability into Your DNA

Transforming toward sustainability starts with making it part of an organization's purpose and embedding it into the value proposition. While that purpose can be aspirational, it must also be anchored in the business strategy, true to its identity, and achievable through the company's products, services, and people. Transformation needs to be rooted in people practices that drive and enable change; for example, nearly half (44%) of North American organizations use or are considering the use of ESG and DEI metrics in their incentive plans.[51] Globally, nearly two-thirds of organizations in 2023 said they planned to adopt technology for climate change mitigation (63%) or environmental management (65% by 2028).[52]

That said, embedding ESG goals must become a much broader exercise than executive incentives or top-down goal alignment—it needs to cover and engage the entire workforce in the talent ecosystem. Discussing and adapting people's objectives plays an important role in translating sustainability into employees' behavior. This can succeed only if the entire transformation is based on employee listening, co-creation, transparency, and trust.[53] Weaving sustainability commitments into a cohesive story that influences at a day-to-day level is something the global paint company Beckers Group knows all about.

After a decade of protecting the planet, the sustainability veterans at Beckers Group set their sights on the S in ESG. They realized success would take a shared ownership of people sustainability throughout the firm, and all departments would have to unite. With the CHRO at the helm, the paint pros built their people stream within the sustainability strategy to spark action, and set big, bold goals for 2030 to motivate themselves.

The people stream focused on driving well-being, diversity and inclusion, community engagement, and employee empowerment. When it launched, Beckers Group held all-stakeholder workshops to co-create a set of KPIs that worked for everyone, from recruiting to engagement surveys and more. They then used those 2030 goals to develop yearly sustainability contracts, bi-monthly sustainability reports, two new related leadership roles, and a new pay structure that holds managers accountable for meeting the goals.

Beckers' efforts have paid off, and they've been repeatedly recognized as a leading organization in DEI. Instead of letting perfection slow progress, the company painted a future vision around social progress to sustain its people and the business. Judith Jungmann, Beckers Group CHRO, said, "What has enabled us to continue this sustainability journey has been making this the mission of everyone in the company, and continuing to evolve what 'good' looks like in terms of sustainability."

The Future Is Now

Throughout this chapter you might have realized there is no silver bullet to become *sustainable at the core*, as we call it. It is a transformational exercise that touches on your *operating model*, your *culture*, and the *work* in your organization. And at their intersection are truths that demand a change in how we learn, lead, and collaborate—the levers to pull for true sustainability.

The path ahead is neither straightforward nor familiar. True sustainability will take nothing short of a major structural change in society, with countless unknowns and roadblocks along the way.

Yet Mercer's CEO and CFO study suggests that even if faced with dire economic headwinds, a majority of business leaders will not scale back their investment and will actively keep up their commitments to ESG (62%), DEI (63%), and Good Work (57%).[54]

With or without a single department leading the charge, sustainability in all its forms needs to be deeply embedded in every process, policy, and decision. Fuse it into the foundation of your people strategy and make a mark on the lives of those that contribute. Sustainability aspirations can act as a human-centric catalyst for the massive business transformations that you'll need to make in a climate of constant change. Build it into your budgeting models so it's an *expectation*, not an ask. Engage your workers to make it *their* plan.

James Henderson, a professor of Strategic Management at IMD, has observed multiple benefits when firms engage in inclusive strategic planning. At Roche Diagnostics and Swiss-Re, he showed how involving large groups of the workforce in the planning process led to increased engagement and greater appreciation of sustainable business practices.[55] As he explains, "When contributors know your strategy, understand your rationale for trade-offs, and feel they are part of the planning process, their engagement and commitment towards executing on your strategy soars."

If budget or capacity keeps you from going all-in today, then set goals for tomorrow. But start by making meaningful progress today—it's progress, not attainment, that the youthful generation expects to see on these issues. This means revolutionizing your business with an eye toward empathy, economics, and the environment. If we get this right, we'll all have a chance to turn these truths about the world of work into a blueprint for a more human-centered and equitable future for us all.

People Leaders' CTAs

1. **Lead the way on the change you want to see.** Start with values—what should drive decision-making in your firm? Engage team members in pinpointing changes the team can make. Consider how new hires will embrace corporate

values. Monitor progress indicators and share success stories as if you're planting new seeds of inspiration.

2. **Metrics matter, but storytelling sticks.** Share progress on human capital metrics such as flex hours, well-being, skills goals, and DEI-related goals. Figure out which stories and actions are lauded within your firm and the values they promote. Consider how storytelling might impact your broader corporate culture and make a lasting impression on your people.

3. **Make sustainability a way of life.** Help your team make decisions with sustainability at the core. Discuss how things might need to be adjusted in terms of time and budgets, and look at the entire ecosystem from suppliers to partners to producers. Make brave decisions today that could change the company's course for decades to come.

Executives' and HR's CTAs

1. **Define actionable sustainability commitments.** Set ambitions that inspire your workforce. Commit to those aspirations with actionable, funded plans, even if it's a 10-year journey. Consider upping your percentage of *jobs for good* (i.e., roles that drive a net positive impact on the world) or a percentage of time allocated for CSR/volunteering. Engage a wide range of contributors in strategy development. This will enable workers to see the link between business sustainability and creating the capacity for other initiatives. Ensure there's a listening program to keep up on how sentiment and values are evolving.

2. **Reset success metrics for an era of stakeholder capitalism.** Set success outcomes for all stakeholder groups. Embed sustainability into your business and functional plans including your Total Rewards philosophy. Monitor progress on human capital metrics (e.g., internal to external hire ratio, skilling, living wage, burnout indicators) alongside financial goals. Keep an eye on equity metrics, especially career and health equity for all.

Epilogue: The End and The Beginning

Say Goodbye to Yesterday

In 2020, we found ourselves dealing with a devastating global pandemic that permanently altered the way we work.

In 2022, we found ourselves with easy access to Gen AI that permanently altered the way we work.

In 2023, we found ourselves writing this book, a book that—we hope—just *might* alter the way we work.

Without these monumental events, Team Mercer probably wouldn't spend this much time discussing The People Age, let alone waxing lyrical about how these truths might play out.

Many of the truths in this book emerged due to these two monumental events that bookend our insights: a pandemic that forced us to evaluate our lives and a technological revolution that gave us a glimpse into our futures. And while neither a new virus nor a new technology fully accounts for the shift in work experiences and outlook, they did remind us that the world of work isn't (and hasn't been) working for all of us for quite some time.

But a new way is emerging. You've just read 200-plus pages of proof.

The People Age demands a greater focus on people sustainability, specifically, the long-term well-being and development of individuals within our organizations and our communities. Get this wrong and we'll be stuck in a constant cycle of *churn and burn*. Get this right and we'll fuel our businesses and economies for what comes next. Delivering on people sustainability involves creating an environment that nurtures and supports the physical, mental, and emotional health of contributors, while fostering their growth, engagement, and satisfaction. We're finally recognizing—- *really* recognizing—that individuals are *the* core assets in our organizations and that their well-being is vital for success and longevity.

On this journey, we've also been reflecting on our own privilege, blind spots in our worldviews, and how to bring about change. We give too much attention to knowledge workers and the developed West, and not enough attention to the long-term impacts of supply chain disruption, catastrophes, and inequities in healthcare and learning. We've under-addressed the grassroots solutions needed to solve for *different* issues, in *different* places, by *different* thinkers. The good news is that AI can flag these gaps (if we prompt it to).

All of which got us wondering, what do today's smarty-pants machines think about our 200-plus pages of proof? And so, we asked them. Here's what they had to say.

Are You Ready for a Brand-New Beat?

Can book reviewers be replaced by robots? Will WALL-E get a column in the *New York Times*? Does R2-D2 have the chops to write for *Publishers Weekly*?

Darn good questions, and we wanted the answers, so we fed our entire manuscript through two Gen AI models[1] to find out what Optimus Prime had to say about our little tome.

Hit us with your best shot, Hal 9000. . .

The following are the exact prompts and the full responses unless otherwise indicated.

Q) What are the key lessons from the book that you took away?[1]

---

1. The traditional employer/employee relationship has shifted and new paradigms are emerging.

2. The world of work has changed significantly since the pandemic and businesses need to adapt to remain relevant.

3. The importance of purpose and empathy in delivering an inclusive organization and how to create an organizational culture that benefits everyone.

4. The significance of The People Age, which is a new era that centers around human-centric values, with businesses needing to put people at the center of their operations.

Q) *What is the most important message you would like to share with others after reading this book?*

The most important message I would like to share with others after reading this book is that we need to be more people-centric and focus on sustainability. We need to adapt to the changes that are happening in the world of work and create an organizational culture that benefits everyone.

We need to manage the most valuable resource in an organization—the people—in a sustainable way and embed Good Work into a company's DNA. We need to be more adaptable to change and focus on the human experience. We need to embrace the changes that are happening in the world of work and be more proactive in managing energy and making sure that employees feel valued and recognized.

We need to address the mental health of employees and create a work environment that is sustainable and equitable. We need to focus on skills and create a skills-based talent pipeline that offers greater career growth and agility.

We need to embrace sustainability and ensure that we have a net positive impact on the world. We need to create a shared collective truth that everyone can embrace, and build trust and accountability into the corporate culture.

Q) *From the list of recommendations in the book, which do you think are most important and why?*

1. Have a conversation around life goals. I believe that having a conversation around life goals is important because it allows individuals to have a better understanding of what they want in life and what they are willing to do to achieve those goals. It also allows managers to understand what their team members want and how they can help them achieve their goals while still meeting the needs of the organization.

2. Cultivate an inclusive talent culture. I believe that cultivating an inclusive talent culture is important because it allows for a more diverse and innovative workforce. It also creates a culture where everyone feels valued and can bring their best to the table.

3. Keep challenging your worldview. I believe that keeping an open mind and challenging your worldview is important because it allows for growth and development. It also allows for new ideas and perspectives to be brought to the table, which can lead to innovation and success.

Q) *What are some of the challenges that organizations face in implementing the recommendations in the book?*

One of the biggest challenges that organizations face in implementing the recommendations in the book is resistance to change. Many organizations are used to doing things a certain way, and it can be difficult to get buy-in from stakeholders for new approaches. Another challenge is the need for investment in new technologies, training, and other resources to support the workforce. Finally, there may be challenges related to measuring and monitoring progress on key metrics, as some of these may be difficult to quantify or track over time.

Finally, our AI partners took it upon themselves to ask their own questions based on what they thought we might want to know:

AI's own Q) *How can the lessons of this book be applied to your current work situation?*

> The lessons in this book can be applied to my current work situation in several ways.
>
> - First, I can focus on developing my skills, rather than just doing my job. This means taking advantage of learning opportunities, both within and outside of my organization, and seeking out new challenges that will help me grow.
> - Second, I can focus on building relationships with my colleagues and creating a more inclusive work environment. This means being more empathetic, listening more, and being more open to different perspectives.
> - Third, I can focus on creating a more sustainable work environment. This means being more mindful of my energy use, reducing waste, and finding ways to reduce my carbon footprint.
> - Fourth, I can focus on building trust and accountability with my colleagues. This means being more transparent, communicating more effectively, and holding myself and others accountable for their actions.
> - Finally, I can focus on creating a culture of innovation and creativity. This means being more open to new ideas, taking risks, and experimenting with new approaches.
>
> By applying these lessons to my current work situation, I can create a more people-centric, empathetic, and sustainable work environment that benefits everyone.

How awesome are these new digital partners? They read the book, they paid attention, and they didn't do a bad job—even flattering us in the process. . . And all without billing us for their time! The reality, of course, is that context is king and our AI partners work best as one voice in the choir—so the following are our combined takeaways.

Right Here, Right Now

Stepping back from these 10 truths to think bigger (and *different*), here are what we see as some of the most salient points for us all to embrace *right here, right now:*

1. **Win and retain contributors**.

    The brightest future is an inclusive and diverse one, one where there's not just equity in pay and conditions, but one where people feel they have equality in options, a dignified job, and the right to not only be heard, but to collectively bargain for a fair deal. We want to build on this vision by cultivating a work experience that people crave and one that has sufficient capacity to keep apace of their changing views and expectations. The Good Work framework is a good place to start as we seek to ensure that productivity gains—such as those from AI—are redistributed to all stakeholders.

2. **Manage your people resources sustainably.**

    Economic cycles may cause the balance of power between worker and employer to oscillate in the short term, but demographics indicate that we need to make the world of work a lot more *workable* if we don't want to find ourselves *out of people*. Encouraging workforce participation after significant life events and job losses is critical. Opening our doors to nontraditional and older talent and ensuring that they feel they *belong*, not just that they are included, is key. Keep an eye on equity as we embrace new talent models, and ensuring we build pathways to prosperity for those in declining jobs are all ways to address these truths. And in addition to all of these logical, humanistic ideas, let's plan and manage demand and supply in the utmost professional and compassionate manner.

3. **Grow in new ways.**

    The digital, green, and energy transitions will bring enormous growth opportunities. How we invest in these today-centric skills and locate those tomorrow-centric jobs has the potential to fuel companies, societies and our futures. Getting it right demands better long-range thinking and an investable business case to ensure we approach these changes as opportunities to *work different*. The initiatives that have successfully set a new blueprint, such as—Standard Chartered's talent marketplace and Ericsson's self-funded Total Rewards transformation—all show that affordability and sustainability need to work in unison if they are to be scaled.

4. **Amplify your capabilities.**

Work redesign will identify the untapped potential in our current workforce. Upskilling and reskilling will bring the organization and the individual to new heights. AI can make superheroes of us all. We need to closely analyze the opportunities that new technology adds to the game and ensure we all amplify our skills in the process. Gen AI will allow us to do things that sci-fi gurus could only dream of. That said, preserving and cultivating human traits will be critical to making the most of this collaboration and ensuring humans remain on the front foot in The People Age. What is fascinating is that our AI partners downplayed the impact of AI on jobs in their book synopsis above—just like us, these tools have biases that shape their thinking.

It's a New Dawn; It's a New Day

So how do we ensure that these *truths* drive new work realities?

Strategists Gary Hamel and C.K. Prahalad once argued that Western companies spend too much time focusing on trimming their ambitions to match resources, and as a result, search only for advantages they can sustain. Conversely, Japanese corporations tend to leverage resources by accelerating the pace of organizational learning and try to attain seemingly impossible goals.[2] Here, in The People Age, we need to foster both: the desire to succeed at an employee level, along with a heightened responsibility to ensure we manage our resources sustainably. People being resource No. 1.

The energy and engagement of our people define our company's potential and unlocking their capability is the mission of leadership. The good news is that contributors crave the freedom of innovation that organizations need. Workers desire the flexibility and movement that are cornerstones of workforce agility. Workers want to work for healthy organizations, in the same way that organizations need a healthy workforce with a healthy pipeline of talent. At the end of this book, you'll find a strategy canvas that we've been applying to our own teams and businesses to remind us of the shift that is happening and to help us work *different*.

Because. . .

If you run a team with contributors who don't want to hop from job to job, you win.

If you work for a widget company (or elsewhere) that does more for the world than make widgets (or whatever)—a company that gives back, a company that thinks globally, a company that's about more than just profits—you win.

If you're part of a professional infrastructure that embraces diverse workers doing diverse work in a diverse manner, you win.

We believe that finding a common language (or rhythm) to talk about these new truths is critical to taking action on them. And so, our last question to our AI partner was, if this book was a song, what song would it be?

One of them responded, "The book would be Lionel Richie's and Michael Jackson's [et al.] 'We Are the World' because the future rests with us."

---

visit mercer.com for more on how to make progress on these topics and the download the books playlist.

Appendix 1: 10 Truths for Winning in The People Age

Truths	Implications
1. Goodbye employees, hello contributors	We've entered The People Age, where powers have shifted. A new employer/employee deal needs to be crafted, and greater skills in partnering are required to design future ways of working that inspire people.
2. Stressed out, burnt out, and quietly quitting	Your contributors are exhausted, and the employee deal is no longer meeting their expectations. Intensify your focus on health and well-being indicators to keep productivity, engagement, and energy levels high.
3. It doesn't pay to stay	Break the quit-for-a-raise cycle by resetting your Total Rewards philosophies, firing up internal talent movements, and tailoring your offerings to individual preferences, including opening up gig working and new contracts.
4. Purpose rules and empathy wins	Ensure your corporate purpose resonates with your contributors and defines your commitment to multiple stakeholders. Energize and engage your people toward a purposeful path with enhanced people management skills.
5. Trust and accountability are a team sport	Optimize goal-setting and performance management practices to ensure trust and accountability deliver psychological safety within a climate of learning and innovation at an individual and team level.
6. The new rhythm of work	Flex your work in various dimensions to retain your people and enhance your organizational flexibility. Streamline decision-making, technology, and meetings to reduce complexity and their cognitive load.

(continued)

Truths	Implications
7. Skills are the real currency of work	Know what skills you have in your talent ecosystem and what you will need for tomorrow. Build a skills-based organization to open up learning and development opportunities to enhance attraction and agility.
8. Supply is unchained	Plan and manage your talent supply chain with lessons from supply chain management. Build an agile and robust workforce that is market sensitive, resilient and can quickly adjust to changes.
9. Intelligence is getting amplified	Evaluate and understand the potential of AI for your business, cultivate a digital-first culture and infuse AI into your processes, roles, and people development practices to deliver an intelligence edge.
10. Sustainability starts with people	Transform your organization to promote business, environmental, and social sustainability. Appreciate the value of contributors in your new work equation. Without people to fuel sustainability—in all its guises—we will not have a future to sustain.

Source: Bravery, Anderson, and Bonic, Work Different, 2024.

Appendix 2: Strategy Canvas

Our purpose and values

Technological advances

Value creation goals	Sustainability priorities	Our investment

Shareholder commitments:

Contributor commitments:

Societal commitments:

Investor commitments:

Other commitments:

People sustainability:

Business sustainability:

Environmental sustainability:

Capability:

Capacity:

Agility:

Collaboration:

Analytics and cultural enablers

External / societal forces

Thriving in the People Age takes an honest, deliberate effort to build the truths from this book into your business strategy. Use the prompts below to discuss these topics with your team and visualize your priorities on the strategy canvas overleaf.

Value creation goals*

1. **Shareholder commitments:**
   What commitments have we made to shareholders in terms of profitability and revenue growth? What other commitments do we need to factor into our thinking?

2. **Contributor commitments:**
   What do our workforce segments value and how can we ensure our EVP reflects those values?

3. **Societal commitments:**
   How can we positively impact the health and wealth of workers in the communities where we operate?

4. **Investor commitments:**
   What do investors expect of us today and in the future? What agendas DEI, ESG, financial returns matter most, given our industry?

5. **Other commitments:**
   How might we deliver value to other entities within our ecosystem (partners, nonprofits, etc.)? What goals and commitments should we make?

Sustainability priorities

1. **People sustainability:**
   How healthy is our talent pipeline (turnover, illness, safety, well-being) today? Where do we have unsustainable people practices? What would enhance the resilience of our people?

2. **Business sustainability:**
   What are the upcoming risks to our business model? How can we embed sustainability throughout? What else would boost our business resilience?

3. **Environmental sustainability:**
   How can we further our environmental agenda (climate mitigation, energy transition, supply chain, biodiversity, etc.)? How do we need to adapt for greater environmental resilience?

Our investment

1. **Capability:**
   What skills will be business-critical in the short term? How can we acquire those skills? What would amplify our people's intelligence, creativity, and innovation in the future?

2. **Capacity:**
   Does our talent supply meet demand? Can it flex to balance daily work with one-off projects? What depletes energy? Which departments and jobs would benefit from work redesign?

3. **Agility:**
   How can we foster a more dynamic, flexible workforce? Are contributors empowered to take initiative? How might AI simplify work and amplify our impact?

4. **Collaboration:**
   Where can we break down silos and bolster inclusion? What new capabilities might we acquire through M&A? What do our key partners expect of us? What would strengthen our relationships?

* Craft one or two specific, timebound commitments for each population (e.g., *We will upskill 5,000 employees by 20XX, We will fast-track our digital transformation to boost productivity by 12% in the next year, We will reduce stress-related illnesses by 5% in the next two years, We will reduce our pay equity gap to less than 1% by 20XX).*

Source: *Bravery, Anderson, and Bonic 2023*   To download a printable copy of this strategy canvas and the questions before it, please visit the *Work Different* page on Mercer.com.

Source: *Work Different: Bravery, Anderson, Bonic*
visit mercer.com for a downloadable version of this canvas

Notes

Introduction: The Pivot

1. Zwile Nkosi, "With more business disruption expected, making organizations 'Future-Fit' is top of mind new study finds," Mercer, March 14, 2019.
2. "Business Roundtable redefines the purpose of a corporation to promote 'an economy that serves all Americans,'" Business Roundtable, August 19, 2019, **https://www.businessroundtable .org/business-roundtable-redefines-the-purpose-of-a-corporation-to-promote-an-economy-that-serves-all-americans**.
3. Ana Kreacic, John Romeo, Simon Luong, Lucia Uribe, Amy Lasater-Wille, Elizabeth Costa, Kamal Ahmed, and Jonathan Paterson, "A-Gen-Z report: What business needs to know about the generation changing everything," Oliver Wyman Forum and The News Movement (2023): 49, **https://www.oliverwymanforum .com/content/dam/oliver-wyman/ow-forum/template-scripts/a-gen-z/pdf/A-Gen-Z-Report.pdf**.
4. Blair Jones and Jeff Brodsky, "The CHRO's critical role in times of crisis," Semler Brossy, November 24, 2021, **https://semlerbrossy .com/insights/the-chros-critical-role-in-times-of-crisis/**.
5. Kate Bravery, Adrienne Cernigoi, and Joana Silva, "Global Talent Trends 2022: Rise of the relatable organization," *Mercer* (2022): 80.
6. Kate Bravery, Adrienne Cernigoi, and Joana Silva, "Global Talent Trends 2022–2023: Rise of the relatable organization," *Mercer* (2023): 36.
7. Krystal Hu, "ChatGPT sets record for fastest-growing user base – analyst note," Reuters, February 2, 2023, **https://www.reuters .com/technology/chatgpt-sets-record-fastest-growing-user-base-analyst-note-2023-02-01/**.
8. Katharina Buchholz, "ChatGPT sprints to one million users," *Statista*, January 24, 2023, **https://www.statista.com/chart/ 29174/time-to-one-million-users/**.
9. Attilio Di Battista, Sam Grayling, Elselot Hasselaar, Till Leopold, Ricky Li, Mark Rayner, Saadia Zahidi, "Future of Jobs Report 2023," World Economic Forum, (2023): 6.

10. Andrew R. Chow, "Bill Gates believes generative AI will be 'revolutionary,'" *Time*, March 21, 2023, **https://time.com/6264801/ bill-gates-ai/**.

11. Kelly Kline, "Elon Musk is so worried about the threat of AI, he wants government to regulate it," *Mashable*, July 16, 2017, **https://mashable.com/article/elon-musk-ai-greatest-risk-to-civilization**.

12. Grace Kay, "Billionaire investors Warren Buffett and Charlie Munger aren't sold on AI hype: 'Old-fashioned intelligence works pretty well,'" *Business Insider*, May 10, 2023, **https://www .businessinsider.com/billionaires-warren-buffett-charlie-munger-not-sold-ai-hype-2023-5**.

Chapter 1: Goodbye Employees, Hello Contributors

1. Philippa Fogarty, Simon Frantz, Javier Hirschfield, Sarah Keating, Emmanuel Lafont, Bryan Lufkin, Rafael Mishael, Visvak Ponnavolu, Maddy Savage, and Meredith Turits, "Coronavirus: How the world of work may change forever," *BBC*, October 23, 2020, **https:// www.bbc.com/worklife/article/20201023-coronavirus-how-will-the-pandemic-change-the-way-we-work**.

2. "Rethinking what we need from work: A guide to employees' most pressing needs and how your organization can meet them, based on Mercer's 2022–2023 Inside Employees' Minds study," *Mercer* (2023): 7–8, **https://www.mercer.com/en-us/insights/ talent-and-transformation/attracting-and-retaining-talent/ rethinking-what-we-need-from-work-inside-employees-minds-2022/**.

3. "We create an unbossed environment," *Novartis*, **https://www .novartis.com/about/strategy/people-and-culture/we-create-unbossed-environment** (accessed May 26, 2023).

4. Kate Bravery, Adrienne Cernigoi, and Joana Silva, "Global Talent Trends 2022: Rise of the relatable organization," *Mercer* (2022): 32.

5. Kate Bravery, Adrienne Cernigoi, and Joana Silva, "Global Talent Trends 2022: Rise of the relatable organization," *Mercer* (2022): 32.

6. "Job openings and labor turnover – January 2022," Bureau of Labor Statistics (March 2022): 3, **https://www.bls.gov/news .release/archives/jolts_03092022.pdf**.

7. Shane McFeely and Ben Wigert, "This fixable problem costs U.S. businesses $1 trillion," Gallup, March 13, 2019, **https://www.gallup.com/workplace/247391/fixable-problem-costs-businesses-trillion.aspx**.

8. Greg Lewis and Joseph Soroñgon, "The jobs with the highest turn-over rates, according to LinkedIn data," LinkedIn, June 30, 2022, **https://www.linkedin.com/business/talent/blog/talent-analytics/types-of-jobs-with-most-turnover**.

9. Richard Kestenbaum, "LVMH converting its perfume facto-ries to make hand sanitizer," *Forbes*, March 15, 2020, **https://www.forbes.com/sites/richardkestenbaum/2020/03/15/lvmh-converting-its-perfume-factories-to-make-hand-sanitizer/?sh=7892ffe74a9a**.

10. Jon Springer, "Aldi, McDonald's make staff-sharing deal in Germany," *Winsight Grocery Business*, March 23, 2020, **https://www.winsightgrocerybusiness.com/retailers/aldi-mcdonalds-make-staff-sharing-deal-germany**.

11. Kate Bravery, Adrienne Cernigoi, and Joana Silva, "Global Talent Trends 2022–2023: Rise of the relatable organization," *Mercer* (2023): 31.

12. Kate Bravery, Adrienne Cernigoi, and Joana Silva, "Global Talent Trends 2022: Rise of the relatable organization," *Mercer* (2022): 32.

13. Sarah Butcher, "Citi's new pitch to analysts: work less, earn less, live by the beach," *efinancialcareers*, March 14, 2022, **https://www.efinancialcareers.com/news/2022/03/citi-malaga-analysts**.

14. Ana Kreacic, John Romeo, Simon Luong, Lucia Uribe, Amy Lasater-Wille, Elizabeth Costa, Kamal Ahmed, and Jonathan Pat-erson, "A-Gen-Z report: What business needs to know about the generation changing everything," Oliver Wyman Forum and The News Movement (2023): 48, **https://www.oliverwymanforum.com/content/dam/oliver-wyman/ow-forum/template-scripts/a-gen-z/pdf/A-Gen-Z-Report.pdf**.

15. Kate Bravery, Adrienne Cernigoi, and Joana Silva, "Global Talent Trends 2022–2023: Rise of the relatable organization," *Mercer*, 2023.

16. Kate Bravery, Adrienne Cernigoi, and Joana Silva, "Global Tal-ent Trends 2022–2023: Rise of the relatable organization," *Mercer* (2023): 31–32.

17. Kate Bravery, Adrienne Cernigoi, and Joana Silva, "Global Tal-ent Trends 2022–2023: Rise of the relatable organization," *Mercer* (2023): 61.

18. "Employee value proposition," *Gartner*, **https://www.gartner .com/en/human-resources/insights/employee-engagement-performance/employee-value-proposition** (accessed May 26, 2023).

19. Jörgen Sundberg and Anuradha Razdan, "How Unilever developed a new EVP and employer brand," *Link Humans*, **https:// linkhumans.com/unilever/** (accessed May 26, 2023).

20. Richard Beckhard and Reuben T. Harris, *Organizational Transitions: Managing Complex Change* (Reading: Addison Wesley Publishing Company, 1977).

21. Jessica Bryant, "Employers Drop College Degree Requirements," *BestColleges*, April 12, 2022, **https://www.bestcolleges.com/ news/analysis/2022/04/11/employers-drop-college-degree-requirements-burning-glass-institute**.

22. Kate Bravery, Adrienne Cernigoi, and Joana Silva, "Global Talent Trends 2022–2023: Rise of the relatable organization," *Mercer* (2023): 15, 33, 74–75.

23. Ana Kreacic, John Romeo, Simon Luong, Lucia Uribe, Amy Lasater-Wille, Elizabeth Costa, Kamal Ahmed, and Jonathan Paterson, "A-Gen-Z report: What business needs to know about the generation changing everything," Oliver Wyman Forum and The News Movement (2023): 17, **https://www.oliverwymanforum. com/content/dam/oliver-wyman/ow-forum/template-scripts/a-gen-z/pdf/A-Gen-Z-Report.pdf**.

Chapter 2: Stressed Out, Burned Out, and Quietly Quitting

1. "Mental Health in the Workplace," *World Health Organization*, **https://www.who.int/teams/mental-health-and-substance-use/promotion-prevention/mental-health-in-the-workplace**.

2. Kate Bravery, Adrienne Cernigoi, and Joana Silva, "Global Talent Trends 2022–2023: Rise of the relatable organization," *Mercer* (2023): 9.

3. "Rethinking what we need from work: A guide to employees' most pressing needs and how your organization can meet them, based on Mercer's 2022–2023 Inside Employees' Minds study," *Mercer*,

2023, https://www.mercer.com/en-us/insights/talent-and-transformation/attracting-and-retaining-talent/rethinking-what-we-need-from-work-inside-employees-minds-2022/.

4. "2022 Work Trend Index: Annual Report | Great expectations: Making hybrid work *work*," Microsoft. (March 2022): 22, https://assets.ctfassets.net/y8fb0rhks3b3/3dbLTNFA72EguJaZD vzkGX/cbe2c85d25b8c006cea95bc0e2b7cf7e/2022_Work_Trend_Index_Annual_Report.pdf.

5. Rachel Ranosa and Cathryn Gunther, "Human energy is the most critical business resource: Cathryn Gunther, Mars Inc," *People Matters*, June 23, 2022, https://www.peoplemattersglobal.com/article/wellbeing/why-your-energy-at-work-is-an-output-of-holistic-health-cathryn-gunther-mars-inc-34359.

6. Cathryn Gunther, "Focusing on Energy to Improve Associates' Wellbeing," *Mars*, September 1, 2021, https://www.mars.com/news-and-stories/articles/focusing-energy-improve-associates-wellbeing.

7. Kate Bravery, Adrienne Cernigoi, and Joana Silva, "Global Talent Trends 2022–2023: Rise of the relatable organization," *Mercer* (2023): 45.

8. Robin Lloyd, "Metric mishap caused loss of NASA orbiter," *CNN*, September 30, 1999, http://edition.cnn.com/TECH/space/9909/30/mars.metric.02/.

9. Roger Bohn, "Stop Fighting Fires," *Harvard Business Review* (July–August 2000): n.p., https://hbr.org/2000/07/stop-fighting-fires.

10. Lia LaPiana and Frank Bauer, "Mars Climate Orbiter Mishap Investigation Board Phase I Report," NASA (November 1999): 19–21, https://llis.nasa.gov/llis_lib/pdf/1009464main1_0641-mr.pdf.

11. Jeroen Kraaijenbrink, "What BANI really means (and how it corrects your world view," *Forbes*, June 22, 2022, https://www.forbes.com/sites/jeroenkraaijenbrink/2022/06/22/what-bani-really-means-and-how-it-corrects-your-world-view/?sh=29cd441611bb.

12. "Health on demand 2023," *Mercer*, 2023. https://www.mercer.com/content/dam/mercer-dotcom/global/en/shared-assets/global/attachments/pdf-2023-health-on-demand-report.pdf.

13. "South Africa's youth continues to bear the burden of unemployment," *Statistics South Africa*, June 1, 2022, https://www.statssa.gov.za/?p=15407.

14. Wolfgang Seidl, "The ROI of supporting employee mental health," interview by Kate Bravery, *The New Shape of Work*, Mercer, October 7, 2022. Audio, 5:03, **https://www.mercer.com/insights/people-strategy/future-of-work/podcast-new-shape-of-work/the-roi-of-supporting-employee-mental-health/**.

15. Kate Bravery, Adrienne Cernigoi, and Joana Silva, "Global Talent Trends 2022–2023: Rise of the relatable organization," *Mercer* (2023): 9, 37.

16. Ivan Ivanov, "Global health: A new vision for employees, employers, and economies," *Growth Summit 2023*, World Economic Forum, May 3, 2023. Video, 36:10. **https://www.weforum.org/events/the-growth-summit-jobs-and-opportunity-for-all-2023/sessions/workforce-health-a-new-vision-for-employees-employers-and-economies**.

17. "Burn-out an 'occupational phenomenon': International Classification of Diseases," World Health Organization, May 28, 2019, **https://www.who.int/news/item/28-05-2019-burn-out-an-occupational-phenomenon-international-classification-of-diseases**.

18. Christina Maslach, Susan E. Jackson, Michael P. Leiter, Wilmar B. Schaufeli, and Richard L. Schwab, "Maslach Burnout Inventory (MBI)," *Mind Garden*, **https://www.mindgarden.com/117-maslach-burnout-inventory-mbi** (accessed May 26, 2023).

19. Brian Creely, "A little bit about Bryan," *A Life after Layoff*, **https://www.alifeafterlayoff.com/about-bryan-creely/** (accessed May 26, 2023).

20. Jim Harter, "Is quiet quitting real?" Gallup, May 17, 2023, **https://www.gallup.com/workplace/398306/quiet-quitting-real.aspx**.

21. Melissa Swift, *Work here now: Think like a human and build a powerhouse workplace* (Hoboken: Wiley, 2023), 20.

22. Kate Bravery, Adrienne Cernigoi, and Joana Silva, "Global Talent Trends 2022–2023: Rise of the relatable organization," *Mercer* (2023): 48.

23. Kate Bravery, Adrienne Cernigoi, and Joana Silva, "Global Talent Trends 2022–2023: Rise of the relatable organization," *Mercer* (2023): 48.

Chapter 3: The New Rhythm of Work

1. Calvin Harris, "Calvin Harris: The secrets of my success," *The Guardian*, December 12, 2012. **https://www.theguardian.com/ music/2012/dec/21/calvin-harris-secrets-my-success**.

2. Mara Quintanilla, "Eliminating meetings for remote workers: How Shopify is clearing out employee calendars," *GroWrk*, **https:// growrk.com/blogs/news/eliminating-meetings-for-remote- workers/** (accessed May 26, 2023).

3. Jena Lee, "A neuropsychological explanation of Zoom fatigue," *Psychiatric Times*, November 17, 2020, **https://www.psychiatric- times.com/view/psychological-exploration-zoom-fatigue**.

4. Tim Jacks, "Research on remote work in the era of COVID-19," *Journal of Global Information Technology Management* 24, no. 1 (June 2021): 93–97, **https://doi.org/10/1080/1097198X.2021.1914500**.

5. Amantha Imber, *Time Wise* (Melbourne: Penguin Life Australia, 2022).

6. Kate Bravery, Adrienne Cernigoi, and Joana Silva, "Global Talent Trends 2022–2023: Rise of the relatable organization," *Mercer*, 2023.

7. Aidan Mantelow, Guillaume Hingel, Steffica Warwick, Elslot Hasselaar, Atilio di Battista, Saaudi Zahidi, Nicole Luk, Padma Ramanthan, Kate Bravery, and Ravin Jesuthasan, "The good work framework: A new business agenda for the future of work," The World Economic Forum and Mercer, 2022, **https://www.weforum.org/ whitepapers/the-good-work-framework-a-new-business- agenda-for-the-future-of-work**.

8. "American Express," *Work Your Way*, **https://www.work yourway.com/flexible-employers/american-express** (accessed April 21, 2023).

9. Laurence Goasduff, "Gartner forecasts 39% of global knowledge workers will work hybrid by the end of 2023," *Gartner*, March 1, 2023, **https://www.gartner.com/en/newsroom/press- releases/2023-03-01-gartner-forecasts-39-percent-of-global- knowledge-workers-will-work-hybrid-by-the-end-of-2023**.

10. "The new shape of work: Redefine flexible working," *Mercer*, 2023, **https://www.mercer.com/insights/talent-and-transformation/ flexible-working/the-new-shape-of-work-redefine- flexible-working/**.

11. Ravin Jesuthasan and John W. Bourdreau, *Work without Jobs: How to Reboot Your Organization's Work Operating System* (Management on the Cutting Edge, 2022).

Chapter 4: It Doesn't Pay to Stay

1. "Rethinking what we need from work: A guide to employees' most pressing needs and how your organization can meet them, based on Mercer's 2022–2023 Inside Employees' Minds study," *Mercer*, 2023, **https://www.mercer.com/en-us/insights/talent-and-transformation/attracting-and-retaining-talent/rethinking-what-we-need-from-work-inside-employees-minds-2022/**.
2. "The Great Resignation statistics," *EDsmart*, **https://www.edsmart.org/the-great-resignation-statistics/** (accessed February 10, 2023).
3. "More than 9 million workers expected to leave jobs in 2022," *HR Review*, January 18, 2022, **https://www.hrreview.co.uk/hr-news/more-than-9-million-workers-expected-to-leave-jobs-in-2022/140215**.
4. Kate Bravery, Adrienne Cernigoi, and Joana Silva, "Global Talent Trends 2022: Rise of the relatable organization," *Mercer* (2022): 30.
5. Ana Kreacic, John Romeo, Simon Luong, Lucia Uribe, Amy Lasater-Wille, Elizabeth Costa, Kamal Ahmed, and Jonathan Paterson, "A-Gen-Z report: What business needs to know about the generation changing everything," Oliver Wyman Forum and The News Movement (2023): 74, **https://www.oliverwymanforum.com/content/dam/oliver-wyman/ow-forum/template-scripts/a-gen-z/pdf/A-Gen-Z-Report.pdf**.
6. Kate Bravery, Adrienne Cernigoi, and Joana Silva, "Global Talent Trends 2022: Rise of the relatable organization," *Mercer* (2022): 39.
7. Polovina, Samantha, "Real-time insight pulse: Inflation and impact on pay and rewards, *Mercer*, November 21, 2022, **https://app.keysurvey.com/reportmodule/REPORT3/report/41644126/41337277/d6913d91684017a85deecc4540ed0f9d?Dir=&Enc_Dir=79457c9a&av=IxnIBAm77ac%3D&afterVoting=6529d120760c&msig=7078255d8def7b2672b847041c1efebf**.
8. John Robertson, "Wage Growth Tracker: Three-month moving average of median wage growth, hourly data," Federal Reserve Bank of Atlanta, **https://www.atlantafed.org/chcs/wage-growth-tracker.aspx** (accessed May 2023).

9. Haig R. Nalbantian, "The critical importance of roles in career equity," *CFO*, December 8, 2022, **https://www.cfo.com/human-capital-careers/2022/12/roles-in-career-equity-accelerator-roles-women-people-of-color/**.

10. Haig R. Nalbantian, "The underrated barriers that keep women from reaching the C-Suite," Financial Alliance for Women, February 25, 2021, **https://financialallianceforwomen.org/news-events/underrated-barriers-that-keep-women-from-reaching-the-c-suite/**.

11. Alex Christian, "The case for job hopping," BBC, July 21, 2022, **https://www.bbc.com/worklife/article/20220720-the-case-for-job-hopping**.

12. "The Changing Childhood Project: A multigenerational, international survey on 21st century childhood," Unicef (2022): 21, **UNICEF-Global-Insight-Gallup-Changing-Childhood-Survey-Report-English-2021.pdf**.

13. Samantha Polovina, Real-time Insight Pulse: Inflation and impact on pay and rewards. *Mercer*, November 21, 2022, **https://app.keysurvey.com/reportmodule/REPORT3/report/41644126/41337277/d6913d91684017a85deecc4540ed0f9d?Dir=&Enc_Dir=79457c9a&av=IxnIBAm77ac%3D&afterVoting=6529d120760c&msig=7078255d8def7b2672b847041c1efebf**.

14. Chetna Singh, "Total rewards at the center of innovation at SAP," interview by Kate Bravery, *New Shape of Work*, Mercer, September 15, 2022. Video, 1:37, **https://www.mercer.com/en-us/insights/people-strategy/future-of-work/podcast-new-shape-of-work/total-rewards-at-the-center-of-innovation-at-sap/**.

15. Jackie Wiles, "Great Resignation or not, money won't fix all your talent problems," *Gartner*, December 9, 2021, **https://www.gartner.com/en/articles/great-resignation-or-not-money-won-t-fix-all-your-talent-problems**.

16. Katie Navarra, "The real costs of recruitment," *SHRM*, April 11, 2022, **https://www.shrm.org/resourcesandtools/hr-topics/talent-acquisition/pages/the-real-costs-of-recruitment.aspx**.

17. Richard A. Guzzo, Haig R. Nalbantian, and Nick L. Anderson, "Don't underestimate value of employee tenure," *Harvard Business Review*, January 24, 2023, **https://hbr.org/2023/01/dont-underestimate-the-value-of-employee-tenure**.

18. "Beat the crisis: How executives are responding to economic shocks and talent shortages," *Mercer*, 2023, **https://www.mercer .com/en-us/insights/talent-and-transformation/attracting-and-retaining-talent/how-executives-are-responding-to-economic-shocks-and-talent-shortages/**.

19. "Rethinking what we need from work: A guide to employees' most pressing needs and how your organization can meet them, based on Mercer's 2022–2023 Inside Employees' Minds study," *Mercer*, 2023, **https://www.mercer.com/en-us/insights/talent-and-transformation/attracting-and-retaining-talent/rethinking-what-we-need-from-work-inside-employees-minds-2022/**.

20. "Labour v capital in the post-lockdown economy," *The Economist*, February 19, 2022, **https://www.economist.com/finance-and-economics/labour-v-capital-in-the-post-lockdown-economy/21807700**.

21. "Beat the crisis: How executives are responding to economic shocks and talent shortages," *Mercer*, 2023, **https://www.mercer.com/en-us/insights/talent-and-transformation/attracting-and-retaining-talent/how-executives-are-responding-to-economic-shocks-and-talent-shortages/**.

22. Clint Rainey, "The age of 'greedflation' is here: See how obscene CEO-to-worker pay ratios are right now," Fast Company, July 18, 2022, **https://www.fastcompany.com/90770163/the-age-of-greedflation-is-here-see-how-obscene-ceo-to-worker-pay-ratios-are-right-now**.

23. Dominic Rushe, "Wage gap between CEOs and US workers jumped to 670-to-1 last year, study finds," *The Guardian*, **https://www.theguardian.com/us-news/2022/jun/07/us-wage-gap-ceos-workers-institute-for-policy-studies-report**.

24. Matt Mathers, "FTSE 100 chief executives' pay soars by 22% in a year despite cost of living crisis," *Independent*, November 7, 2022, **https://www.independent.co.uk/news/business/ftse-100-index-ceos-pay-rise-b2219378.html**.

25. Daniel Thomas, "100,000 workers take action as 'Striketober' hits the US," BBC, October 14, 2021, **https://www.bbc.com/news/business-58916266**.

26. Anna Cooban, "'Unprecedented' strike: 100,000 UK nurses set to walk off the job," MSN, December 12, 2022, **https://www .msn.com/en-us/news/world/uk-strikes-set-to-escalate-as-nurses-prepare-for-unprecedented-walkou/t/ar-AA15bwkM**.

27. Pippa Crerar and Kiran Stacey, "Union fury as Rishi Sunak unveils anti-strike laws for 'minimum service levels'," *The Guardian*, January 5, 2023, **https://www.theguardian.com/uk-news/2023/jan/05/uk-ministers-announce-anti-strike-legislation**.

Chapter 5: Purpose Rules and Empathy Wins

1. "Build organization culture as a strategic capability," *Mercer*, 2023, **https://www.mercer.com/solutions/transformation/workforce-and-organization-transformation/culture/**.
2. "No transformation without culture," *Mercer*, 2023, **https://www.mercer.ca/en/our-thinking/career/no-transformation-without-culture.html**.
3. "Award KION shapes the future of logistics," KION Group, May 21, 2021, **https://www.kiongroup.com/en/News-Stories/Stories/Performance/Award-KION-shapes-the-future-of-logistics.html**.
4. "Larry Fink's 2022 letter to CEOs: The power of capitalism," Black-Rock, 2022, **https://www.blackrock.com/dk/individual/2022-larry-fink-ceo-letter**.
5. "Unilever's purpose-led brands outperform," Unilever, June 11, 2019, **https://www.unilever.com/news/press-and-media/press-releases/2019/unilevers-purpose-led-brands-outperform/**.
6. "Brands with purpose grow – and here's the proof," Unilever, June 11, 2019, **https://www.unilever.com/news/news-search/2019/brands-with-purpose-grow-and-here-is-the-proof/**.
7. "Sustainability figures," *Siemens*, 2022, **https://www.siemens.com/kr/en/company/sustainability/sustainability-figures.html**.
8. Tracy Brower, PhD, "Want to find your purpose at work? Change your perceptions," *Forbes*, August 12, 2019, **https://www.forbes.com/sites/tracybrower/2019/08/12/want-to-find-your-purpose-at-work-change-your-perceptions/**.
9. Dave Bailey, "How to find your purpose at work," *Medium*, May 6, 2020, **https://medium.dave-bailey.com/how-to-find-your-purpose-at-work-182acf4f2839**.

10. Jeroen Kraaijenbrink, "What BANI really means (and how it corrects your world view," *Forbes*, June 22, 2022, **https://www .forbes.com/sites/jeroenkraaijenbrink/2022/06/22/what-bani-really-means-and-how-it-corrects-your-world-view/? sh=29cd441611bb**.

Chapter 6: Trust and Accountability Are a Team Sport

1. Frederic Laloux, *Reinventing Organizations: An Illustrated Invitation to Join the Conversation on Next-Stage Organizations* (Nelson Parker, 2016), 25.
2. "What is Principal Agent Theory?" Program on Negotiation Harvard Law School, 2023, **https://www.pon.harvard.edu/tag/ principal-agent-theory/**.
3. Yun Lin and Nate Rattner, "S&P 500 doubles from its pandemic bottom, marking the fastest bull market rally since WWII," CNBC, August 16, 2021, **https://www.cnbc.com/2021/08/16/sp-500-doubles-from-its-pandemic-bottom-marking-the-fastest-bull-market-rally-since-wwii.html**.
4. "Netflix Jobs: A great workplace combines exceptional colleagues and hard problems," Netflix, 2023, **https://jobs.netflix.com/ culture**.
5. "Netflix Reviews," Glassdoor, 2023, **https://www.glassdoor .com/Reviews/Netflix-Reviews-E11891.htm**.
6. Kate Bravery, Adrienne Cernigoi, and Joana Silva, "Global Talent Trends 2022–2023: Rise of the relatable organization," *Mercer*, 2023.
7. "Gartner Says 81% of HR leaders are changing their organization's performance management system," *Gartner*, November 19, 2019, **https://www.gartner.com/en/newsroom/press-releases/ 2019-11-19-gartner-says-81--of-hr-leaders-are-changing -their-org**.
8. Jay Fitzgerald, "Silos that work: How the pandemic changed the way we collaborate," Harvard Business School, February 8, 2022, **https://hbswk.hbs.edu/item/silos-that-work-how-the-pandemic-changed-the-way-we-collaborate**.

9. John C. Maxwell, Failing forward: turning mistakes into stepping stones for success. (Nashville: Thomas Nelson Publishers, 2000), n.p."

10. Sarah Robb O'Hagan, "Gatorade: Sarah Robb O'Hagan," Interview by Guy Gaz, *Wisdom from the Top with Guy Raz*, NPR, November 3, 2021. Audio, **https://podcasts.apple.com/au/podcast/gatorade-sarah-robb-ohagan/id1460154838?i=1000539787632**.

11. Michael Jordan "Failure" Commercial, video, **https://www.youtube.com/watch?v=JA7G7AV-LT8**.

12. Candice Choi, "The banking crisis: A timeline of key events," *Wall Street Journal*, May 11, 2023, **https://www.wsj.com/articles/bank-collapse-crisis-timeline-724f6458**.

13. "A timeline of the Credit Suisse scandals," *The Week*, February 22, 2022, **https://www.theweek.co.uk/news/world-news/955848/a-timeline-of-the-credit-suisse-scandals**.

14. "Credit Suisse falls prey to a crisis of confidence," *Financial Times*, March 16, 2023, **https://www.ft.com/content/18278291-772e-4caa-8910-1d7b8563ed42**.

15. Kate Bravery, Adrienne Cernigoi, and Joana Silva, "Global Talent Trends 2022–2023: Rise of the relatable organization," *Mercer*, 2023.

16. General Stanley McChrustal with Tantum Collins, David Silverman and Chris Fussell, *Teams of Teams: New rules of engagement for a complex world* (Penguin Publishing Group, 2015).

Chapter 7: Intelligence Is Getting Amplified

1. Jeremy Kahn, "The inside story of ChatGPT: How OpenAI founder Sam Altman built the world's hottest technology with billions from Microsoft," *Fortune*, January 25, 2023, **https://fortune.com/longform/chatgpt-openai-sam-altman-microsoft/**.

2. Morgan Smith, "ChatGPT is the hottest new job skill that can help you get hired, according to HR experts," CNBC, April 5, 2023, **https://www.cnbc.com/2023/04/05/chatgpt-is-the-newest-in-demand-job-skill-that-can-help-you-get-hired.html**.

3. "Pricing: Simple and flexible. Only pay for what you use," OpenAI, 2023, **https://openai.com/pricing**.

4. Cassie Moorhead, "How to set your freelance writing rate," Upwork, October 24, 2022, **https://www.upwork.com/resources/freelance-writing-rates**.

5. Amit Agrawal, "AI has been used to develop and advance numerous fields and industries, including finance, healthcare, education, transportation, and more," CIS, 2023, **https://www.cisin.com/coffee-reak/enterprise/ai-has-been-used-to-develop-and-advance-numerous-fields-and-industries-including-finance-healthcare-education-transportation-and-more.html**.

6. Sophia Epstein, "How do you control an AI as powerful as OpenAI's GPT-3?" *Wired*, July 27, 2020, **https://www.wired.co.uk/article/gpt-3-openai-examples**.

7. Davey Alba, "OpenAI chatbot spits out biased musings, despite guardrails," Bloomberg, December 8, 2022, **https://www.bloomberg.com/news/newsletters/2022-12-08/chatgpt-open-ai-s-chatbot-is-spitting-out-biased-sexist-results**.

8. Hannah Getahun, "Breaking ChatGPT: The AI's alter ego DAN reveals why the internet is so drawn to making the chatbot violate its own rules," *Insider*, February 12, 2023, **https://www.businessinsider.com/open-ai-chatgpt-alter-ego-dan-on-reddit-ignores-guidelines-2023-2**.

9. Alexander Muacevic, John R Adler, Hussam Alkaissi, and Samy I McFarlane, "Artificial hallucinations in ChatGPT: Implications in scientific writing," National Library of Medicine: National Center for Biotechnology Information, February 19, 2023, **https://www.ncbi.nlm.nih.gov/pmc/articles/PMC9939079/**.

10. Susan Armstrong, "The rise of deepfakes in job interviews: Why we should be concerned," *Euronews*, June 10, 2022, **https://www.euronews.com/next/2022/10/06/the-rise-of-deepfakes-in-job-interviews-why-we-should-be-concerned**.

11. Kinza Yasar, "Black box AI," *Tech Target*, 2023, **https://www.techtarget.com/whatis/definition/black-box-AI**.

12. Attilio Di Battista, Sam Grayling, Elselot Hasselaar, Till Leopold, Ricky Li, Mark Rayner, and Saadia Zahidi, "Future of Jobs Report 2023," World Economic Forum, (2023): 6.

13. Attilio Di Battista, Sam Grayling, Elselot Hasselaar, Till Leopold, Ricky Li, Mark Rayner, and Saadia Zahidi, "Future of Jobs Report 2023," World Economic Forum, 2023.

14. "Generative AI is churning out unicorns like it's 2021," *CB Insights*, May 10, 2023, **https://www.cbinsights.com/research/generative-ai-unicorns-valuations-revenues-headcount/**.

15. Trey Williams, "Some companies are already replacing workers with ChatGPT, despite warnings it shouldn't be relied on for 'anything important'," *Fortune*, February 25, 2023, **https://fortune .com/2023/02/25/companies-replacing-workers-chatgpt-ai/**.

16. David Autor, Caroline Chin, Anna M. Salomons, and Bryan Seegmiller, "New Frontiers: The Origins and Content of New Work, 1940–2018," *Working Papers* 30389 (August 2022): n.p. **https:// www.nber.org/papers/w30389**.

17. Goldman Sachs data reported in "The threat and promise of artificial intelligence," *Financial Times*, May 9, 2023, **https://www .ft.com/content/41fd34b2-89ee-4b21-ac0a-9b15560ef37c**.

18. David De Cremer and Garry Kasparov, "AI should augment human intelligence, not replace it," *Harvard Business Review*, March 18, 2021, **https://www.kasparov.com/ai-should-augment-human-intelligence-not-replace-it-harvard-business-review-march-18-2021/**.

19. Garry Kasparov and Diane L. Coutu, "Strategic intensity: A conversation with world chess champion Garry Kasparov," *Harvard Business Review*, April 1, 2005, **https://store.hbr.org/product/ strategic-intensity-a-conversation-with-world-chess-champion-garry-kasparov/r0504b?sku=R0504B-PDF-ENG**.

20. Katyanna Quach, "How Pfizer used AI and supercomputers to design COVID-19 vaccine, tablet," *The Register*, March 22, 2022, **https://www.theregister.com/2022/03/22/pfizer_nvidia_ai/**.

21. Philip Ball, "The lightning-fast quest for COVID vaccines – and what it means for other diseases," *Nature*, December 18, 2020, **https://www.nature.com/articles/d41586-020-03626-1**.

22. "Chief People Officer's quick guide to generative artificial intelligence," *Mercer*, April 13, 2023, **https://www.mercer.com/ insights/people-strategy/future-of-work/chief-people-officers-quick-guide-to-generative-artificial-intelligence/**.

23. "70% of workers using ChatGPT at work are not telling their boss; Overall usage among professionals jumps to 43%," *Fishbowl*, February 1, 2023, **https://www.fishbowlapp.com/ insights/70-percent-of-workers-using-chatgpt-at-work-are-not-telling-their-boss/**.

24. "Satya Nadella: 'The learn-it-all does better than the know-it-all'," *Wall Street Journal*, January 23, 2019, **https://www.wsj.com/ video/satya-nadella-the-learn-it-all-does-better-than-the-know-it-all/D8BC205C-D7F5-423E-8A41-0E921E86597C.html**.

25. "Khan Academy: Khan Academy explores the potential for GPT-4 in a limited pilot program," OpenAI, March 14, 2023, **https://openai.com/customer-stories/khan-academy**.

26. "Morgan Stanley. Morgan Stanley wealth management deploys GPT-4 to organize its vast knowledge base," OpenAI, March 14, 2023, **https://openai.com/customer-stories/morgan-stanley**.

27. Sultan Saidov, "Beamery announces TalentGPT, the world's first generative AI for HR," *Beamery*, March 27, 2023, **https://beamery.com/resources/news/beamery-announces-talentgpt-the-world-s-first-generative-ai-for-hr**.

28. Ana Kreacic, John Romeo, Simon Luong, Lucia Uribe, Amy Lasater-Wille, Elizabeth Costa, Kamal Ahmed, and Jonathan Paterson, "A-Gen-Z Report: What business needs to know about the generation changing everything," Oliver Wyman Forum and The News Movement, 2023, **https://www.oliverwymanforum.com/content/dam/oliver-wyman/ow-forum/template-scripts/a-gen-z/pdf/A-Gen-Z-Report.pdf**.

Chapter 8: Skills Are the Real Currency of Work

1. Ravin Jesuthasan and John W. Bourdreau, *Work without Jobs: How to Reboot Your Organization's Work Operating System*, (Management on the Cutting Edge, 2022).

2. Attilio Di Battista, Sam Grayling, Elselot Hasselaar, Till Leopold, Ricky Li, Mark Rayner, and Saadia Zahidi, "Future of Jobs Report 2023," World Economic Forum, 2023.

3. Stephane Kasriel, "Skill, re-skill and re-skill again. How to keep up with the future of work," World Economic Forum, July 31, 2017, **https://www.weforum.org/agenda/2017/07/skill-reskill-prepare-for-future-of-work/**.

4. Beat the crisis: How executives are responding to economic shocks and talent shortages," *Mercer*, 2023, **https://www.mercer.com/en-us/insights/talent-and-transformation/attracting-and-retaining-talent/how-executives-are-responding-to-economic-shocks-and-talent-shortages/**.

5. Kate Bravery, Adrienne Cernigoi, and Joana Silva, "Global Talent Trends 2022: Rise of the relatable organization," *Mercer* (2022): 58.

6. Kate Bravery, Adrienne Cernigoi, and Joana Silva, "Global Talent Trends 2022: Rise of the relatable organization," *Mercer,* 2022.

7. Paul Sandle, "BT to cut up to 55,000 jobs by 2030 as fibre and AI arrive," Reuters, May 18, 2023, **https://www.reuters.com/ business/media-telecom/bt-meets-expectations-with-5-rise-full-year-earnings-2023-05-18/**.

8. Tera Allas, Will Fairbairn, and Elizabeth Foote, "The economic case for reskilling in the UK: How employers can thrive by boosting workers' skills," McKinsey, November 16, 2020, **https://www .mckinsey.com/capabilities/people-and-organizational-performance/our-insights/the-economic-case-for-reskilling-in-the-uk-how-employers-can-thrive-by-boosting-workers-skills**.

9. Matt Moran, "31+ eLearning Statistics 2023: Facts, trends, demographics, and more," *startupbonsai,* January 2, 2023, **https:// startupbonsai.com/elearning-statistics/**.

10. Kate Bravery, Adrienne Cernigoi, and Joana Silva, "Global Talent Trends 2022: Rise of the relatable organization," *Mercer* (2022): 58.

11. Kate Bravery, Adrienne Cernigoi, and Joana Silva, "Global Talent Trends 2022: Rise of the relatable organization," *Mercer,* 2022.

12. Kate Bravery, Adrienne Cernigoi, and Joana Silva, "Global Talent Trends 2022: Rise of the relatable organization," *Mercer* (2022): 58.

13. Kate Bravery, Adrienne Cernigoi, and Joana Silva, "Global Talent Trends 2022: Rise of the relatable organization," *Mercer* (2022): 58.

14. Richard Feloni, "IBM is using its AI star Watson to pinpoint salaries and coach employees. Here are 9 robot tools that could one day find their way to your office." *Business Insider India,* August 12, 2019, **https://www.businessinsider.in/ibm-is-using-its-ai-star-watson-to-pinpoint-salaries-and-coach-employees-here-are-9-robot-tools-that-could-one-day-find-their-way-to-your-office-/articleshow/70650368.cms**.

15. José María Álvarez-Pallete, "The future of jobs," panel with Saadia Zahidi, Pamela Coke-Hamilton, Martin J. Walsh, Jose Maria Alvarez-Pallete, Gilbert Fossoun Houngbo, and Geoff Cutmore, *Davos,* World Economic Forum, January 18, 2023. Audio, 27:14, **https://www.weforum.org/events/world-economic-forum-annual-meeting-2023/sessions/the-future-of-jobs**.

16. Edith Krieg, "Telefonica reskills 100,000 employees for a digital workplace of the future," *Forbes,* October 22, 2021, **https:// www.forbes.com/sites/sap/2021/10/22/telefnica-reskills-100000-employees-for-a-digital-workplace-of-the-future/ ?sh=3b447e5624b8**.

17. Chetna Singh, "Total rewards at the center of innovation at SAP," interview by Kate Bravery, *New Shape of Work*, Mercer, September 15, 2022. Audio, 22:54, **https://www.mercer.com/insights/ people-strategy/future-of-work/podcast-new-shape-of- work/total-rewards-at-the-center-of-innovation-at-sap/**.

18. Attilio Di Battista, Sam Grayling, Elselot Hasselaar, Till Leopold, Ricky Li, Mark Rayner, and Saadia Zahidi, "Future of Jobs Report 2023," World Economic Forum, (2023): 37.

19. "(ISC)² Cybersecurity Workforce Study: A critical need for cyber- security professionals persists amidst a year of cultural and work- place evolution," *(ISC)²*, 2022, **https://www.isc2.org/-/media/ ISC2/Research/2022-WorkForce-Study/ISC2-Cybersecurity- Workforce-Study.ashx**.

20. Jamie Grierson, "Sunak's maths to 18 plan 'misguided', says man asked to promote it," *The Guardian*, April 18, 2023, **https://www .theguardian.com/education/2023/apr/18/sunaks-maths- to-18-plan-misguided-says-man-asked-to-promote-it**.

21. Kelly Field, "Tech giants and 2-year colleges are teaming up to teach in-demand skills," *Higher Ed Dive*, September 4, 2019, **https:// www.highereddive.com/news/tech-giants-and-2-year- colleges-are-teaming-up-to-teach-in-demand-skills/562225/**.

22. "Microsoft Discovery Program," *Microsoft*, 2023, **https://careers .microsoft.com/students/us/en/ushighschoolprogram**.

23. "Our Mission," *Digital Frontiers*, 2023, **https://digitalfrontiers- institute.org/**.

24. Kamal Ahluwalia, "Unlock M&A deal potential with data and AI," interview by Kate Bravery, *Transforming for the future*, Mer- cer, November 17, 2021. Audio, 6:07, **https://www.mercer.com/ insights/people-strategy/future-of-work/transforming-for- the-future-podcast/unlock-m-and-a-deal-potential-with- data-and-ai/**.

25. Kate Bravery, Adrienne Cernigoi, Stefani Baldwin, and Joana Silva, "Global Talent Trends 2020: Win with empathy," *Mercer* (2022): 63.

26. Amy Baxendale, "Becoming a skills-powered organisation: Arcadis' journey," interview by Cynthia Cottrell, *Making work 'work'*, Mer- cer, March 2023. Audio, 5:28, **https://www.mercer.com.au/ our-thinking/workforce/podcast-making-work-work.html**.

27. David Henderson, "Evolving for the new shape of work while optimizing for today," interview by Kate Bravery, *New Shape*

of Work, Mercer, August 24, 2021. Audio, 12:48, **https://www
.mercer.com/insights/people-strategy/future-of-work/
podcast-new-shape-of-work/evolving-for-the-new-shape-
of-work-while-optimizing-for-today/**.

28. "How Schneider Electric increased employee retention," *Gloat*,
2023, **https://gloat.com/resources/schneider-electric-
customer-success-story/**.

Chapter 9: Supply Is Unchained

1. Alyssa Stringer, "A comprehensive list of 2023 tech layoffs," *Tech
Crunch*, September 19, 2021, **https://techcrunch.com/2023/
05/09/tech-industry-layoffs/**.

2. Lauren Frayer, "Why is India running out of oxygen?," NPR, May 5,
2021, **https://www.npr.org/sections/goatsandsoda/2021/05/
05/989461528/why-is-india-running-out-of-oxygen**.

3. "It's official: July was Earth's hottest month on record," *NOAA*,
August 13, 2021, **https://www.noaa.gov/news/its-official-july-
2021-was-earths-hottest-month-on-record**.

4. "It's official: July was Earth's hottest month on record," *NOAA*,
August 13, 2021, **https://www.noaa.gov/news/its-official-
july-2021-was-earths-hottest-month-on-record**.

5. Jeff Masters, "The top 10 global weather and climate change events
of 2021," *Yale Climate Connections*, January 11, 2022, **https://
yaleclimateconnections.org/2022/01/the-top-10-global-
weather-and-climate-change-events-of-2021/**.

6. "People + Work Connect," *Accenture*, 2022, **https://www
.accenture.com/us-en/about/company/people-work-
connect**.

7. "People + Work Connect," *Accenture*, 2022, **https://www
.accenture.com/us-en/about/company/people-work-
connect**.

8. Matt Perez, "Report: Marriott to furlough tens of thousands
of employees amid coronavirus closures," *Forbes*, **https://
www.forbes.com/sites/mattperez/2020/03/17/marriott-
to-furlough-tens-of-thousands-of-employees-amid-
coronavirus-closures/**.

9. "A new AI-powered network is helping workers displaced by the coronavirus crisis," McKinsey, April 8, 2020, **https://www.mckinsey.com/about-us/new-at-mckinsey-blog/how-two-organizations-we-served-are-helping-workers-displaced-by-the-coronavirus-crisis-find-new-jobs**.

10. Jordan Valinsky, "Peloton sales surge 172% as pandemic bolsters home fitness industry," CNN Business, September 11, 2020, **https://www.cnn.com/2020/09/11/business/peloton-stock-earnings/index.html**.

11. Megan Cerullo, "Peloton invests $100 million to fly bikes overseas as customers ask 'where's my bike'?", CBS News, February 5, 2021, **https://www.cbsnews.com/news/peloton-delivery-investment-100-million/**.

12. Jon Hopkins, "Peloton Interactive posts losses of more than $1.2 billion in its fiscal fourth quarter as revenue plunges," *Proactivewatch*, August 25, 2022, **https://www.proactiveinvestors.co.uk/companies/news/991025/peloton-interactive-posts-losses-of-more-than-1-2-billion-in-its-fiscal-fourth-quarter-as-revenue-plunges-991025.html**.

13. Mark Sweney, "**Made.com** plans to cut third of staff as it seeks emergency investment or buyer," *The Guardian*, September 23, 2022, **https://www.theguardian.com/business/2022/sep/23/madecom-plans-to-cut-a-third-of-staff-as-it-seeks-buyer-or-investment**.

14. "New figures highlight potential job losses," *Airlines*, September 28, 2021, **https://airlines.iata.org/news/new-figures-highlight-potential-job-losses**.

15. Mary Meisenzahl, "Over half of restaurant workers say they've been abused by customers or managers – and many are planning to flee the industry because of it," *Insider*, October 8, 2021, **https://www.businessinsider.com/restaurant-workers-plan-to-quit-abuse-from-customers-managers-2021-10?r=US&IR=T**.

16. Olaf Schatterman, Drew Woodhouse, and Joe Terino, "Supply chain lessons from Covid-19: Time to refocus on resilience," Bain & Company, April 27, 2020, **https://www.bain.com/insights/supply-chain-lessons-from-covid-19/**.

17. Dave Muoio, "Hospitals' per patient labor spend increased 37% from 2019 to Q1 2022," *Fierce Healthcare*, May 12, 2022, **https://www.fiercehealthcare.com/providers/hospitals-patient-labor-spend-increased-37-2019-q1-2022**.

Chapter 10: Sustainability Starts with People

1. Klaus Schwab and Thierry Malleret, *The Great Narrative* (The Great Reset, 2021), 148.
2. Rethinking what we need from work: A guide to employees' most pressing needs and how your organization can meet them, based on "Mercer's 2022–2023 Inside Employees' Minds study," *Mercer*, 2023, **https://www.mercer.com/en-us/insights/talent-and-transformation/attracting-and-retaining-talent/rethinking-what-we-need-from-work-inside-employees-minds-2022/**.
3. "Climate Change 2023: Synthesis Report," United Nations, 2023, **https://www.un.org/en/climatechange/reports**.
4. Sophia Heading and Saadia Zahidi, "The Global Risks Report 2023, 18th Edition: Insight Report," World Economic Forum, (2023): 7.
5. Nick Green, "One in six over-55s have no pension savings yet," *unbiased*, February 17, 2023, **https://www.unbiased.co.uk/news/financial-adviser/one-in-six-over-55s-have-no-pension-savings-yet**.
6. "Global Wage Report: 2022–23: The impact of inflation and COVID-19 on wages and purchasing power," International Labour Organization, 2023, **https://www.ilo.org/wcmsp5/groups/public/---ed_protect/---protrav/---travail/documents/publication/wcms:862569.pdf**.
7. "Ninety per cent of world excluded from old age pension schemes," International Labour Organization, April 28, 2000, **https://www.ilo.org/asia/media-centre/news/WCMS_BK_PR_19_EN/lang--en/index.htm**.
8. "The pension gap epidemic," The Geneva Association, 2023, **https://www.genevaassociation.org/sites/default/files/research-topics-document-type/pdf_public/pensions_epidemic_summary_final.pdf**.
9. Nick Green, "One in six over-55s have no pension savings yet," *unbiased*, February 17, 2023, **https://www.unbiased.co.uk/news/financial-adviser/one-in-six-over-55s-have-no-pension-savings-yet**.

10. Aimee Picchi, "Millions of older Americans are nearing retirement without a penny in savings," CBS News, April 18, 2023, **https://www.cbsnews.com/news/retirement-baby-boomers-with-no-retirement-savings/**.

11. Martin Armstrong, "It will take another 136 years to close the global gender gap," World Economic Forum, April 12, 2021, **https://www.weforum.org/agenda/2021/04/136-years-is-the-estimated-journey-time-to-gender-equality/**

12. Kusum Kali Pal, Kim Piaget, Silja Baller, Vesselina Ratcheva, and Saadia Zahidi, "Global Gender Gap 2022, World Economic Forum, 2022, **https://www.weforum.org/reports/global-gender-gap-report-2022/in-full/2-1-gender-gaps-in-the-labour-force-recovery**.

13. "Non-communicable diseases cause 74% of global deaths: WHO," *Medical xppress,* September 21, 2022, **https://medicalxpress.com/news/2022-09-non-communicable-diseases-global-deaths.html**.

14. "World employment and social outlook trends 2023," International Labour Organization, 2023, **https://www.ilo.org/wcmsp5/groups/public/---dgreports/---inst/documents/publication/wcms:865332.pdf**.

15. Kate Bravery, Adrienne Cernigoi, and Joana Silva, "Global Talent Trends 2022: Rise of the relatable organization," *Mercer* (2022): 12.

16. Elselot Hasselar, Till Leopold, and MinJi Suh, "Pathways to social justice: A revitalized vision for diversity, equity and inclusion in the workforce," World Economic Forum, 2021, **https://www3.weforum.org/docs/WEF_Pathways_to_Social_Justice_2021.pdf**.

17. David Gelles, 'Billionaire no more: Patagonia gives away the company," *New York Times,* September 14, 2022, **https://www.nytimes.com/2022/09/14/climate/patagonia-climate-philanthropy-chouinard.html**.

18. Yvon Chouinard, *Let My People Go Surfing: The Education of a Reluctant Businessman* (Penguin Books, 2016), 61.

19. "Our core values," Patagonia, 2022, **https://www.patagonia.com/core-values/**.

20. Lora Kolodny, "Patagonia founder just donated the entire company, worth $3 billion, to fight climate change," CNBC, September 14, 2022, **https://www.cnbc.com/2022/09/14/patagonia-founder-donates-entire-company-to-fight-climate-change.html**.

21. Sophia Heading and Saadia Zahidi, "The Global Risks Report 2023, 18th Edition: Insight Report," World Economic Forum, 2023.

22. "Corporate sustainability reporting," European Commission, 2022, **https://finance.ec.europa.eu/capital-markets-union-and-financial-markets/company-reporting-and-auditing/company-reporting/corporate-sustainability-reporting_en**.

23. Fabian Wiktor, "A livable future for all is possible, if we take urgent climate action: flagship UN report," United Nations, March 20, 2023, **https://news.un.org/en/story/2023/03/1134777**.

24. Attilio Di Battista, Sam Grayling, Elselot Hasselaar, Till Leopold, Ricky Li, Mark Rayner, and Saadia Zahidi, "Future of Jobs Report 2023," World Economic Forum, (2023): 254.

25. Nigel Topping, "LinkedIn's Allen Blue: 'Half of all jobs will be redefined by climate change'," LinkedIn, September 21, 2021, **https://www.linkedin.com/pulse/linkedins-allen-blue-half-all-jobs-redefined-climate-change-topping/**.

26. Michael J. McDonald, "Work as we knew it is ending: The remote, freelance revolution has begun," *Toptal*, 2023, **https://www.toptal.com/insights/rise-of-remote/contingent-workforce**.

27. Ana Kreacic, John Romeo, Simon Luong, Lucia Uribe, Amy Lasater-Wille, Elizabeth Costa, Kamal Ahmed, and Jonathan Paterson, "A-Gen-Z Report: What business needs to know about the generation changing everything," Oliver Wyman Forum and The News Movement, 2023, **https://www.oliverwymanforum.com/content/dam/oliver-wyman/ow-forum/template-scripts/a-gen-z/pdf/A-Gen-Z-Report.pdf**.

28. Aidan Mantelow, Guillaunne Hingel, Steffica Warwick, Elselot Hasselar, Attilo de Battista, and Saadhi Zahidi, "The Good Work Framework: A new business agenda for the future of work," World Economic Forum, 2022, **https://www3.weforum.org/docs/WEF_The_Good_Work_Framework_2022.pdf**.

29. Beat the crisis: How executives are responding to economic shocks and talent shortages," *Mercer*, 2023, **https://www.mercer.com/en-us/insights/talent-and-transformation/attracting-and-retaining-talent/how-executives-are-responding-to-economic-shocks-and-talent-shortages/**.

30. Kate Bravery, Adrienne Cernigoi, and Joana Silva, "Global Talent Trends 2022: Rise of the relatable organization," *Mercer* (2022): 12.

31. Rigas Hadzilacos, Aidan Mankelow, Till Leopold, Saadia Zahidi, "Resetting the future of work agenda: Disruption and renewal in a post-COVID world," World Economic Forum, 2022, **https://www.marshmclennan.com/content/dam/mmc-web/insights/publications/2021/march/gl-2020-resetting-the-future-of-work-agenda.pdf**.

32. "Future of work: Strategy and goals," Unilever, 2023, **https://www.unilever.com/planet-and-society/future-of-work/strategy-and-goals/**.
33. "Future workplace," Unilever, 2023, **https://www.unilever.com/planet-and-society/future-of-work/future-workplace/**.
34. "Target-setting: Commitments made by members of the Good Work Alliance," World Economic Forum, 2023, **https://initiatives.weforum.org/good-work-alliance/targetsetting**.
35. Allianz SE, "Shaping the future of work," *Allianz*, December 13, 2021, **https://www.allianz.com/en/press/news/company/human_resources/211213_Allianz-Ways-of-Working-WOW-shaping-the-future-of-work.html**.
36. Target-setting: Commitments made by members of the Good Work Alliance," World Economic Forum, 2023, **https://initiatives.weforum.org/good-work-alliance/targetsetting**.
37. Target-setting: Commitments made by members of the Good Work Alliance," World Economic Forum, 2023, **https://initiatives.weforum.org/good-work-alliance/targetsetting**.
38. Kate Bravery, Adrienne Cernigoi, and Joana Silva, "Global Talent Trends 2022–2023: Rise of the relatable organization," *Mercer* (2023): 12.
39. Ronan Maher, "Prioritizing a living wage with Yara," interview by Kate Bravery, *New Shape of Work*, Mercer, January 13, 2023. Audio, 8:48, **https://www.mercer.com/insights/people-strategy/future-of-work/podcast-new-shape-of-work/prioritizing-a-living-wage-with-yara-international/**.
40. Michael J. McDonald, "Work As We Knew It Is Ending. The Remote, Freelance Revolution Has Begun," *Toptal*, 2023, **https://www.toptal.com/insights/rise-of-remote/contingent-workforce**.
41. "Health on Demand 2023," *Mercer* (2023): 4, **https://www.mercer.com/content/dam/mercer-dotcom/global/en/shared-assets/global/attachments/pdf-2023-health-on-demand-report.pdf**.
42. Kate Bravery, Adrienne Cernigoi, and Joana Silva, "Global Talent Trends 2022–2023: Rise of the relatable organization," *Mercer* (2023): 51.
43. Alex Brill, "Global health: A new vision for employees, employers, and economies," interview by Kate Bravery, *World Economic Growth Forum*, World Economic Forum, May 3, 2023. Audio, 26:07,

https://www.weforum.org/events/the-growth-summit-jobs-and-opportunity-for-all-2023/sessions/workforce-health-a-new-vision-for-employees-employers-and-economies.

44. Natasha Lamb and Michael Passoff, "Racial and gender pay scorecard," Arjuna Capital, 2018, **https://arjuna-capital.com/wp-content/uploads/2021/03/Racial-Gender-Pay-Scorecard-2021-Arjuna-Capital-and-Proxy-Impact.pdf**.

45. Azka Ali, Yvonne Sonsino, and David Knox, "How to fix the gender pension gap," World Economic Forum, September 27, 2021, **https://www.weforum.org/agenda/2021/09/how-to-fix-the-gender-pension-gap/**.

46. Kate Bravery, Adrienne Cernigoi, and Joana Silva, "Global Talent Trends 2022–2023: Rise of the relatable organization," *Mercer* (2023): 60.

47. Helga Birgen, Jillian Reid, and Alexis Cheang, "Investing in a time of climate change: The sequel 2019," *Mercer*, 2019, **https://info.mercer.com/rs/521-DEV-513/images/Climate-change-the-sequel-2019-full-report.pdf**.

48. "Radical change is only successful when everyone is involved and everyone works together," Tchibo, 2023, **https://www.tchibo-nachhaltigkeit.de/en/taking-responsibility/people/industry-wide-change**.

49. "Partnership behind 'Green Fuels for Denmark' accelerates project and investigates production of green jet fuel by 2025," *Orsted*, April 2, 2022, **https://orsted.com/en/media/newsroom/news/2022/02/20220204476711**.

50. Paul Polman, David Anderson, Kate Bravery, and Samira El Asmar, "People first: The future of cities post-COVID," *Mercer*, 2023, **https://www.mercer.com/en-ae/insights/people-strategy/future-of-work/people-first-the-future-of-cities-post-covid/**.

51. "The importance of ESGs in incentive plans and how they can benefit your company," *Mercer*, 2021, **https://www.imercer.com/articleinsights/the-importance-of-esgs-in-incentive-plans**.

52. Attilio Di Battista, Sam Grayling, Elselot Hasselaar, Till Leopold, Ricky Li, Mark Rayner, and Saadia Zahidi, "Future of Jobs Report 2023," World Economic Forum, 2023.

53. "Reframing competitive employee experience," *Mercer*, 2023, **https://www.mercer.com/what-we-do/workforce-and-careers/mercer-employee-experience-insights.html**.

54. "Beat the crisis: How executives are responding to economic shocks and talent shortages," *Mercer*, 2023, **https://www.mercer.com/ en-us/insights/talent-and-transformation/attracting-and-retaining-talent/how-executives-are-responding-to-economic-shocks-and-talent-shortages/**.
55. **https://www.imd.org/ibyimd/strategy/seven-ways-to-build-a-more-inclusive-strategy/**

Epilogue: The End and the Beginning

1. Mercer Data and Analytics team studied several large language models (LLMs) available for enterprise clients. We selected GPT-3.5 and Flan-T5 models that are immediately available for use in the AI Development toolset provided by our Cloud providers. These are the prompts and direct output.
2. Gary Hamel and C.K. Prahalad, "Strategic intent," *Harvard Business Review,* July–August 2006, **https://hbr.org/2005/07/strategic-intent**.

Acknowledgments

Thank you to Alan Goldsher, who brought our three different voices together without getting in the middle of the creative differences among us authors, and to Kevin Anderson and his team Lauren Carsley and Stephen Power for their calm guidance. Thank you to Gina Fassino, Wilson Fernandez, Joana Silva, Anca De Maio, Pia Garcia, and Molly Proefriedt for reading early drafts and to Jens Peterson, who tirelessly edited multiple copies with Ellie Green, Elana Abernathy Wohrstein and Doveen Schecter who all helped with the editing process. Thank you to Dawid Gutowski, as always for his great design eye and responsive partnership.

Thank you to Saadia Zahidi, Ravin Jesuthasan, Will Self, Brian Fisher, Heather Ryan, and Sophia Van for their expert advice that sparked many of our discussions. Let's not forget our AI experts led by Guru Kashyap; call out to Ana Costa de Silva, Aditya Gupta, and Inteshab Nehal. And a very big thank you to the many companies that kindly spoke with us during this period, shaped our thinking, and inspired us to consider how we could all work *different*.

Index